The
Nurture
Revolution

The
Nurture
Revolution

GROW YOUR BABY'S BRAIN AND
TRANSFORM THEIR MENTAL HEALTH
THROUGH THE ART OF NURTURED PARENTING

Greer Kirshenbaum, PhD

balance

New York Boston

Balance
Hachette Book Group
1290 Avenue of the Americas
New York, NY 10104
GCP-Balance.com
Twitter.com/GCPBalance
Instagram.com/GCPBalance
First Edition: June 2023

Balance is an imprint of Grand Central Publishing. The Balance name and logo are trademarks of Hachette Book Group, Inc.

The publisher is not responsible for websites (or their content) that are not owned by the publisher.

The Feelings Inventory (page 269) and the Needs Inventory (page 274) are copyright © 2005 by Center for Nonviolent Communication. Used by permission.

The Hachette Speakers Bureau provides a wide range of authors for speaking events. To find out more, go to hachettespeakersbureau.com or email HachetteSpeakers@hbgusa.com.

Balance books may be purchased in bulk for business, educational, or promotional use. For information, please contact your local bookseller or the Hachette Book Group Special Markets Department at special.markets@hbgusa.com.

Library of Congress Cataloging-in-Publication Data has been applied for.

ISBNs: 978-1-5387-0933-7 (Hardcover); 978-1-5387-0935-1 (ebook)

Printed in the United States of America

LSC-C
Printing 1, 2023

To all the babies and all the nurturers—past, present, and future.

May you be held, seen, heard, understood, and supported so that you may experience more freedom, more joy, more connection, and more awe. May you feel your nurtured infancy inside you, and may it set you free to continue cycles of nurture that will heal humanity and planet Earth.

CONTENTS

Contents

Introduction

WELCOME TO THE NURTURE REVOLUTION

When I became pregnant in 2018, I imagined I'd take daily walks and practice prenatal yoga. I would eat healthy food and meditate daily, enjoy acupuncture and massages. I would be active but also Zen. No stress, all joy and peace. I wished to be cared for by midwives who would nurture my emotional well-being and honor my transition into motherhood. During labor and birth, I would be tended to by a doula who would support me emotionally and physically. Labor would start on its own once I was full term. I'd labor at home, supported by my doula, as long as possible, and then drive to the hospital where I'd have an unmedicated, vaginal birth. I wanted my husband to catch our baby and put him on my chest right away. I wanted to see if my baby would do a breast crawl, then I would hold my baby skin-to-skin for hours and breastfeed when my baby was ready. I would take my baby home right away and feed and sleep on cue as we recovered.

Instead, I found out at twelve weeks that I had complete placenta previa, which is when the placenta grows completely over your cervix, blocking the baby's way out. It also causes bleeding during pregnancy. My health care was immediately transferred from midwives to high-risk obstetricians who cared only for my physical well-being, scared me, and hurt me emotionally. I couldn't walk very far or practice prenatal yoga or I would have bleeds. In fact, I barely moved throughout my pregnancy. I also happened to be enmeshed in an intensely stressful family crisis during this time, with lots of anger and sadness to navigate. I tried to buffer the stress I was experiencing as best I could. I received acupuncture and massage, took naps, engaged in daily mindfulness practices, slowed down, and accepted support from a wonderfully nurturing birth doula.

My surgical birth was planned for thirty-four weeks, six weeks before full term. I was going to have a premature baby and a cesarean birth—a major stressor for my baby and major abdominal surgery I'd need to heal from. My baby was taken away from me immediately at birth and I wasn't able to see him for over twenty-four hours. During our stay in the hospital, the doctors warned me of the potential risks to my baby's brain and development from being born so early. After his birth, for ten days my baby was in the neonatal intensive care unit (NICU), where I could only hold him for one hour every three hours. I could not sleep over in the hospital and I was discouraged from breastfeeding.

Despite the early stress my baby experienced in utero, the separation at birth, and the risks associated with premature birth, I was optimistic about my infant's development. As a neuroscientist who specializes in infant neurobiology and mental health, I knew the power that my nurturing would have on his infancy. In the field of neuroscience, we define infancy as birth to three years old, as these are the years when the brain is in a unique immature state where the growth of critical brain circuits is most influenced by experience. When the doctors told me about the increased risks associated with prematurity, I knew that what they *weren't* saying was that these risks are disproportionately higher among babies who do not go on to receive nurtured caregiving in infancy and beyond. I knew the outcomes those doctors shared have significant risk in the context of low-nurture baby care and the inherent higher stress that comes with low nurture. I also knew that most research outcomes of premature babies or babies born with other risks, like delayed development, derive from babies who experience low nurture.

In contrast, I knew that I was going to use every second I could of my son's infancy, day and night, to buffer the effects of the early stress he and I experienced and to build his brain as strong as possible with nurture. I was confident that the nurture I provided in infancy would not only mitigate all of the effects of a stressful pregnancy, birth, prematurity, and NICU stay, but also grow an incredibly resilient brain for both my baby and myself. I knew that by providing high nurture, I would be bathing my baby's brain in nurturing hormones and neurotransmitters like oxytocin, dopamine, and endorphins, and as a result his brain would have extremely high neuroplasticity and a very low risk of poor outcomes. I knew that high nurture would also be an opportunity for me to change *my* brain toward better mental health.

I didn't begin my neuroscience career researching the infant brain. My initial scientific goal was to develop new treatments for poor mental health in adults. These days nearly everyone, myself included, is affected by mental health struggles. We experience it either personally or vicariously through family and friends. In the lab, my dream was to develop a new medication capable of relieving the pain and suffering caused by the most common mental health concerns: anxiety, depression, addiction, and chronic stress. I spent many years researching and studying the cells, genetics, circuits, and behaviors that underlie depression, mania, anxiety, learning, and sleep disorders.

Over my career, research identifying infancy as the foundation of mental health proliferated and got my attention. I accumulated a collection of more and more astonishing research illuminating the importance of early life experience in shaping mental and physical health, and even overall lifelong success. One day it dawned on me: Neuroscience had already uncovered a powerful medicine for alleviating mental health struggles, but the answer wasn't and couldn't be a pill. It was a preventive experiential approach: When babies receive nurturing care in the first three years of life, it builds strong, resilient brains—brains that are less susceptible to poor mental health for life. Nurture has a dramatic impact on genetics and the development of an infant's stress system. With nurture in infancy, genetics that increase risk are mitigated and the stress system grows to be regulated and resilient, which leads to a cascade of changes in the brain and body to boost lifelong health.

Nurture as a preventive medicine against mental health issues is well known among scientists, therapists, and infant health workers. We talk about it in meetings, conferences, and in our published work. But few share this information with parents—who need it the most. There is an enormous and widening knowledge gap between experts and the public. The parents I've worked with were awash in advice, products, and promises, but they had no idea what science had already confirmed. Everyone who has a baby, and everyone who has been a baby, has the right to this information. Billions of public dollars have been spent on quality cutting-edge research, resulting in thousands of rigorous scientific studies, yet the results remain locked away in the ivory tower, inaccessible to those who have funded it and can benefit from it. Unfortunately, it requires an advanced degree or years of experience to "speak" science, and few scientists have time to translate their work to the public.

So I left the lab determined to apply this preventive medicine to the world. I trained to work with families as a doula—the first neuroscientist doula, in fact—and got to work teaching families about nurturing neuroscience in pregnancy, birth, and infancy. My academic training includes a BSc in neuroscience from Dalhousie University, where I learned a foundation in how the brain develops and functions and how to assess and interpret scientific research; a PhD in neuroscience and medical science from the University of Toronto, where I learned hands-on how genetics and experience interact to form mental health, as well as how to plan, execute, and interpret research; and a postdoctoral fellowship in integrative neuroscience at Columbia University, where I learned from the world's leading scientists in infant mental health and brain development. Next, I was educated in infant-parent relationships and infant mental health by leading researchers and practitioners at the New York University Medical School Institute for Psychoanalytic Education, the Yale Child Study Center Minding the Baby program, the Toronto Psychoanalytic Society and Institute, and Infant and Early Mental Health Promotion at the Hospital for Sick Children in Toronto. I became a neuroscience- and evidence-based infant and family sleep specialist and educator. And I began educating and supporting parents on growing their babies' brains with nurture. I called my approach

"Nurture Neuroscience." I created a unique professional training to certify infant and family sleep professionals to work with a neuroscience- and mental health–informed approach.

Giving birth to my own baby gave me a real-life education as I learned that we can't control everything when it comes to parenthood. You might dream of breastfeeding but find lactation impossible, or you might want to stay home but your job demands that you return quickly, or you might imagine tons of support postpartum but feel alone, or like me you may have had a stressful pregnancy and a birth that was entirely out of your hands. We're all being failed socially, too, because many of us live in countries lacking any real institutional support for parenting our infants—things like parental leave, childcare support, access to supportive medical and postpartum caregivers, and so much more. However, whatever our experience and limitations, infants benefit from *any* amount of nurturing their caregivers provide, whether those caregivers be biological parents, adoptive parents, parents by surrogacy, parents with infertility, those who had difficult pregnancies, parents with mental health struggles, those who have experienced traumatic births, parents who were nurtured themselves, parents who personally experienced low nurture, parents who work full-time, stay-at-home parents, single parents, grandparents, aunts, uncles, or any other type of caregiver. All nurture is nourishing for our babies' brains. No matter our circumstance, we all have nurturing superpowers to bathe our babies' brains in the hormones and neurotransmitters that build healthy and resilient permanent brain structures.

THE MENTAL HEALTH REVOLUTION IS BUILT IN INFANCY

Nurturing our babies' brains is a movement to revolutionize mental health to impact larger systems in our world. Mental health doesn't impact individuals in isolation. Our families, communities, and nations at large are impacted by the mental health of their members. We are in a mental health crisis with wide-ranging effects on humanity and our planet. We are also in possession of knowledge to dramatically shift this crisis and create new cycles of intergenerational mental wellness. Lifelong mental health starts with infant mental health.

Mental health struggles are prevalent, growing, and difficult to treat. Many of our struggles begin in childhood or adolescence,[1] and at least one out of every five adults in the United States and Canada experiences poor mental health at any time.[2] Over a lifetime, it's estimated that 50–80 percent of individuals experience a period of poor mental health.[3] Pharmaceutical treatments absolutely can help, especially in combination with therapy, but overall they have not improved our collective mental health. More people take prescriptions than ever before, but outcomes have not improved. We need a better strategy. We need to tackle the sources of mental unwellness, instead of only responding to the results. Mental unwellness causes profound suffering not only to those directly struggling, but to their family and friends as well. It influences all of the individuals who make up our public institutions, and how we care about each other and the planet.[4]

Worse, mental health is in decline for future generations. Mental health struggles are impacting children at younger ages and more intensely. Collectively, more and more of us are becoming deeply stressed and are deeply suffering.[5] We can continue down this path, or we can take a sharp turn toward healing and health. We can revolutionize our treatment of infants in the early years and give them future health. Mental health. Physical health. More empathy, more connection, more peace.

For a long time, I and other researchers were confident that we could find genes and targets in the brain that caused anxiety, depression, and addiction and design effective pharmaceuticals. It turns out that mental wellness and mental illness are much more complicated than we hoped. We have yet to discover a drug and target combination capable of bringing relief. Psychotherapy, psychedelic-assisted psychotherapy, Somatic Experiencing therapy, internal family systems, compassionate inquiry, and other therapies are effective, but they are also expensive, inaccessible, hard to navigate, and take a long time to work. Even the most resourced individuals can have a near-impossible time accessing effective therapy. We are far from designing a simple cure that targets the intricate system that is mental health.

Here's what we do know: Mental health is made up of complex emotional and cognitive brain circuits, largely formed by relationships in early life, from conception to about age three.[6] We know that these brain circuits are made up of billions of cells and trillions of connections. We know that brain circuits for mood, depression, anxiety, addiction, and resilience are all built between conception and age three and last for life.[7] Figure 1 shows critical brain circuits that are created in early life, which include the brain areas called the amygdala, hypothalamus, hippocampus, and prefrontal cortex. They are the foundation for all brain functioning, including mental health, relationships, and cognition, the equivalent of the foundation of a house.[8] We know that responsive relationships in early life build these brain areas to be resilient and healthy, and able to prevent mental unwellness.

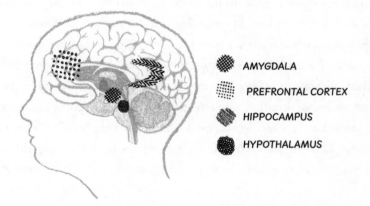

Figure 1.
Overview of major brain areas that underlie lifelong mental health that are built by experience in infancy.

From a neuroscience perspective, mental and emotional wellness are rooted in a resilient stress system. Such a system adaptively responds to pertinent internal and external threats and, importantly, is also capable of recovering from stress with relative ease. In other words, it assures that you don't perceive threats when none exist. When you are faced with a pertinent threat, you're able to calm down relatively quickly afterward; you don't stay in a heightened or activated state after a threat passes. This means that a resilient stress system protects the brain against frequent or prolonged stress that leads to mental unwellness such as symptoms of depression, anxiety, and addiction.

We have a golden opportunity to create mental wellness in infancy. A nurturing relationship with at least one caregiver is the best preventive treatment we have to relieve mental unwellness and boost mental wellness. In order to build a brain that is resilient, healthy, and able to withstand adversity later in life, babies need brain-nurturing experiences while they are developing.[9] The incredible thing is that our nurturing extends beyond our babies as well: Their resilient brain health is genetically transmitted to their children, too. We are creating a blueprint for mental health for future generations, a profoundly meaningful legacy of healing. When I ask parents what they want for their children, they usually say excellent physical and mental health, empathy, self-confidence, self-worth, intelligence, morality, values, a sense of humor, healthy relationships, success in learning and school, success in work, reaching their individual potential, excelling at what they love, life satisfaction, happiness, discovery of a passion or meaning, kindness, generosity, security. The foundation of all of these attributes is a resilient stress system. Nurture builds such a system. When we help our babies reach their potential in developing their infant brain, we are helping them live up to and actualize their potential.

THE NURTURE REVOLUTION

The idea of nurture may seem simple, but it is in fact a radical departure from what I call low-nurture culture, which is prevalent in places like the United States, Canada, the United Kingdom, and Australia, and I've seen it expanding into many parts of the world that previously had higher-nurture practices for babies—China, Spain, Brazil, and India among them. Low-nurture cultures lack support or acknowledgment of the rights and needs of parents and babies. They pressure parents to abandon their neurobiology and become low nurturers. For at least the last hundred years, brought on in large part by societal changes during the Industrial Revolution that needed citizens to be workers not nurturers, the advice from doctors, most of whom have not birthed, fed, or taken care of babies, has been to separate a baby at birth, separate them at night, teach independence, teach "self-soothing," avoid holding too much, avoid spoiling, avoid feeding too much or too long; don't comfort or "give in," don't validate emotions, but do modify behaviors with punishments ranging from violence to shame to isolation.[10] It goes against our gut feelings and instincts not to nurture our babies, but we've also learned to suppress or dissociate from our gut feelings.

Low-nurture cultures are so entrenched that few if any of us were nurtured as babies, and few of us have the protection or gift of nurture in our brains. Few of us are as resilient as we could be or have good mental health. This certainly makes it harder to provide this type of care to our infants. We don't have the resilient stress response we're hoping to gift to our babies, and it's hard to give something we ourselves never received.

It's made even harder when society still doesn't see the value in taking a nurturing approach to infants and the people caring for them. I will never forget the first time I told a client, "You are allowed to hold your baby as much as you want," and she burst into tears of joy, so relieved that she didn't have to keep following her pediatrician's orders to leave her screaming baby alone in his bassinet. I've worked with other families who told me they lie to their friends or pediatricians because they are ashamed about how much they hold and respond to their babies. This is heartbreaking, and it's also bad advice that directly contradicts what we know about raising healthy, resilient humans. It is time for a paradigm shift from the outdated behavioral model that says you have to train babies to be independent and "well behaved" to a nurture approach that shows parents how powerfully their love and care builds health and resilience in their babies' brains and stress systems.

Science has shown us without a doubt that nurture is what infants need to thrive as adults, and no matter how you were parented or where you are in your parenting or mental health journey, nurture is something we can all learn and practice. It's also something our parent brains are uniquely wired for, as you'll soon see. I'm going to help you tap into your parenting instincts for nurture. Science-backed nurturing is where parental instincts and science come together. With nurture as your North Star, you can release some of the vigilance and worry that come with parenting. Nurture is always there to guide you, no matter the situation.

Some of the suggestions I make for how to practice nurtured parenting may be familiar to those of you who follow attachment parenting. Developed by Dr. William Sears and Martha Sears in 1993, attachment parenting aims to create a secure attachment relationship between parent and baby through methods like breastfeeding, babywearing, and bed-sharing.[11] However, the use of neuroscience to help us get in touch with and feel confident in our parenting instincts, while also advocating for practices that encourage a close relationship with our babies, is unique. The recommendations in this book come from what we know builds the brain and what we know are clear outcomes from building the brain. As a result, nurtured parenting goes beyond attachment practices to also be deeply interested in parents' and babies' internal worlds, rooted in the healthy functioning of their stress systems, and what develops their complex brain structures.

Armed with this information, parents can effect a sea change in mental health for the next generation. If parents understand how nurturing early experience transforms lives, the next generation will have tremendously better mental health, not to mention better physical health and success. It's a gift of resilience and health we can give the next generation simply by following our intuition to care for our young. Ending cycles of intergenerational trauma from low-nurturing parenting and starting cycles of intergenerational resilience is a big priority for many parents.

The research I share in this book is so solid and irrefutable that it will free you from ongoing debates with your mother-in-law about responding to your baby's cries or trying fifteen different approaches to infant sleep. We have research to guide us to what is best for our children's lives. We know that experience in pregnancy, birth, and infancy impacts health for life, and we have the knowledge to make the experience nurturing, positive, and enriching. Responding to infants respectfully and reliably physically builds a strong brain, mind, and body on many measurable levels.

HOW TO USE THIS BOOK

In part 1, chapters 1–4, I'll show you what's special about the infant brain, the science of how nurture builds the infant brain and the stress system, how this affects genetic expression, and what's special about the parent brain, too. In part 2, I offer practical support for nurturing your infant through your presence, empathy, relationship and connection, stress support, and sleep. In chapter 5 we'll delve into two foundational concepts of nurture: presence and empathy. Then we'll work through the six infant states of consciousness: quiet alert, which we support with nurtured connection in chapter 6; active alert and crying, which we support by nurturing stress in chapter 7; and drowsy, quiet asleep and active asleep, which we support with nurtured sleep in chapter 8.[12] We'll go deep into each of these states so that in every situation you find yourself, you can forge a nurturing path forward. In each chapter I focus on the underlying concepts that will help you nurture in your own way, whether you do skin-to-skin immediately after birth or your baby is in the NICU, whether you breastfeed or chestfeed or tube feed or bottle feed, and whether you're newly pregnant or parenting a two-and-a-half-year-old.

As a parent myself, I know it's not enough to say that nurture is the answer. Most of us carry our own baggage from the ways we were parented, feel pressure from our communities, and face structural inequalities that make parenting that much harder. Many of us find it overwhelming and insulting to be told that parenting is intuitive. So in the final chapter of part 2, chapter 9, I'll give you practices to develop your nurturing instincts and regulate your own nervous system.

Throughout the book, we'll work our way through the thirty myths (see page xxii) that dominate low-nurturing parenting and replace them with the truth about the power of your nurture to grow your infant's brain. At the end of the book you'll find lots of resources where you can get quick support and practical lists to bring to your birth or hang on your fridge.

NO PERFECT BRAIN

Whenever I was hit with an obstacle during my pregnancy and birth that was out of my control—and now as the parent of a three-year-old—I had faith that the nurture I could influence would be a powerful part of the story. In pregnancy, that looked like meditating, napping or resting, prioritizing sleep, relaxing with a book or a show, and even starting to write this book! All are things that make me happy and helped manage the ongoing stress I was experiencing. When I was able to meet my baby, I held him skin-to-skin, latched him, and ensured we had quiet, intimate time together. In the NICU I did everything I could to hold and breastfeed my baby as much as possible. Then, when I brought my baby home, I had all of the influence. I could take care of him my way. I was confident that all of the nurture I would give my baby would build his brain.

There is no such thing as a perfect brain. Perfection is not the goal, not for our children and not for us as parents. What happens to us shapes us. We can't control everything about pregnancy, birth, postpartum, or parenting, but we can influence how much we nurture. Applying the research I share in this book is the best chance we currently have to improve the mental and physical health of our children and the whole of society. We have the tools to maximize our children's potential and minimize challenges like susceptibility to anxiety, depression, addiction, and poor physical health. Nurturing, positive early life experience is a gift that lasts a lifetime.

We no longer have to worry that we are spoiling our babies, are encouraging them to be "clingy" and too dependent, or are developing bad habits by holding, kissing, cuddling, or reliably responding to them. We have the science to show that nurture is not only good for our babies, but also offers them the best chance at having all the things we wish for them as they grow into adults: mental and physical health, healthy relationships, success in school and in work. We can inform our parenting choices with solid scientific research to maximize our children's health. The next generation of infants is sure to see enormous benefits.

LOW-NURTURE MYTHS

For generations, we have been lied to about what to expect about our babies, their development, and their needs. The roots of these beliefs are capitalist and patriarchal and they are still infiltrating everything we believe about babies. We've been so heavily influenced by belief-based, low-nurture information that starting a nurture revolution means unlearning deeply ingrained myths and replacing them with knowledge-based, neuroscience-backed information. Understanding the evidence frees you from feeling you and your baby have to conform to these unrealistic and dangerous myths. When you unlearn them, you let yourself be a part of your own life rather than an echo of these doctor-perpetuated myths.

Below are thirty influential myths that promote low nurture, followed by the reality. They will appear in context throughout the book. You'll notice that these myths encourage us to believe that babies need to be separated and not responded to by their caregivers and that their experiences and feelings don't matter. The nurture revolution turns these notions on their head, showing us that closeness, responsiveness, and honoring infant experiences and feelings are the path to good mental health and resilience.

Myth 1: *Infants don't remember anything, so experience in infancy doesn't really matter.*
Reality: The infant brain has a huge capacity for memory. Memories from infancy are stored in the brain as implicit memory, which makes up the emotional brain, the unconscious mind, and the foundation for lifelong mental and physical health.

Myth 2: *Responding to cries spoils an infant or teaches an infant to be dependent.*
Reality: Responding reliably strengthens a baby's emotional brain circuits, helps them grow confidently independent, and gives them the gift of stress regulation for life.

Myth 3: Babies can and need to learn to self-soothe, which means go from a state of *high stress to a state of safety on their own.*
Reality: Babies cannot self-soothe because they do not have the brain parts to do so until way beyond infancy.

Myth 4: *Babies are resilient, so experience in infancy doesn't matter.*
Reality: Experience in infancy matters. It interacts with genes to influence mental health.

Myth 5: *We can't make a difference to our baby's mental health outcomes if our baby inherits mental health genetics and intergenerational trauma through epigenetics.*
Reality: Nurture makes an impact on inherited DNA and epigenetics to reduce or silence mental health effects.

Myth 6: *Everyone falls in love with and knows what to do with their baby right away.*

Reality: Lots of time touching, smelling, and looking into your baby's eyes slowly builds your love, knowledge, and relationship with your baby.

Myth 7: *Having a baby impairs your brain function.*
Reality: Having a baby changes your brain to give you nurturing superpowers.

Myth 8: *Being with my baby is doing nothing.*
Reality: Being with my baby is vital brain-building, circuit-sculpting, cycle-starting activism for my baby's future.

Myth 9: *Only pay attention to your baby's stress and emotions when there's a reason for them.*
Reality: All of your baby's stress and emotions need to feel welcome and safe.

Myth 10: *Since my baby will be with a grandparent, a nanny, or at daycare, I should reduce my care at home to prepare them.*
Reality: Providing my baby with as much nurture as possible when we are together is what they need to build their brain.

Myth 11: *You need to buy things for your baby's brain development.*
Reality: Your presence is the key to your baby's brain development.

Myth 12: *I need swings, seats, and containers to take care of my baby. My baby needs lots of classes and socialization to thrive.*
Reality: The sensory experiences from my body are the only thing my baby needs.

Myth 13: *I should feed my baby on a schedule.*
Reality: Feed your baby when their body is experiencing physiological signals of hunger and showing hunger cues.

Myth 14: *Breastfeeding or body feeding past six or twelve or twenty-four or thirty-six months is extra, spoiling, or for no reason.*
Reality: Breastfeeding or body feeding at six or twelve or twenty-four or thirty-six months is brain-building and nurturing.

Myth 15: *Holding a baby is doing nothing.*
Reality: Holding a baby is seriously hard and brain-building work.

Myth 16: *Newborn babies are happy with a swaddle, hat, pacifier, and bassinet.*
Reality: Newborns are happy on someone's skin, chest-to-chest, covered by a blanket—no swaddle, hat, pacifier, or bassinet needed.

Myth 17: *Babies' stress and emotions don't matter and can be ignored.*
Reality: Babies feel transformational stress and a huge range of emotions that influence how their brains and bodies develop.

Myth 18: *If we respond to our crying, clinging babies, we teach them that that behavior is good, so they learn to cry and cling more.*
Reality: When we respond to crying and clinging, babies cry less, and we build the infant brain to be more independent later.

Myth 19: *There's no difference if I hold my crying baby; they're crying anyway.*
Reality: Holding my crying baby provides a nurture bath to their brain regardless of how long they cry.

Myth 20: *Babies need to sleep from 7 p.m. to 7 a.m., with four hours of napping daily.*
Reality: There is a huge range of sleep needs for babies, and in a safe, comfortable sleep environment my baby will sleep the amount that their brain needs.

Myth 21: *Night waking in babies who are three to thirty-six months old is harmful or unnecessary.*
Reality: Night wakings are part of infant sleep, and babies stop waking at night as their brain develops.

Myth 22: *Babies have sleep regressions and need sleep training to learn to sleep again.*
Reality: Babies are always progressing. When they have a massive change in brain development they often have more wakings, and when it passes sleep becomes more settled as the brain develops further.

Myth 23: *Sleep training is the answer to your night waking concerns.*
Reality: If you are concerned about your baby's night waking, investigate medical or sensory processing issues.

Myth 24: *There are set bedtimes, wake times, and naptimes for your baby.*
Reality: Your baby's brain will tell you when they are tired and will take the amount of sleep that it needs to grow.

Myth 25: *You should use minimum input to help your baby back to sleep.*
Reality: It is beneficial to provide the most comforting and easiest method to soothe your baby at night.

Myth 26: *Stop feeding in the night at three, six, twelve, twenty-four, or thirty-six months.*
Reality: Babies can be thirsty or hungry in the night throughout infancy, from zero to three years and beyond.

Myth 27: *Babies need to be in their own room at four, six, twelve, twenty-four, or thirty-six months.*
Reality: Babies tell us when they feel safe enough to sleep alone.

Myth 28: *Babies need to learn to sleep without contact.*
Reality: Many babies require contact to feel safe enough to sleep.

Myth 29: *Your baby or child needs to outgrow connection at bedtime in infancy or childhood.*
Reality: Bedtime is a precious time where nurtured connection and nurtured sleep overlap. Children will tell you when they no longer want to connect at bedtime.

Myth 30: *You have to have all of your inner work sorted out before becoming a parent.*
Reality: Becoming a parent is a unique opportunity to learn about your stress system and do inner work within the relationship with your baby.

PART I

Chapter 1

A SEASON FOR NURTURE

Did you know that a baby's brain needs to experience visual input from the eye in order to develop brain areas for sight? If a baby's brain doesn't receive visual input from the eye in the sensitive time of infancy, they develop lifelong visual impairments.[1] My first lesson in neuroscience is one I want all parents to know: Infancy, from birth to age three years, is a season to grow the brain through experience.

My career in neuroscience has taught me that this connection goes far beyond sight. The development of many systems in the brain are time-sensitive. For many systems in the brain, infancy is a special, once-in-a-lifetime time period to build health and resilience that will serve our babies for their entire lives. For the first three years of their lives, infants undergo a wildly sensitive season of development, during which their brains are quite literally built by sensory, motor, social, and emotional experience. The infant brain possesses tremendous neuroplasticity, meaning it has great flexibility and an immense capacity to be shaped by experience.[2] The other seasons of great neuroplasticity for the brain are adolescence, when we mature into adults; and matrescence and patrescence, when we mature into parents.

When it comes to mental health, infant neuroplasticity is most notable in the stress system, which is vital to mental health. The development of the stress system influences other parts of what I call the "emotional brain," including neurotransmitter systems, gut health, cognitive systems, and even DNA. Mental health arises from complex interactions and interconnectivity in the emotional brain. Each part of the emotional brain is affected by experience in infancy—we help our babies' brains grow through the kind of care we give them. When we are nurturing, we build health into the emotional brain at every level.

HOW YOUR BABY'S BRAIN GROWS

Your baby's brain and mind become astoundingly more complex minute to minute, day to day, and week to week. The human brain is a physical organ made up of vast and interconnected neuron and glial cells. All brains—from newborn to adult—have about 160 billion brain cells.[3] Babies are born with nearly all of their brain cells, but their brains are about 75 percent smaller than adult brains.[4] The infant brain gets bigger in the first three years of life both by growing an incredible mass of connections between cells and by adding proteins to specialize cells.[5] During this period, the infant brain makes up to one million connections per second, guided by both genetics and experience, nature and nurture.[6] In a quick ten-minute meal, for example, your baby's brain will make up to 600 million new connections—and in a day their brain will form up to eight trillion six hundred and forty billion connections! In figure 2 you can see that the cells in a newborn brain have very few connections among them and few specialized proteins. From birth to three years, brain cells grow dense connections, and they grow in complexity by adding proteins. This rapid development is astonishing to witness. When I watch a baby roll over for the first time or share a smile with someone, I imagine the beautiful new connections sparking in their brain like little microscopic fireworks.

The infant brain doubles in size in the first year of life. It goes from 25 percent of an adult size to 50 percent of an adult size. By age three the infant brain is about 80 percent the size of an adult brain. By age five it is 90 percent of an adult brain, but it takes up to age twenty-five for 100 percent of the adult brain to be formed.[7] Take a look at figure 3 to

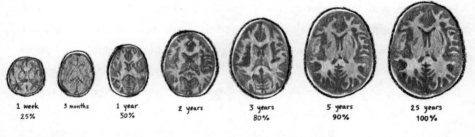

Infant Brain Development
ONE MILLION CONNECTIONS PER SECOND

| Newborn | 1 month | 6 months | 3 years | 3+ years | 3+ years |

Figure 2.

The progression of your infant's brain cells from birth, when they are sparsely connected, to incredibly dense connections at three years old. After three years of age the most frequently used brain circuits are covered in protective cells and then circuits that were not used frequently are eliminated by pruning.

| 1 week | 3 months | 1 year | 2 years | 3 years | 5 years | 25 years |
| 25% | | 50% | | 80% | 90% | 100% |

Figure 3.

The infant brain has rapid growth in the first three years. Images of relative brain size at one week, three months, one year, two years, three years, five years, twenty-five years.

appreciate how rapidly the size of the infant brain increases between one week to three months, one week to one year, one year to two years, and two years to three years. In the image, you'll also see that after three to five years old, the brain grows, but not as dramatically as it does from birth to three years.

I want parents to understand this process so they can clearly understand the opportunity for great brain flexibility and great nurturing possibilities in the first three years of life, when the infant brain is connecting like wildfire.

Both connectivity and protein growth are significantly influenced by experience.[8] This time of dense growth is the key to why the infant brain is unique. We only have access to this neuroplasticity in the first three years of life. Although the brain does maintain some plasticity as we age, so we can later build on the systems that were formed in infancy (this is the basis of most therapy), it's nothing like the plasticity we have in infancy, where we're quite literally building the foundation of the brain and the systems associated with it.[9]

In figure 2, the panels labeled "3+" represent the end of infancy. At the end of infancy, the period of rapid growth ends. The brain initiates new cell growth that works to keep and solidify the circuits that were used the most in the first three years. In the first "3+" panel, inhibitory brain cells and protective glue-like brain cells, known as the extracellular matrix, begin to grow, in order to keep the brain circuits that were most used in infancy. The growth of these cells signals the close of the season of special neuroplasticity in the infant brain. It is very hard—though not impossible, as you'll see—to change brain connections once the protective cells grow. The final panel labeled "3+" represents pruning, a brain mechanism that eliminates connections that were not used repeatedly in infancy. At the same time, at the close of infancy, the mechanisms that specialize cells by adding proteins end for many systems, like stress and neurotransmitter systems.[10]

The special season of neuroplasticity or flexibility of the infant brain is one of humanity's biggest gifts. It gives us the ability to adapt to our environment and customize our brains for the world we live in, so we can be better prepared to survive in it. Humans live on every continent, in nearly every habitat on Earth, because our infant brains can morph and adapt almost anywhere.

NURTURING EXPERIENCES GROW
RESILIENT BRAINS

Because of the highly flexible nature of infant brains, this time represents our biggest opportunity to build health into the brain. This may feel overwhelming—don't we already have more than enough pressure and responsibility, and too little support, in raising our children? Do we really need yet another approach to childrearing, as if our friend groups and social media feeds weren't flooded with tons of advice for the best way to parent? I get it; I'm a parent, too. I want to reduce your anxiety, your confusion, and your to-do list. What I want to offer you is simpler and more straightforward. It's incontrovertibly supported in neuroscience. The most powerful tool we have for building healthy brains in infancy is not perfection, or any strict rules or requirements, or any product you need to buy. It's quite simply nurture. Nurture has the tremendous power to grow a baby's brain by connecting and shaping resilient emotional brains that enjoy improved mental wellness. Inside the brain, nurture leads to resilient stress systems, resilient protein expression from DNA, and resilient emotional systems—all of which make up mental wellness.

During infancy, brain cells are called "excitatory," meaning they easily send messages to one another to build connections and build cells. Neuroscientists call communication between brain cells "firing" because the connections are so fast. The most frequently used connections during infancy are the ones that stay in the brain. As mentioned, in the process of pruning, those unused or not often used connections are eliminated. A good example of this phenomenon is in the auditory system. At birth, infants' brains can process and learn sounds from every language on the planet. If an infant is exposed to the sounds of languages with phonemes that are distinct from their native language, such as a Vietnamese infant hearing English-language sounds, their brain wires in those sounds so they can hear and produce them later in life. However, if babies don't hear non-native phonemes in early life, they are literally unable to hear and produce those sounds as adults. A native English speaker can approximate Vietnamese-language sounds, but they won't be able to hear or produce an identical phoneme unless they've been exposed to them in infancy. This is because after infancy the auditory system prunes its connections, and the unused ones are eliminated.[11]

Pioneering neuroscientists Donald Hebb and Carla Shatz famously taught us, "Neurons that fire together wire together and those that don't won't."[12] For infant brains, this means that whatever repeated consistent experiences we give them quite literally build their brain connections and brain proteins. We can help build their brains for health and wellness through consistent experiences of nurture. Think of nurture as the dense connections and proteins shown in the three-year-old panel of figure 2 or the immense brain growth shown in figure 3; it's the preventive medicine that acts to shape the brain, the mind, and mental health for generations to come.[13]

If there were specific genes or proteins in the brain that could improve mental health, scientists could develop medications to target them and successfully treat those issues, but there are no simple answers here. Instead, it's become clear that mental health arises from complicated circuits between billions of cells and trillions of connections, largely formed in infancy.[14] Until we can untangle trillions of connections, the most effective "pill" we have to improve mental health is wiring the infant brain with nurture. It's not by accident that most pharmaceuticals for mental health struggles come with the advice that they be used in conjunction with talk therapy and other healing modalities.[15] This is to help the brain's intricate connections rewire through the combination of increased neuroplasticity from medication and brain rewiring from healing experiences, because mental health is not an isolated function in our bodies. It's largely due to how well our stress system functions, or how well our brain and nervous system respond to stress and then return to states of safety. But it's also due to how our thinking brain and our emotional brain developed in infancy, to our DNA and to epigenetics (meaning genetic markers we inherit), to our neurotransmitters, and even to our gut health. Not one of these acts alone; all the parts are elegantly interconnected and together they make up mental health.

But while good mental health is a complex combination of all of the above, the beautiful gift of infancy is that nurture works in all of these areas to build resilient stress systems and emotional brains in our babies.

When infants grow up with reliably nurturing caregivers, their brains are bathed in what I call a nurture bath—the infant brain releases a cocktail of hormones and neurotransmitters beginning with oxytocin and followed by a cascade of dopamine, serotonin, endorphins, and GABA—which helps them develop resilient emotional brain circuitry.[16] When their brains soak in this nurture bath, or oxytocin cascade, their emotional systems develop great capacities to handle stress, emotion, relationships, and conflict—to be resilient. When the emotional brain is resilient, the whole brain can then devote resources to exploration, curiosity, thinking, creativity, forming relationships, and playing. All of these activities build the brain in an enriching way, at every age. With resilient emotional brains, babies, children, adolescents, and adults can spend more time being reflective, social, cognitive, creative, attentive, and flexible—the states that bring us joy, empathy, connection, and meaning. Resilient emotional brains also create healthy states of safety in our body. This manifests as a relaxed heartbeat, relaxed muscles, low inflammation, healthy blood flow to our vital organs, regulated digestive and immune systems, slower aging of the body's cells or telomeres, and high-quality restorative sleep. This safety state protects the body from illnesses like heart disease, cancer, and diabetes, as well as digestive problems and neurological disorders. Simultaneously, this safety state powerfully provides protection from anxiety and depression.

Many of us spend a lifetime in therapy or in meditation centers or yoga classes cultivating a resilient emotional brain. Over years and a lot of work (and money), we try to change our emotional brains from reactive into resilient so that we can better handle stress, emotions, and relationships, and so that we spend less time feeling anxious, depressed, lonely, and dependent on substances, and in better health. But our babies can skip this endeavor; we can build resilience in their emotional brains now to last a lifetime. Every time you lovingly hold your baby and look into their eyes, every time you guide your baby from stress to calm, and every time you lie down beside your sleeping baby, their brain releases a beautiful cascade of hormones and neurotransmitters that bathe their emotional brain in connections, proteins, and DNA for lifelong health. When you are a reliable source of nurture, your baby's brain can come to rely on bathing in those nurturing hormones. This primarily helps them grow a resilient stress system, which is the foundation of a resilient emotional brain, health, and wellness. The downstream effects of this are myriad. As you'll see in the following chapters, these nurturing hormones and neurotransmitters develop the stress system, which goes on to develop the entire emotional brain, including:

- Stress reactivity, in the amygdala, hypothalamus, hippocampus, and prefrontal cortex
- Cognition, by way of the prefrontal cortex
- Empathy and emotional intelligence, in the insula and orbitofrontal cortex
- Sociability, relationships, and parenting behavior, through oxytocin and estrogen
- Reward and addiction, through dopamine
- Neurotransmitter systems, for mood, like serotonin, norepinephrine, GABA, and glutamate
- Gut health, by supporting more diverse microbes that promote mental health

Nurture is truly an awesome gift we can give to our babies' brains. It is the source of everything we wish for our babies, the seed that grows an authentic, stable self, a center that holds, as well as ease, confidence, self-worth, and wellness. Nurture is entangled in every meaningful part of life: the people we love and who love us, our relationships, feelings, emotions, mood, health, success, and confidence. Nurture grows the parts of ourselves that carry us through adversity, lift us up, and bring us true joy. It provides access to the states of consciousness we all need and want.

Disorders Associated with Chronic Stress States

The opposite of a resilient emotional brain is a reactive brain. Many of us are sick, mentally and physically, from spending the majority of our lives in a reactive state. We are chronically in stressed states with unprocessed emotions. Rather than an oxytocin cascade, our emotional brains are often flooded in what I call cortisol cascades, composed of stressful hormones like cortisol, adrenaline, norepinephrine, and glutamate. This is an uncomfortable and painful place to live. We are anxious, depressed, addicted, scared, disconnected, dissociated, and in pain. This state gives rise to acts of selfishness, greed, aggression, and low empathy. It has deeply hurt us and our planet. Many of us also suffer from physical illnesses rooted in a reactive stress system: heart disease, cancer, autoimmune disorders, digestive disorders, and diabetes, to name a few. The way dysregulated stress systems manifest is different for everyone. In my family it looks like migraines, allergies, asthma, anxiety, depression, and alcoholism. Here are some of the issues that can emerge from living in a chronic state of stress:

- Vigilance, anxiety, depression, and other mental health struggles
- Poor sleep and insomnia
- Relationship problems
- Heart disease and stroke
- Cancer
- Diabetes
- Irritable bowel syndrome and other digestive issues
- Headaches and migraines
- Autoimmune disorders
- Allergies
- Neurological disorders
- Chronic pain

When we say nurture and positive early life experiences make an impact, we are talking about saving mental and physical lives.[17]

WHAT IS NURTURE?

When I say "nurture," it is to express an intention: deliberate time spent in a physical and emotional relationship with your baby. You respect your baby. You listen to and trust their cues and communication. Your goal is to be a supportive, reliable, and safe person for your baby. You intend to meet your baby's physical needs and to be aware of their emotions, acting as a source of calm and regulation when needed. It also means providing repair when you don't get it right. We are never seeking perfection. Repair is a part of nurture; being able to say "I'm sorry" also builds your baby's brain.

Your nurturing, attuned presence helps regulate your baby's stress and emotions. Your touch provides their brains with a nourishing oxytocin cascade. Your eye contact stimulates their thinking brain, and your words help them understand emotions. Your hugs help support their sleep. In all these ways and more, your loving presence puts your baby's brain and nervous system into a state where it is primarily bathed in hormones that favor the development of a robust emotional system, which favors the development of lifelong mental health.

Your baby needs you to be reliably present, but you're not always going to read their cues accurately or be in a space to be a regulated and attuned presence for them. We absolutely cannot and will not always get it right 100 percent of the time; no relationship is in sync all the time. There will be times you aren't paying attention, act impulsively, or react from anger, fear, or anxiety. When you don't get it right, you can repair it by apologizing, just like you would in any relationship. You don't have to be perfect, you just have to be in the relationship with your baby. Nurture transforms the brain when it happens in our relationship reliably—when our babies can rely on us to be nurturing or to repair when we are not.

Since parents and baby are part of nurture, the whole family is part of the support and change to create a nurture revolution. I'm not talking about self-sacrifice or forcing yourself to do things you find uncomfortable, miserable, or boring; there are as many ways to nurture as there are parents, and I'll help you find your unique way with lots of practical suggestions in part 2. This is nuanced work. At the heart of all nurture is the intention to be present, attuned, and close. To be a source of calm. To say, with your presence, "I'm here. I see you. You are important to me. You're safe." In a low-nurture culture that erroneously tells us to separate, limit presence and teach independence; to let them cry it out, not to spoil, to make them "self-soothe," your gentle presence is indeed a radical act.

Nurture Is Remembered

You may think that none of this will matter because babies don't remember anything from their early years, and you certainly wouldn't be alone in that thought. The idea that infants don't remember anything, so experience in infancy doesn't really matter, is a common misconception. I've heard this from even the most informed and open-minded baby specialists, such as neonatologists, pediatricians, lactation consultants, and pediatric therapists. It is time to unlearn myth number 1, *Infants don't remember anything, so experience in infancy doesn't really matter.* This belief stems from a lack of clarity around memory. Memory means that an event occurs to permanently change brain cells and brain function. There are many forms of memory, including explicit and implicit memories.[18] We tend to focus only on explicit memory, which includes autobiographical memories of conscious events in our lives—the "what," "where," "when," "who" memories. Within infancy, the brain does form autobiographical memories, so infants have memories of events while they are infants. However, as adults we experience infantile or childhood amnesia, in which years after infancy we are unable to recall events in infancy from zero to three years. This is thought to be due to a rapidly developing hippocampus in infancy.[19] It is true that most people don't seem to remember events that took place in infancy, like their first bite of food or their first step, because our long-term memories for events begin to form around age three to four years.

However, a sizable amount of memory from infancy is stored in the brain as implicit memory, and this makes up the unconscious mind.[20] The massive growth of the infant brain means that a ton of memories and critical brain areas are formed in babyhood. Lifelong memories are encoded into the structure of the stress and emotional systems, and on top of DNA by epigenetics, which are formed in infancy. In infancy the brain creates non-autobiographical implicit memories like sensory, motor, and emotional memory. So while babies may not remember discrete events from their infancy, they will remember how to eat, how to walk, and, importantly, their DNA, stress systems, and emotional systems will remember how the people they love made them feel.

I like to adapt a Maya Angelou quote to illustrate this point: "[Babies] will forget what you said, [babies] will forget what you did, but [babies] will never forget how you made them feel." Babies do not forget how they were nurtured. We may have limited recollection of early life, but nurturing experiences change our DNA, stress systems, and emotional systems and stay in our brains. So in fact, the reality is that the infant brain has a huge capacity for memory. We can best support our babies when we understand how powerful this period of life truly is.

Your presence, relationship, communication, play, laughs, and responsiveness with your baby in their first three years are transformative to the brain they will have for the rest of their life. As I will remind you often, you do not need to be perfect. Any amount you nurture benefits your baby. And repair is always possible for those inevitable moments (or days, or periods) when anger, frustration, or busy schedules get the best of us; in fact, repair is an important aspect of nurture—it helps build resilience. Your baby needs you to be your wonderful imperfect self. They benefit when you have intentions to be nurturing, and they benefit when you offer repair when it's needed.

Nurture Is Hard Work, and It Matters

This gift of flexibility in infancy also makes human babies extremely vulnerable. Human infants require the most parental care of any species on Earth. Nurture is hard work. The constant needs of infants can be overwhelming. I have certainly felt this way. On top of this, many of us did not have our own needs met as babies and children, and it is new territory to be in a responsive, secure relationship.

So when you feel challenged by nurture, this is why: You are doing something profound. You are doing tremendous work building a brain, the most complex thing in existence besides perhaps the universe. You are building countless brain cells and receptors in your baby's brain with your brain. This is intense, deep work and something to truly be proud of and celebrate.

Part of nurture is taking advantage of the neuroplasticity in our new parenting brains and taking care of ourselves as parents. Nurturing a baby is not meant to be done by one person—we need our partners, family, friends, and professional caregivers to take part in our baby's lifelong well-being. When one person is doing most of the baby care, we want this person to be supported and nurtured by others as well. There are two vital layers of support for a baby. The first layer is the mother or primary caregiver(s) who takes care of the baby, while the second layer consists of those who take care of the mother or primary caregiver(s). Both are necessary yet often the second layer is lacking.

I want you to know that your hard work of nurturing matters. It is everything to your baby. It is brain-shaping and life-changing. Your child will benefit from your parenting throughout babyhood, childhood, adolescence, adulthood, and maybe as a parent themselves one day. Even more powerfully, your nurture will benefit your potential grandchildren, great-grandchildren, and so on. Nurturing one baby profoundly nurtures the future. Psychologist Louis Cozolino writes, "We are not the survival of the fittest. We are the survival of the nurtured."[21] The future is survival of the nurtured.

Chapter 2

BABIES NEED TO BORROW YOUR BRAIN

Picture an infant, a child, an adolescent, an adult, and a parent all relaxing on a couch together. Someone pushes a button and a speaker suddenly blares loud music. While each individual experiences the exact same sound, very different circuits are activated in each of their brains, because they are all at distinct stages of life. Their reactions might look something like this: The infant, whose brain circuits can't interpret the sound or regulate stress, vocalizes to seek out a caregiver for safety and to help regulate their stress. The child, whose brain circuits have the knowledge that the noise is not harmful, covers their ears as they have learned the motor skill to block the noise. The adolescent's brain is wired to seek out risk taking, so they might love loud songs and turn up the volume even higher. The adult, whose brain finds the music aversive, gets up to lower the volume. Finally, the parent's brain is connected for childcare, so they go to their infant and protect the infant's little ears from the loud sound, and then likely go lower the volume if need be. This isn't a personality test; their reactions differ because the connections in their brains differ. What it begins to show is how drastically different our brains are at different times in our development.

The differences among these reactions matter for parenting because infants' brains have specific needs in order to thrive. While the child, the adolescent, and the adult are capable of managing their own response to the loud music, the infant looks to their caregiver to assure them that all is well, to make sense of the sound they hear, and to calm them—literally to shut off their stress response by soothing them. We also see that the caregiver's brain is wired to respond and protect, which we'll explore in chapter 4.

Because of the way the human brain develops, during infancy, babies cannot manage their stress and emotions on their own. When adults lend babies their brain and are nurturing, the infant brain bathes in that cocktail of nurturing hormones and neurotransmitters, beginning with oxytocin release and followed by dopamine, serotonin, endorphins, and GABA.[1] When infants' brains can rely on their caregivers to reliably support the oxytocin cascade, they can grow resilience that lasts for life. If infants lack social interactions and are left alone with stress, the feeling is unbearably painful and their brain is bathed in the cortisol cascade of stressful hormones, as we discussed in the previous chapter. If this happens repeatedly for long periods, their brain circuits can be influenced for life to be reactive—wired to have an overactive or underactive stress system. The outcome depends on the age when stress happens and what kind of stressor occurs.[2] Low nurture leads to wiring for vulnerability to anxiety, depression, hypervigilance, mental health struggles, and more.[3]

This means that babies need reliable access to you, a parent or caregiver, for what I call an external emotional brain; they need a caregiver who can reliably regulate their stress, support their emotions, and meet their needs. In order to build the healthiest brain, your baby needs to borrow your mature brain functions during the important early years of their life. The infant brain develops in the relationship with the adult brain. It borrows the adult brain to develop regulation, sociability, cognition, and health.[4]

If you've ever held space for a toddler who needed you during a meltdown, this might sound obvious—but the prevailing low-nurture parenting of our time encourages us to put unrealistic expectations concerning independence and separation, managing emotions, and rational thinking, among other things, on infants. These emotional processes can only be supported by complex brain circuits that infants simply do not yet have. Until they do, they need to use yours.

THE THREE STAGES OF INFANT BRAIN DEVELOPMENT

The infant brain develops from the bottom to the top in three stages that relate to nurturing mental health. Survival brain circuits, or the brain stem, are at the bottom of the brain and develop first, beginning in pregnancy and into the first year of life. Emotional brain circuits, or the limbic system, make up the center of the brain and develop extensively in pregnancy and infancy up to age three. Emotional brain circuits become especially flexible again in the periods of adolescence and in parenthood. Thinking brain circuits, or the prefrontal cortex, are at the top of the brain and develop throughout infancy and all the way up to age twenty-five and beyond (see figure 4).[5]

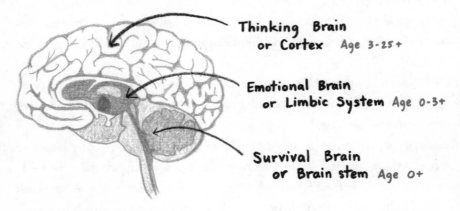

Thinking Brain or Cortex Age 3-25+

Emotional Brain or Limbic System Age 0-3+

Survival Brain or Brain stem Age 0+

Figure 4.

The survival brain is developed at birth and helped by nurture. The emotional brain develops between zero and three years and is critically shaped by nurture. The thinking brain develops between three and twenty-five years and is shaped by the emotional brain.

The infant brain's unique composition includes functioning survival brain circuits, immature and developing emotional brain circuits, including the stress system, and emerging thinking brain circuits. The immaturity of emotional and thinking brain circuits is our opportunity to grow nurture into the brain. In the first three years of life, genetics and experience guide brain cells in these circuits to connect, which matures the brain and the abilities of an individual.

All of these brain circuits develop in relationship to one another—survival brain circuits are like a building manual to nurture emotional brain circuits. Emotional brain circuits are a foundation on which the thinking brain is built. Thinking brain circuits are shaped throughout infancy and only begin to exert regulation of the stress system in the brain after infancy. They continue to develop through childhood, adolescence, and adulthood up to twenty-five years old, and throughout are highly influenced by the abilities of emotional brain circuits. Listening to the survival brain builds a resilient emotional brain, and resilience in the emotional brain creates a strong foundation for the thinking brain to develop.[6]

While each part is interdependent on the others, it's emotional brain circuits, and specifically the stress system, to which I want to pay particular attention, because its development is crucial for lifelong mental health. To build a strong brain to support a successful mind, experience in infancy must be attuned to the development of this part of the brain. Nurture in infancy primarily interacts with the stress system. Parents are an integral part of their baby's stress system, specifically by lending their brain to their baby in connection, to regulate stress and in sleep. When an infant's stress system is regulated by nurture, it leads to transformation of the stress system directly, which in turn transforms the development of all other areas in the emotional brain, like DNA, epigenetics, social systems, reward systems, neurotransmitter systems, and cognitive systems.

By primarily targeting the stress system, nurture in infancy builds the cells, receptors, and circuits in the entire emotional brain for resilience. Knowledge of the infant brain is critical to confidently understanding what babies need and how we can give them what they need. When we know about the infant brain, we can trust our intuition to be responsive and be confident that our nurture is powerful. The infant brain is grossly misunderstood, and this has led to very unrealistic expectations for babies and shame for parents. Understanding the three phases of infant brain development helps us see how we play a role in growing an infant's emotional brain circuits through the stress system, toward resilience and mental health. This understanding restores human rights and dignity to babies, sets neurobiologically normal expectations, and celebrates parents. We can only expect infants to use the brain circuits that they have developed.

Survival Brain Circuits

The first phase is the development of survival brain circuits. When you first meet your newborn, their survival brain circuits, centered in the brain stem, are the most highly developed and functioning part of their brain. The cells in this part of the brain are well connected into complex circuits at birth compared to other brain areas where cells are not well connected. Babies are born with well-developed survival circuits to equip them for two things: to sustain life and to be in relationships. Infants' brain circuits can successfully direct their body to sustain life. To breathe air, pump blood, feed, digest, eliminate waste, and sleep. (Surprise! Babies know how to sleep, but we'll get to that later.) These bodily functions are one half of what infants need to stay alive and thrive. The other half is to be in intimate relationships with parents and caregivers. Thanks to their survival brain circuits, infants can participate in relationships with parents and caregivers by orienting to loved ones' smells or sounds or faces, making eye contact, seeking closeness, and communicating. (Yes, even newborn babies have many ways of communicating, and we will learn to speak baby later on.) Survival brain circuits keep babies alive physically and invite us in to nurture and enliven them emotionally in relationships. Both the physical and emotional are vital. All infant communication is valid and important. Babies need us to respond to it. When we listen and respond to the cues from survival brain circuits, we nurture the next phase of brain development: the emotional brain circuits.

Survival brain circuits function at birth but also continue their development in early life. For example, infants can breathe, circulate blood, and sleep at birth, but patterns of breathing, heartbeat, and sleep become more regular with age. The development of survival brain circuits is known as hardwiring; genetics heavily guides the development of survival brain circuits, but experience with caregivers can help this process as it happens. Through nurture, caregivers stabilize and regulate survival brain circuits in infants. Infants breathe better, pump blood better, sleep better, and absorb nutrients better when they are held by caregivers. While experience may not hugely influence the development of connections in survival circuits, it helps them carry out their functions until they fully develop.

I work with many families who believe that they need to teach their newborns to do things that work against the biology of survival brain circuits. For example, many parents believe they need to teach babies to lie alone in a bassinet in order to "create independence," or to teach babies to stop crying by ignoring their cries. Wanting to be close and held is what your baby's survival biology needs in order to be regulated. Separation from caregivers is a threat to a baby's survival and activates their brain circuitry to cry or cling. Compared to the warm, soothing, and dynamic presence of a parent where all body systems are regulated, the bassinet or sitting alone is a static quiet lonely unregulated place—and many infants don't like it at all and will signal their stress by vocalizing every time. You can't train a baby's survival system to stop having needs and cueing for relationship.

Your baby's survival circuits tell you, "Hold me, look into my eyes, talk to me, keep me close, regulate my stress, help me with my emotions, help me with sleep, and I will explore and come back to you when I need you." When parents can understand and hear this communication clearly with no distortions and know that it is biologically normal and beneficial to listen to the survival circuits, then nurturing follows.

Emotional Brain Circuits

The second phase of infant brain development is the development of emotional brain circuits, which begin to grow in the womb and continue to develop for the first three years of life—as intensely as up to one million connections per second in speed. Emotional brain circuits are the star of the show of infancy, the prime place where nurture transforms the brain to lay the foundation for lifelong health. Infancy is defined as zero to three years largely because this is the season when the emotional brain is immature, developing, and incredibly sensitive to experience. When you respond to your baby's survival circuits unconditionally, you are doing the life-changing, brain-building work of building resilient emotional brain circuits.

Emotional brain circuits are built from DNA and epigenetics and include the stress system, social systems, reward systems, neurotransmitter systems, and cognitive systems. We'll explore DNA and epigenetics in depth in chapter 3. Emotional brain circuits process how we perceive and respond to stress, our moods, our emotions, our thinking, and our relationships—put together, emotional brain circuits make up our mental health. Experience shapes how emotional brain circuits are formed and how they connect with later-developing thinking brain circuits.

Experiences in infancy critically shape emotional brain circuits that underlie and shape the development of the entire brain, nervous system, mind, and body of an individual. The most extreme example of the effects of nurture on the emotional brain comes from orphans who experienced a total absence of nurture. They were fed, clothed, changed, and bathed, but spent the whole day and night in a crib in a state of emotional neglect. One might think that babies in this situation would cry all day, but the opposite was the case: These babies were silent. Their needs were ignored so a survival mechanism to shut down was activated and they stopped signaling for help. This total lack of nurture profoundly shaped their stress systems to be blunted, their emotional brains to be highly susceptible to mental health struggles and cognitive impairments, and their brains to be smaller and with fewer connections compared to the brains of typically developing children. This type of care led to poor impulse control, social withdrawal, problems with coping and regulating emotions, low self-esteem, tics, tantrums, stealing and self-punishment, intellectual impairments, and low academic achievement. Many of these babies were adopted, and then received nurture. The closer to birth they were adopted, the better their emotional system was able to rewire; when adopted after two or three years old, the season of nurture was over and it was much more difficult to rewire the emotional system through nurture.[7] However, if these babies are adopted and nurtured by adoptive parents throughout their childhood and adolescence, their brain and stress system are able to undergo repair in adolescence.[8]

Emotional brain circuits are "softwired" in infancy and early life. This means that genetics and experience have a fundamental impact on forming complex brain circuits. After the season of nurture, emotional brain circuits become much more hardwired, or difficult to change with experience. This is why experience in infancy matters and lasts forever. Nurture gets baked in during infancy, and you can't add the sugar after the cake is baked. Emotional brain circuits have higher neuroplasticity again in adolescence and in matrescence or patrescence—when we become parents. These are two other opportunities where we might get special access to alter the brain circuits that are formed in infancy.

The primary way nurture acts is in the brain's stress system. Infants need to borrow their parents' mature brains to manage their stress states and boost their safety states when they're awake and asleep. Daytime and nighttime nurture lowers stress hormones like the cortisol cascade and releases safety hormones like the oxytocin cascade. This combination of low stress hormones and high safety hormones is the nurture bath that goes on to direct most other parts of the emotional brain to develop resiliency. When nurture acts in the stress system in infancy, the stress system itself builds resilience, DNA is influenced, neurotransmitter systems develop to support mental health, and gut health develops to support overall health. The infant survival brain tells us when babies need help with their stress systems. You'll know your baby feels stress when they cling to you to keep you close or they cry for you to bring you closer. You can trust your baby's need for closeness; they're telling you that they need your help to calm and regulate, communicate, sleep, or to care for a physical need.

Another way nurture acts is in the social systems in the brain. Infants need to borrow their parents' mature brains for social interactions like face-to-face communication and emotional learning. Social interactions in infancy build social brain circuits and stress regulation circuits in the prefrontal cortex. Emotional learning builds emotional circuits in the brain so that babies learn to be comfortable experiencing emotions. The infant survival brain gives us cues to know when babies are open to social interaction and emotional learning. When babies are social, they look into our eyes, babble or coo or talk, make noises, gesture, move their bodies, and make faces at us. They are working hard to be in a social relationship. When we reciprocate these interactions, we build up their social systems. When we see our babies experiencing emotions, we can help them navigate their feelings, which also builds up their social systems.

In infants, emotional brain circuits are immature, unconnected, and built by constantly learning from experience. This means that infants are not able to handle their own stress or emotions. The relationship experienced between the infant and their caregivers, through thousands of interactions, develops and connects the brain cells to physically shape the structure and function of the stress system and thereby emotional brain circuits. The most important impact a parent will have on their child is the formation of the stress system to shape emotional brain circuits.

Since emotional brain circuits are not even close to fully developed in infants, and infants clearly need to regulate their stress and emotions often, they need a way to accomplish emotional regulation. Amazingly, the presence of a caregiver provides the infant with the emotional input they need. When the presence of a parent or caregiver brings an infant from a state of stress to a state of calm it is called social buffering or co-regulation. Co-regulation is the only route to calm for infants. We unequivocally cannot expect infants to accomplish emotional regulation or stress recovery on their own, what is commonly known as "self-soothing" or self-regulation. The brain circuits that do this job are in the thinking brain and they don't work yet—infants absolutely need a caregiver to do the job. We must lend infants our adult brain's ability for regulation.

Unconditional access to an external emotional brain is a necessary and integral part of a baby's biology until they grow their own. The circuitry of their emotional brain just begins to mature around three years old, but it is still quite immature, and it strengthens more and more over time. Each individual child has their own developmental trajectory and the intensity and frequency of need for an external emotional brain varies from person to person. There is no set age or prescription for when this will happen. Just like everything we will discuss in this book, we need to get this information from our children. When they need regulation, they will send out cues from their survival brain, and when they can regulate on their own, they will do it on their own. Nurture is trusting the communication from our baby's survival and emotional brain circuits and trusting our abilities to regulate our children.

Access to an external emotional brain is the essential fundamental human right for infants. The ability to access regulation with the infant brain shapes who we are in the most important ways. The need for regulation from others is universal, and it is what infants are focused on and preoccupied with. When a baby can't engage a caregiver in communication or get help to lower their stress or manage emotions or have help with sleep, it is excruciating and intolerable. Babies then create strategies in an attempt to manage the lack of help with their stress. Not getting help with stress leads to the need for survival mechanisms that help with pain at the time but can hurt their mental health and their relationships as they get older.

If babies are nurtured and have a reliable external emotional brain, their brain develops to have strong self-regulation mechanisms. Their brain also develops circuitry to seek out co-regulation from others when it is needed in life. Self-regulation and co-regulation are both very healthy ways to handle stress that promote mental health. Seeking out others when stressed is known as a secure attachment style, which develops in parallel to a resilient stress system.[9]

If babies find that access to caregivers as an external brain is unreliable, their brain can become hypervigilant as a survival mechanism.[10] They become wired to watch, observe, and stay close to their caregiver with the goal of being able to predict when the caregiver might give them access to the vital regulation input they need. This is at the expense of feeling safe and secure enough to focus on exploration, play, and creativity. As a result, the brain bathes in stress and can develop in a way that is reactive and hard to self-regulate. It can develop circuitry toward hypervigilance in other important relationships as well. Difficulty self-regulating combined with hypervigilance in relationships often leads to difficulties with mental health. Hypervigilance toward others when stressed is known as an insecure anxious attachment style, which develops in parallel to a reactive stress system.[11]

If babies experience a caregiver or an external emotional brain that rejects them, and they can't access stress regulation at all, their brain can develop a survival mechanism of avoidance of the caregiver and dissociating or shutting down from stress.[12] This might look like the baby avoiding the caregiver and acting like everything is fine when they are in fact stressed. This is so that the caregiver will like that the baby doesn't have needs and will approach them with their external brain. The brain bathes in stress and can develop a reactive stress system where it is hard to self-regulate. It can develop circuitry toward avoidance in other important relationships, which is not an effective strategy to manage stress and mental health. Avoidance toward others when stressed is known as an insecure avoidant attachment style, which develops in parallel to a reactive stress system.[13]

Babies can have different caregivers who respond to them differently, and can develop more than one way of seeking out co-regulation when stressed. However, having one reliably responsive caregiver or external brain in their life is enough to build the stress system toward resilience.

The need for an external brain is typically the highest in infancy, and reduces throughout childhood, adolescence, and adulthood as the thinking brain matures, but the truth is that this need never fully resolves. We don't expect humans to never need other humans. Adults of all ages seek out a loved one in times of stress and get great comfort and co-regulation through close relationships. Humans are social creatures, and our minds connect and work together. Humans do poorly in isolation because we calm and regulate each other. We need co-regulation to handle strong emotions, both positive and negative, throughout our lives. You might have sought out your own parents for comfort into adulthood, because even though your emotional brain circuits are quite developed, one can always use the extra boost of parental presence.

Not only does the parent, an external emotional brain, act as replacement brain circuitry for infants, but the quality and quantity of the external emotional brain—the parent or caregiver's own co-regulation process—acts to teach the infant's brain about the world and shape the infant's emotional brain circuits. If an infant has a reliable caregiver or reliable external emotional brain, their own emotional brain circuits grow resilient, which also influences their cognitive brain to be exploratory and curious. If an infant has an unpredictable or inattentive caregiver or lacks an external emotional brain, their own emotional brain circuits can become reactive, which also influences their thinking brain to be focused on threats.

The myth that *responding to cries spoils an infant or teaches an infant to be dependent* is one of the biggest untruths of our current low-nurture culture. Let's clear this up directly: Paying attention to your infant's communication and cries does not spoil them or make them dependent. Here we unlearn myth 2. Replace it with the knowledge that <u>responding reliably strengthens a baby's emotional brain circuits, helps them grow confidently independent, and gives them the gift of stress regulation for life</u>. In fact, if a parent responds to cries sometimes but not other times in an effort to make their child not spoiled and independent, they might influence their child's emotional circuits to be less regulated and need more external regulation in the future. In this way, the effort to force a child to be independent can make them more dependent and potentially clingier and more anxious or defiant and avoidant. Developing a strong emotional brain in infancy is vital and parenting is absolutely fundamental to the growth and development of your child's emotional brain circuits.

The Thinking Brain

The third phase is the development of thinking brain circuits. These circuits are distributed in complex networks in the brain and centered in the prefrontal cortex. Similar to emotional brain circuits, cells in thinking brain circuits are mostly unconnected at birth and form complex circuits and connections via experience. The thinking brain's growth period begins just after the emotional brain, around three years, and its development depends on how emotional brain circuits have developed to function.

Self-regulation skills begin to emerge after the first three years of infancy and continue to mature up to twenty-five years of age. These are the brain circuits that babies need to borrow from you. Thinking brain circuits in the prefrontal cortex develop after emotional brain circuits and are influenced by how the emotional circuits develop. When the stress system develops resilience in infancy, thinking brain circuits can also grow to be resilient, flexible, and healthy. They can grow great abilities for self-regulation, curiosity, planning, thinking, creativity, problem solving, and emotional intelligence.[14]

Thinking brain circuits are responsible for many complex processes, including regulating powerful emotions, developing personality traits, future planning, complex decision making, social behavior, complex thinking, and complex planning. The tasks performed by thinking brain circuits are generally called executive functions.

Thinking brain circuits are softwired, meaning that genetics and experience shape the circuits that make up the thinking brain. However, unlike survival brain circuits and the emotional brain circuits, thinking brain circuits do not become quite as rigid or hardwired. They maintain the ability to change throughout life, through neuroplasticity. To create change here requires focused, repeated work.

The development of emotional brain circuits has a huge impact on how thinking brain circuits work. A resilient emotional brain coexists with high activity and thinking power in the thinking brain. A reactive emotional brain shuts off the thinking brain, making it difficult for it to function. Nurtured resilient emotional brain circuits will support a powerful thinking brain and create a regulated brain. Imagine yourself in a high-stress situation, like being called into your boss's office. A resilient emotional brain circuit would feel the stress or threat—"Am I going to get fired? Did I do something wrong?"—and then the thinking brain will quickly come online to regulate you—"I can handle whatever my boss has to say." Low-nurtured emotional brain circuits will be influenced to be more stressed and reactive, and less able to support the thinking brain. Specifically, when emotional brain circuits are activated, thinking brain circuits are inhibited and unable to work. This might look like hiding in the bathroom and avoiding your boss all week. It's like you get stuck in the threat state.

We need regulated emotional brain circuits to give our thinking brain opportunities to function. If the emotional brain develops to be adaptive, the cognitive brain can develop complex and flexible functions that support learning, curiosity, and relationships. If the emotional brain develops to be reactive, the thinking brain can be impaired, and its functions become limited.

Thinking brain circuits have many important connections with emotional brain circuits, and the circuits function together intimately. When emotional brain circuits are regulated, the two areas are in balance: Both are used for most tasks. However, when emotional brain circuits get highly activated by an emotion, it creates a brain imbalance and can shut off the thinking brain and impair all aspects of thinking.[15] If emotional brain circuits develop to be adaptive, they can quickly restore the brain balance, recover from an emotional experience, and thinking brain circuits can come back online quickly. If emotional brain circuits develop to be reactive, they can't restore brain balance or recover from an emotional experience quickly, and it may take a long time for thinking brain circuits to come back online, if at all. For example, imagine taking a test that you have studied well for. You answer all of the questions quickly and efficiently thanks to the balanced activity in your emotional brain and thinking brain. Then you see a question that is really, really hard. You immediately become fearful and launch a stress response. With adaptive emotional brain circuits, you can recover from stress relatively fast and start working out the question. With reactive emotional brain circuits, you may panic until your time is up, never getting your brain in a state to think clearly.

Since thinking brain circuits are so interdependent with emotional brain circuits, the best strategy to achieve a regulated brain is to first develop an adaptive emotional brain in infancy or through therapy after infancy. With an adaptive emotional brain, the thinking brain is free to carry out all of its thinking, decision making, and intelligence operations. Mental wellness is all about balance between emotional brain circuits and cognitive brain circuits.

ZOOMING IN ON THE EMOTIONAL BRAIN: THE NEUROBIOLOGY OF THE STRESS SYSTEM

The foundation of the emotional brain is called the stress system, which includes the parts of your brain that control your body's stress response. It is responsible for your brain and body being in a stress state or a safety state. It's necessary to dig a little deeper into the stress system to show just how crucial it is for good mental health, how important the emotional brain is, how nurture in infancy supports the development of a functioning, resilient stress response for life, and how we can rewire our stress systems as we become parents. I'll try not to veer too far into jargon.

The neurobiology of our stress system is our foundation for mental wellness, physical health, connected relationships, and success. When it grows to be regulated, we benefit by living more in safety states, recovering from stress efficiently, and enjoying mental and physical health. When it grows to be reactive, we suffer by living more in stress states, experiencing slow recovery from stress and vulnerability to mental and physical health struggles.

A regulated stress system is a healthy stress system. It is the root of all health and thriving: brain health, mind health, heart health, liver health, foot health—everything health. Conversely, a reactive stress system is the root of all illness. A reactive stress system can be experienced as either a chronically elevated or a chronically suppressed stress system, depending on the intensity of early life stress and its timing. Both elevated and suppressed stress systems are linked to mental and physical illness.

The fundamental brain circuits of the stress system are centralized specifically in the amygdala, the hypothalamus, the hippocampus, and the prefrontal cortex. As parents, it's important to understand what each of these brain areas does in the stress system, because when we nurture and respond to our babies, we are physically building all of these fundamental systems in the brain. When I see a baby being nurtured, I think, "This is so exciting; their amygdala is so happy right now." When I see a baby's stress or communication being rejected, I think, "I'm so worried; their amygdala is on fire right now." Furthermore, as parents, our infancies shaped these structures in our own brains, and they continue to impact our lives and our parenting. We can boost our mental health and our parenting approach in adulthood by practicing techniques that target many of these structures to influence their activity toward a more regulated stress system (see chapter 9).

An intact adult stress system has three basic steps: an alarm, a gas pedal, and a brake pedal (see figure 5). The amygdala is like **an alarm** for the stress system. It receives information from our senses that there is an external threat in the environment, or from our mind or body that there is an internal threat. It says, "HEY! Stop everything, there is a threat here!" Nurture in infancy develops the amygdala alarm to be adaptive, sound an alarm to pertinent threats, and grow adaptive connections to the thinking brain. When you are nurturing, you are directly building the amygdala.[16]

The hypothalamus is like a **gas pedal** for the stress system. It releases stress signals like cortisol and adrenaline to the brain and body, so we are mentally and physically ready to respond to a threat. It says, "OKAY! Transform the brain and body into a stress state to respond to the threat!" Nurture in infancy leads to epigenetic changes to grow the hypothalamus to release adaptive amounts of stress signals.[17]

The hippocampus and the prefrontal cortex function like a **brake pedal** for the stress system. When appropriate, they inhibit the amygdala and hypothalamus to slow and stop the stress response. When stopped, the stress system becomes regulated and the brain and body go into a safety state. They say, "HEY! The threat is gone, stop the stress, back to safety." Nurture in infancy grows these areas to be efficient at stopping stress.[18]

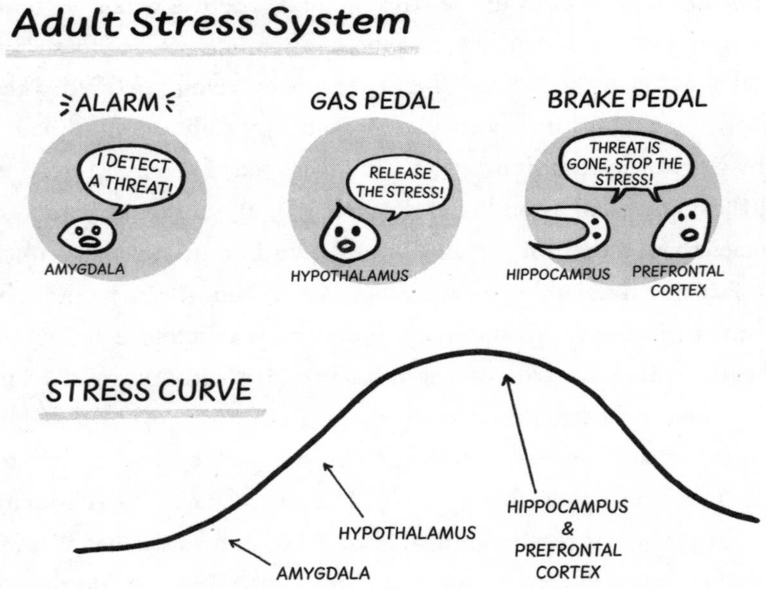

Adult Stress System

Figure 5.
The adult stress system.

Babies, with their unique and special brains, have an immature and developing stress system (see figure 6). Babies have a functioning yet developing amygdala **alarm** that can say, "HEY! Stop everything, there is a threat here!" They have a functioning yet developing hypothalamus **gas pedal** that can say, "OKAY! Get into a stress state to respond to the threat!" But babies do not have a **brake pedal** in their stress system. Their hippocampus and prefrontal cortex are developing and are not able to stop stress.[19]

So how do babies stop their stress and return to a safety state? Nurture. The emotional and sensory experience and calm presence of a regulated parent or caregiver is the missing piece of the infant stress system. When they are nurtured, an oxytocin cascade releases and acts on the infant's stress system to stop stress and simultaneously build the system toward resilience. Nurture also provides the stressed infant brain a regulated calm adult brain that can mirror the calm state to the infant. Infants need nurture to recover their stress system and get into safety states—nurture acts in the moment to stop the stress system. This is how you function as an external brain to your baby. You are an absolutely necessary and integral part of their stress system.[20] You can unlearn myth 3, *Babies can and need to learn to self-soothe, which means go from a state of high stress to a state of safety on their own.* Replace it with: <u>Babies cannot self-soothe because they do not have the brain parts to do so until way beyond infancy.</u>

Parents and caregivers are also an external brain to babies by buffering the stress response. Amazingly, in babies, nurture reduces activation of the stress system. When young babies are lovingly held by parents, oxytocin inhibits the stress system, and the amygdala is silenced, which prevents the stress system from getting activated. Infants don't have stress responses when close to parents. They can cry and show distress, but the oxytocin that nurture gives them buffers the stress response internally.

When infants are flooded by stress and no one helps, their bodies eventually go into a freeze state where they are quiet and still, and then a dissociative state because they cannot tolerate the intensity of the stress, and finally a sleep state. This is an advantageous survival mechanism in

Baby Stress System Alone

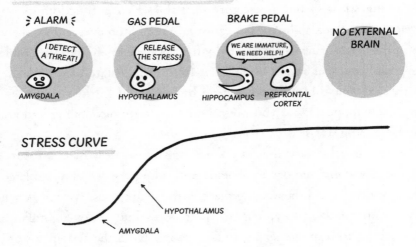

Baby Stress System with External Brain

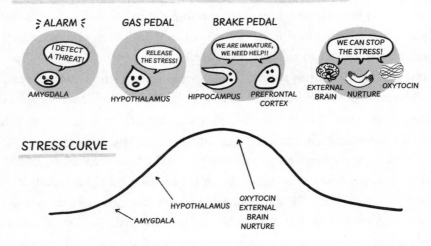

Figure 6.

The baby stress system alone and with an external brain.

evolutionary terms, because if a baby cries and no one is there to help, they will be more likely to survive any predators if they shut down and sleep. However, when this is a repeated and regular experience it does influence the stress system to grow to be reactive.[21]

In addition to being the only way to stop stress for babies, parents and caregivers are an external brain by interacting with babies. When we provide a regulated nurturing presence, communicate with babies, and support their exploration, we grow their prefrontal cortex and future capacity to stop stress with self-regulation.

Critically, nurture does not only act in the moment as an external emotional brain to prevent or regulate the stress system in infants. Nurture, through thousands of experiences with a calm, regulated, and loving external brain in infancy, sets the conditions and builds the efficiency of the stress system that babies will rely on for life. Nurture in infancy leads to changes in the amygdala, hypothalamus, hippocampus, and prefrontal cortex to create an adaptive alarm signal and strong brake pedal for the stress system so that stress states are brief and efficient.[22] The efficiency of the stress system built in infancy is what underlies resilience or vulnerability to mental health struggles. The efficiency of the stress system becomes the foundation for all brain growth that comes after infancy.

Imagine that the stress system in infants floats and incubates in a "brain bath." There are hormones in the brain bath that fundamentally shape how the stress system develops (see figure 7). Parents and caregivers influence what hormones are in the brain bath. We build our baby's brain by orchestrating the hormones their brain floats in when we connect, support stress, and nurture sleep. When the infant brain is bathing in nurturing hormones like oxytocin in states of safety and in states of stress, it is influenced to grow to be resilient. When stress rises and falls with the help of a parent, the brain also grows to be resilient. When the infant brain is incubating in low-nurturing hormones, like low oxytocin, in states of safety and states of stress, it is influenced to grow to be reactive. When stress rises and remains high for a long time, the brain is influenced to grow reactive. These hormonal brain baths direct the developing neurobiology of the amygdala, hypothalamus, hippocampus, and prefrontal cortex on how to grow, as well as neurotransmitter systems, cognitive systems, the gut brain axis, and DNA (see figure 8).

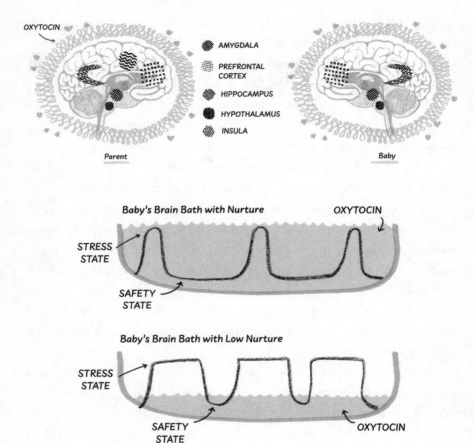

Figure 7.

Top: When parents provide nurture, the parent brain and the baby brain get bathed in oxytocin cascades. **Middle:** When infants' brains are bathed in nurturing hormones like oxytocin, their brains grow resilience in both safety states and stress states. Their stress hormones rise and fall quickly, an ideal pattern to promote the growth of the stress system toward resilience. **Bottom:** When infants' brains are bathed in low-nurturing hormones like low oxytocin, their brains grow toward reactivity in both safety and stress states. Their stress hormones rise and stay high, which is not ideal to promote the growth of the stress system.

Baby Brain in Nurture Bath

Stress System

 AMYGDALA ADAPTIVE

 HYPOTHALAMUS ADAPTIVE

 HIPPOCAMPUS HIGH STOP RECEPTORS

 PREFRONTAL CORTEX
HIGH ABILITY TO INHIBIT STRESS

Cognitive Systems

 FLEXIBLE, CURIOUS, EXPLORATORY
SUPPORT RESILIENCE & FUTURE NURTURING

Gut Health

 DIVERSE MICROBES

DNA

EPIGENETICS
that support RESILIENCE
& FUTURE NURTURING

Baby Brain in Low-Nurture Bath

 AMYGDALA HYPERALERT

 HYPOTHALAMUS HIGH STRESS RELEASE

 HIPPOCAMPUS LOW STOP RECEPTORS

 PREFRONTAL CORTEX
LOW ABILITY TO INHIBIT STRESS

 RIGID, VIGILANT, NARROW
SUPPORT REACTIVTY & LOW FUTURE NURTURING

 LOW-DIVERSITY MICROBES

 EPIGENETICS
that support REACTIVITY
& LOW FUTURE NURTURING

Figure 8.

When babies' brains are bathed in a nurture bath, it influences the development of the stress system, neurotransmitter systems, cognitive systems, gut health, and DNA toward resilience. When babies' brains are bathed in hormones from low nurture, the systems are developed toward reactivity and vulnerability.

When a caregiver acts as an external emotional brain as much as possible, they are directly bathing the developing amygdala, hypothalamus, hippocampus, and prefrontal cortex in a nurture bath. In a bath of nurturing signals, all of the circuitry in the stress system is influenced to grow to be resilient and adaptive.

BEING IN A RELATIONSHIP WITH YOUR BABY

All of this amazing development starts with a pretty simple task: listening and responding to your baby. Their survival brain will tell you what your baby needs, primarily that they need to be close to you, or want to communicate with you, or want to sleep near you, or as they grow past the newborn phase and into toddlerhood they'll need your help with their emotions and exploration. When you understand the communication of the survival brain and offer your baby your mature brain to help them feel calm and make it safe for them to feel their emotions, you build the emotional brain and stress system to be resilient. Resilience in the emotional brain then lays the foundation for all of the complex circuits in the thinking brain to grow resilient, too. The result of this nurtured development is essential for our babies' mental health and freedom.[23]

Chapter 3

NURTURED NATURE

When Michelle was newly pregnant, she reached out to me, concerned that her child would inherit the mental health issues that ran in her family. Her grandmother Lorraine remembered hearing her own mother crying in bed at night, overwhelmed by the strain of mothering in poverty. A few years later, Lorraine was forced to drop out of high school to care for her younger siblings after her mother died. When Lorraine had her first baby, Michelle's mother, Violet, Lorraine was sent away to an institution for three months due to a "nervous condition." Michelle herself struggled with depression and anxiety for much of her life. She'd been in therapy since high school and went on and off antidepressants several times. "I don't want my baby to deal with this, too, but I feel like the odds are stacked against her," she told me.

I work with many families like Michelle's—families who are deeply concerned about their child inheriting the mental health struggles they or their ancestors had. I know it can feel overwhelming. As I shared earlier, I am not an exception to this reality, as my family has a long history of intergenerational trauma and mental health issues. Frankly, someone who does not have mental health challenges or trauma in their family of origin is the exception, not the rule.

Bathing our babies' brains in nurturing hormones builds a resilient emotional brain, but what if we inherit poor mental health through our DNA? When Michelle and I began working together I asked her to do an exercise with me. Together we imagined her baby's brain growing like a seed planted in the earth. First, we looked at all the trauma, mental illness, and struggle in her baby's ancestry; this is like the seed's roots. Then I showed her the power of nurture to interact with this ancestry to change course toward resilience. All the snuggles and kisses; every time Michelle held, talked to, attuned with her baby; every time their eyes met—every single drop of nurture is like providing that seed with good soil conditions, regular, indirect sunlight, and nourishing rain that can help her child grow a healthy brain, whatever legacies she may inherit. While DNA is always present, nurture interacts with DNA in a number of critical ways, giving us significant power over the outcomes of gene expression.

In the season for nurture, we aren't just building our babies' brains with nurturing experience; we also have a huge influence on the expression of the genes involved in mental health. In other words, when we nurture our babies, we influence their DNA. We influence the DNA that builds a baby's brain cells, proteins, and brain circuits to create mental wellness. The nurturing effect on genetics is the first step to growing resilient brain cells, brain circuits, and brain structures.

You are likely familiar with the idea of "nature versus nurture"— the long-standing argument over what makes us who we are: What is encoded in our DNA? Our inherited, unchanging selves, or the highly variable experiences we have in and of the world? Despite the way this debate rages on in popular culture, scientists know that the brain is built by a very complex interplay between nature and nurture over time. Human beings are not just genetics or just experiences; we are both. The brain connections that make up your baby's stress system and lifelong mental health are built by a mixture of nature and nurture. It is always a dance between genetics and experience that can lead to resilience.

This is what I showed Michelle and what I'm going to show you— that yes, her child was inheriting DNA that predisposed her to mental health struggles. We don't have influence over that. However, Michelle can have a huge and profoundly positive influence over how her baby is nurtured. This is the essence of the nurture revolution. The way we nurture our children's nature is essential to their lifelong mental health, especially during sensitive times in brain development like infancy when the brain is in a special state to be shaped by experience.

HOW NURTURE INTERACTS WITH NATURE

There are three important puzzle pieces that make up your baby's stress system, emotional system, lifelong mental health, well-being, and resilience on the genetic level. Nurture in the first three years of life has a profound impact on all of the pieces. They are:

1. The genetic code or DNA they inherit
2. Whether or not they inherit "orchid"—or sensitive—genes in their genetic code
3. The epigenetic markers on their DNA that reflect intergenerational experience with stress or resilience

In the following sections, we'll take a look at each of these, which express just how revolutionary nurture can be.

The Genetic Code or DNA

Within my family, I know that the past three generations have experienced depression, anxiety, addiction, attention deficit disorder, schizoaffective disorder, and bipolar disorder. Chances are that your family also has a history of diagnosed or undiagnosed symptoms of poor mental health. This is pretty heavy stuff. However, neuroscience research shows us that any history we might inherit can be reduced or silenced when combined with nurture. It's important to remember, too, that we can also inherit resilience and nurturing, and we have the ability to start brand-new cycles of inherited resilience in our babies.[1]

Let's take a look at DNA. We inherit genetic material in the form of deoxyribonucleic acid (DNA) from our biological parents at conception when sperm and egg fuse together. DNA provides building instructions for proteins that make up our cells, and our cells then make up all of the organs in our brains and bodies. In other words, DNA contains the biological instructions to build our entire bodies during development.

In most body parts, like the heart or liver, DNA builds the organ's structure from start to finish with little input from experience. This means that to a large extent, a baby heart is a little version of an adult heart, and a baby liver is a little version of an adult liver. However, the brain is an exception, because its structure is built by both DNA and experience. In pregnancy and infancy, DNA builds the brain's basic structure, and then experience builds and strengthens important genes, proteins, cells, and circuits in the brain.[2]

Our DNA influences how all of our body parts function, including our brain. We know of several genes or genetic mutations that increase the risk for many mental health issues, but we don't know of any single gene that causes a mental health issue or determines that someone will have one. Experience, specifically the amount of nurture, plays an important role here. We do know that mental health is inherited on a spectrum. On one end are individuals who inherit DNA that builds their brains to be very resilient to mental health issues. These individuals may experience low nurture and grow up to be resilient. On the other end are individuals who inherit DNA or DNA mutations that build their brains to be susceptible to mental health issues. These individuals may experience low nurture and grow up to be vulnerable to stress and mental health struggles. Each of us exists somewhere along this spectrum.[3]

One of the most powerful discoveries in neuroscience is that wherever an individual is on the spectrum of inherited mental health, nurturing experience in pregnancy and infancy can boost mental health. Conversely, low-nurturing experience in early life can boost inherited mental health difficulties. For example, the *DISC1* gene is a genetic mutation prevalent in families with psychiatric symptoms. We studied this in my PhD laboratory; our lab replicated the *DISC1* mutation in animal models to study the impact of early experience on mental health. Inheriting a mutation in the *DISC1* gene could increase vulnerability to psychiatric symptoms, but only when there was low nurture or another major stressor in early life. When animal models inherited the *DISC1* mutation and had high nurture as babies, they did not develop psychiatric symptoms.[4] The act of nurturing bathed the infant brain in hormones that could silence the functional expression of this genetic mutation. There are many other examples of this phenomenon with many other genes, but the take-home lesson is that nurture can reduce or silence the power of these genes.

In some cases, mental health struggles persist even in the most nurturing environments—in other words, a baby who had a highly nurturing early life could still develop mental health struggles because their genes still made them vulnerable. In these cases, nurture can still reduce the influence of genetics and it is possible that several generations of nurture could incrementally shift mental health.

Orchids and Dandelions

If you've ever wondered why children raised similarly in the same household can grow up to have very different mental health outcomes, among the many factors that can contribute to the difference is that some children in the family may be more sensitive to experience than others because of the genes they inherit. While all the children may experience the same stressors, some may have inherited DNA that makes them more sensitive to experience, while others may have inherited DNA that makes them less sensitive. We call the DNA that makes us more sensitive to experience "orchid" genes, because like orchid flowers they need a specific nurturing environment in order to flourish; while we call DNA that makes us less sensitive to experience "dandelion" genes, because just as dandelions can grow in almost any environment, those with dandelion genes can develop good mental health regardless of experience.

How sensitive an infant is to either nurturing or stressful experience is inherited in DNA on a spectrum. On one end of the spectrum are individuals who inherit DNA that builds their brains to be extremely sensitive to experiences in pregnancy and infancy. On the other end are individuals who inherit DNA that builds their brains and minds to be less sensitive to experiences in pregnancy and infancy. Research has identified specific genes that are very sensitive to experience in infancy. Like their floral namesake, the health, success, and growth of children with orchid genes are dependent on a positive nurturing environment. For example, the serotonin transporter gene (*SLC6A4*), is a known orchid gene. This gene is part of the serotonin neurotransmitter system, which contributes to mental health. If a specific version of this gene is inherited, an infant will be very sensitive to experience in infancy and childhood. In particular, low nurture in infancy can double the chance of developing depression in life but nurture in infancy keeps the chance of developing depression at the level of an average person. Nurturing experience for a child with this gene can protect them from a high chance of depression and all of the challenges that accompany it.[5]

Alternatively, children in possession of dandelion genes can grow and thrive in almost any environment. Since we don't test infants for DNA mutations or orchid genes and will likely never know if our child has one, it is critical that we provide every child with nurturing experience in early life to maximize their chances at good mental health. All infants should be treated as though they have orchid genes and given nurturing experiences as much as possible.

Figure 9 shows two babies on a spectrum of mental health. Baby A is born with genetics that influence their mental health baseline toward the susceptible end. They receive nurture, and this moves them closer to the resilient end. Baby B has genetics that influence their mental health baseline to the middle of the spectrum. They receive nurture, which moves them closer to the resilient end. Both babies are significantly influenced by nurture, and both benefit, yet they don't end up at the same place. This is what doing our best looks like and why nurture has different outcomes in different people.[6]

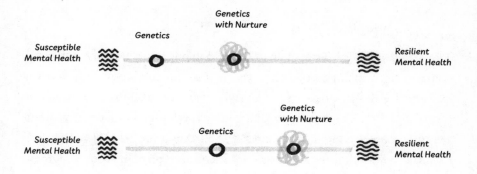

Figure 9.

Baby A and Baby B are born with different genetics and levels of resilience; however, nurture moves both babies toward further resilience.

Another well-known orchid gene is the dopamine receptor (*DRD4*). This gene is part of the dopamine neurotransmitter system, which contributes to mental health outcomes. If a specific version of this gene is inherited, infants are extremely sensitive to how their parents respond to their cues. If parents respond sensitively, these infants develop typically. However, if parents show low sensitivity, these infants grow up with an increased chance of showing externalizing behaviors like aggression and hyperactivity as well as an increased chance of developing attention-deficit/hyperactivity disorder, or ADHD.[7]

As time goes on, science will likely uncover more and more DNA mutations and orchid genes, but we already have enough information to act. We know that many infants inherit genes that make them very sensitive to parenting and experience in early life, and, importantly, we can do something about this by offering children positive experience in infancy in order to give them the best chance in life. Please unlearn myth 4, *Babies are resilient, so experience in infancy doesn't matter*, and replace it with: <u>Experience in infancy matters. It interacts with genes to influence mental health.</u>

Epigenetic Markers on DNA

The study of epigenetics in parenting behavior is relatively new—it's come to light in the last twenty years.[8] *Epi-* means "above" or "on top of," and studies in this area have revealed many proteins that attach on top of our DNA that change our gene expression. Epigenetic proteins are like volume controls for genes: When they bind to DNA, they can turn the volume up on a gene to produce more protein from a segment of DNA, or they can turn the volume down and shut down protein production from a segment of DNA. Think of the caterpillar, chrysalis, and butterfly. They all have the same DNA, but they look different. This is because some genes are "turned on" and others are "turned off" at different stages. A caterpillar and chrysalis have the genes that make proteins for wings switched off, while the butterfly has the wings genes turned on. Another example is our organs: Your liver has the liver genes turned on and the other organ genes silenced, and your heart has the heart genes turned on and liver genes turned off.

Experiences in early development and in the season of nurture lead to epigenetic changes in our babies. Nurturing experiences across early development can change the volume on specific mental health genes in our baby's DNA. Nurture creates epigenetic and gene expression changes to boost mental health in our babies. We also know that stressful experiences across early development change the volume on specific mental health genes in our baby's DNA. Stressful experiences can lead to epigenetic and gene expression changes to make mental health more vulnerable for our babies. There are many experiences our babies will have that we cannot influence, especially those in early development, but we can create epigenetic markers on their DNA with the nurture that we can influence.[9]

Our babies are exposed to emotional experiences that change their epigenetics and gene expression at two specific times. The first occurs during early development in utero, and the second in infancy, or the first three years of life. Emotional experiences include trauma of any kind, including: low nurture, emotional abuse, physical abuse, sexual abuse, war, genocide, famine, immigration, enslavement, and crime. Adverse infant experiences are proposed to include a lack of: carrying, physical contact, breastfeeding or feeding with contact, presence of caregivers, co-sleeping, co-regulation, and mirroring emotions.[10] These experiences may leave epigenetic markers on DNA to increase susceptibility to mental unwellness. Emotional history also includes experiences of resilience, strength, and wellness. These are the experiences we will create with nurture that can leave epigenetic markers on DNA to contribute to mental wellness. It is an intriguing way in which the experience of previous generations lives on and gets passed on.

Development begins much earlier than we might imagine, when our babies exist as sperm and egg cells. Sperm cells contain epigenetic markers that reflect the emotional experiences in Dad's life. If Dad experienced low nurture in infancy or bullying or trauma in his life, his sperm can have epigenetic markers in the stress system to pass on a reactive stress system. If Dad experienced a nurtured infancy, his sperm can have epigenetic markers in the stress system to pass on a regulated stress system. If Dad experienced a mix of stressful and nurturing emotional experiences, his epigenetic markers will reflect that.[11]

The story on the biological mother's side is even more complex. A baby inherits both their maternal grandmother's and their mother's emotional experiences via epigenetics. This is an incredible way that experience is passed on in the maternal line. I feel a very deep connection to my maternal grandmother; she was always my safe, nurturing person, and I lived in her and took on her experiences. Similarly, my son has lived inside his maternal grandmother. All of a female baby's gametes, or egg cells, are created while she is growing inside her mother's womb. When your mother was in your grandmother's uterus, half of your DNA was also there. In a sense, you are your age plus your mother's age old. We exist for about five months inside our grandmother as an egg—and epigenetic markers can form from her emotional experience. For example, if our grandmother experienced low or high nurture, or stress or trauma, it can influence our epigenetics. To this end, the way we support women and pregnant people has real consequences for future generations. Our egg also collects our biological mother's experiences throughout her life until our birth. Our mother's emotional experiences, with high or low nurture or stress or trauma, influence the egg's epigenetic markers. Finally, if we are a mother or pregnant person who is pregnant with a female baby, we are also carrying any potential grandchildren and passing on our emotional experience.[12]

We do not have influence over the experiences biological parents might pass on to babies through epigenetics. Many of us as biological mothers and fathers have histories of low nurture or trauma or stress, and these can be in our sperm and egg cells. Adoptive parents, parents by sperm or egg donor, or parents by surrogacy may or may not know the emotional experiences their babies inherit by epigenetics. The point is, in our currently low-nurturing culture, many of our babies will inherit epigenetic markers that turn up the volume on susceptibility to reactive stress systems that impact mental health. However, we can combat this because we can have an enormous influence over the second occasion in which our babies are exposed to experience that changes their epigenetics—the first three years of life. When we nurture in pregnancy and infancy, we can create new epigenetic markers in our babies that foster resilience and mental wellness. As I practice this as a parent, I have seen profound cycle-breaking and cycle-starting firsthand in my family. I was raised with a lot more nurture than my parents received, and I am raising my child with even more nurture and more resilience. I see this in all of the families I work with—so many of us are beginning to lay down epigenetic markers for health in our babies. We are the first generation with the knowledge of how to nurture to transform the human genome to forever change mental health.[13]

Groundbreaking research in animal models and humans has found that nurturing experience in infancy leads to epigenetic changes in fundamental brain systems for mental health, like the stress system and social systems. It shows that when babies receive high nurturing, they receive epigenetic markers on genes that turn up the volume on proteins in the brain for resilience, mental wellness, and nurturing behavior.

Epigenetic changes for resilience appear on genes in every part of the stress system. In the amygdala, epigenetic changes happen in a gene for a protein called brain-derived neurotrophic factor (BDNF) to shape the amygdala alarm to be adaptive.[14] In the hypothalamus, epigenetic changes happen in several genes, including a gene for a hormone called corticotropin-releasing hormone (CRH), so cells release less stress hormone, leading to a more adaptive stress response.[15] In the hippocampus, epigenetic changes appear in a gene called *GR1*, or the glucocorticoid receptor, to make the stop signal stronger.[16] In the prefrontal cortex, epigenetic changes in BDNF make the stop signal stronger.[17] The oxytocin system also has epigenetic changes that regulate the stress system.[18] The epigenetic changes in high-nurtured babies protect mental health by creating brain systems with regulated stress systems and a lower risk for anxiety and depression.

Epigenetic changes for nurturing behavior happen in the social system on a gene in the estrogen system (*NR3A1*), and in a gene in the oxytocin system (*OXTR*).[19] The epigenetic changes influence babies to grow up to be parents who provide high nurturing for their babies. So the cycle of nurture and resilient mental health continues. We are nurturing our children and our grandchildren.

NURTURING FOR THE FUTURE

We may inherit legacies of trauma, violence, poor mental health, and low nurture in our DNA, but we are not completely powerless against genetics. Experience matters in infancy, and nurture can help our babies grow resilient, healthy brains. And when we nurture our babies, we are also creating a legacy of nurture that gets passed on to future generations. By nurturing the baby in front of us, we are nurturing the future health of humanity and the planet. You can unlearn myth 5, *We can't make a difference to our baby's mental health outcomes if our baby inherits mental health genetics and intergenerational trauma through epigenetics,* and replace it with the knowledge: <u>Nurture makes an impact on inherited DNA and epigenetics to reduce or silence mental health effects.</u>

Nurture is revolutionary activism. If we have lived lives with low nurturing and mental health struggles, which many of us have, we can start a beautiful change toward new cycles of intergenerational epigenetics of health and nurture with our babies. We likely will not do it all in one generation, but by doing our best to nurture, we are moving nurture forward and beginning a new cycle. We can be more nurturing than our parents, our babies can be more nurturing than us, their babies can be even more nurturing, and so on. The change one nurturing parent can make is staggering and legacy-creating.

Chapter 4

SUPERPOWERS OF THE PARENT BRAIN

You're in the middle of a meeting and suddenly can't recall the word for "book" and instead are motioning with your hands. "It works like this," you say as you open and close your palms and fumble around with random descriptors. "It's full of information and stories." Or maybe you walk into a room and don't know why you're there or what you were looking for. This is probably familiar: You are in the middle of a conversation and realize you haven't heard a single word the other person has said. We call it "mom brain" or "dad brain" or "parent brain"— frequently forgetting information that used to come easily, like where you put your keys. You might feel like you're in a fog much of the time. Many parents come to me exasperated by this feeling—mothers, birthers, and primary caregivers, in particular, feel impaired and as if their brain and thinking patterns have changed. I know this feeling all too well; for most of my son's infancy, I'd have to stop my husband and say, "I know you were talking, but I didn't hear a word." I needed my husband's help remembering anything non-baby-related. As the primary caregiver, I was completely focused on my baby's well-being and all of the mental math of taking care of a baby.

If you're experiencing this, too, you're not imagining it, and it's not just sleep deprivation—from a brain perspective, quite a lot is going on. Your cognition is not gone. Your brain is different in many ways. Mainly, its attention is focused on your baby, not word recall or conversations or the location of your sunglasses. Research has discovered and continues to observe the emergence of new and specialized parenting brain circuits that organize when we become parents—circuits that non-parents do not have.[1] While the parent brain doesn't function like your adult brain did before children, it is special for and specific to nurturing babies.[2] The way our brain is organized is one of the things we lose and simultaneously gain as we become parents. This may be cause for both grief and celebration. Our parenting brains orient us to thoughts, feelings, and behaviors to keep our babies safe and promote their optimal brain development. As parents, we really are changed forever on a molecular, cellular, and circuit level. So, yes, what is known as mom brain and dad brain is very real. My hope is that I can help you hold your head up high and say, "Yeah! I have mom [or dad] brain. I have new superpowers!"

On Gender and the Parent Brain

To date, anatomical parental brain changes have been observed in three groups of parents:

1. Biological mothers who are cisgender females and primary caregivers
2. Biological fathers who are cisgender males and secondary caregivers
3. Biological and adoptive fathers who are cisgender homosexual males and primary caregivers

Anatomical parental brain changes have not yet been studied in:

1. Biological or adoptive mothers who are cisgender females who do not give birth and are primary or secondary caregivers
2. Adoptive parents who are primary and secondary caregivers
3. Parents who have a baby by surrogacy who are primary or secondary caregivers
4. Queer parents who are biological parents, adoptive parents, or parents by surrogacy, in primary caregiving and secondary caregiving groups

Including all of these groups in future studies is very much still needed. The research community does not have a long history of studying parents and infants in any domain, and especially in emotional health. The first study to look at anatomical brain changes in biological mothers happened in 2016, so we are just at the beginning.[3] The lack of study is revealing about how much society cares and prioritizes the emotional health and well-being of parents and babies—it doesn't.

This chapter is largely gender- and heteronormative-specific because, unfortunately, we are limited by the lack of research at the time of writing. However, parents in overlooked groups can still find that all of the research we do have points to the conclusion that all parents, regardless of caregiver type or biological relation, have dramatic brain changes to support caregiving and nurturing.[4]

NURTURE CHANGES THE PARENT BRAIN

The existing research shows two important things: First, everyone who becomes a parent—regardless of how, regardless of their gender, and regardless of their status as primary or secondary caregiver—undergoes massive brain changes. Second, parent brains experience bigger changes, and gain more abilities for parenting, in proportion to the amount of time parents spend nurturing their baby in the very beginning of life. The first few months of being a parent are a sensitive period, a season for the development of the parent brain where nurture is essential to change your parenting brain to benefit you and your baby.

Signals from the baby are what changes our brains, beginning either in pregnancy, as a mother or birthing parent, or throughout the first few months postpartum as nonbirthing parents. As parents we all need patience and time to go through this process. Primary caregivers, who spend the most time with the baby and provide the most nurture, have the biggest parental brain changes and the strongest parenting nurturing superpowers. You can unlearn myth 6, *Everyone falls in love with and knows what to do with their baby right away*, and replace it with: <u>Lots of time touching, smelling, and looking into your baby's eyes slowly builds your love, knowledge, and relationship with your baby.</u>[5]

Secondary caregivers, who spend less time with their baby than the primary caregiver, also gain brain changes and abilities to nurture babies, but the amount that their brain changes and their parenting superpowers critically depend on the amount of time they spend with the baby in the early days, about the first twelve to sixteen weeks.[6] This research underscores the importance of parental leave for all parents for a minimum of three to four months postpartum. Parent brain development and its ability to change is in a sensitive period, and these changes go on to influence parenting for life. Research also suggests that nonparents, called alloparents, who spend lots of time nurturing babies experience brain changes for nurturing. This can include family members, friends, doulas, and nannies. I attribute my many years as an alloparent babysitting my baby cousins and my time as a doula for beginning to transform my parenting brain—which was helpful when I had my own baby.

The brain transformation that occurs when we become parents is as massive as the changes that occur in the adolescent brain that transform the brain from a child's into an adult's. Researchers who study these changes in the brain use the term *matrescence* to describe the changes they've observed in pregnant biological mothers who are cisgender females. They use the term *patrescence* to describe the changes they've observed in fathers who are cisgender males, both biological and adoptive. See the box on page 52 regarding the groups yet to be studied.

Studies show that matrescence and patrescence are tremendous periods of brain change and neuroplasticity for adults—the biggest ones we know of in adulthood. This is an opportunity to create new healthy brain circuits for parenting and an opportunity to change our own emotional brain circuits that underlie our mental health. The more we nurture our babies, stay close to them, and respond to them in early life, the more oxytocin we receive. More oxytocin leads to bigger parent brain changes and enhanced abilities to nurture our babies and ourselves.[7]

Honoring the Transformation

While parenthood is accompanied by powerful physical shifts that help us care for our babies, these changes can also make this a fragile time for our mental health. Ideally these brain changes would be accompanied by constant emotional and physical support from elders, family members, and friends. It would involve acknowledgment, ceremony, processing, observing, and understanding. For most of us, however, this is far from reality. Low-nurture cultures in particular do not widely embrace or support this change. They certainly do not give the transformation into a parent the reverence that it deserves. They do not provide any societal support for us parents. So while we push for better from society, doctors, and workplaces, it is up to us to get informed and start asking for and creating what we need as parents.[8]

Becoming a parent changes us deeply. It changes our brains, our behavior, our thoughts, our hormones, our biology, and our bodies. With awareness and knowledge, this can be a beautiful gift—specialized brains to take care of and bond with our infants, a new period of neuroplasticity where we might find healing for ourselves. Despite the cultural pressure to "bounce back," there is no going back. Doing so would be like a teenager going back to being a child, or a child going back to being a baby. Our brains and minds are shaped for parenting, dramatically. But we can ride this wave and allow it to transform us for the better, allow it to shape us toward nurture, responsivity, and emotional connection with our babies, and to be healthier overall.

GETTING TO KNOW YOUR CHANGING PARENT BRAIN

Matrescence leads to major changes in the brain to augment special abilities for parenting. It occurs through sex hormones like estrogen, progesterone, oxytocin, prolactin, and glucocorticoids that change throughout pregnancy, birth, and early infancy.[9] Research shows that throughout pregnancy, the mother or pregnant person develops complex new brain circuits, while brain volume gets smaller in specific areas. It might sound alarming that some brain areas shrink, but it is actually a good thing, in terms of neuroscience. The brain areas that get smaller are actually being refined to enhance function for parenting. If I scanned your brain for anatomy, you would see all of the parts that got more efficient as you became a parent. Then if I scanned your brain for function while showing you a picture of your baby, those same parts would be the only ones that light up. There's an incredible overlap between the parts of your brain that change and the parts that are specific for nurturing your baby. This means that mothers and birthing people develop specialized brain circuits to nurture our babies beginning in pregnancy. Mothers or primary caregivers who don't give birth experience these changes after the baby is born.[10]

Throughout pregnancy, cells from the baby enter the pregnant person through the umbilical cord. These cells make their way into the pregnant person's brain and enhance brain areas for parenting behavior, lactation, and bonding. The baby's cells can also enter the pregnant person's body and repair organs like the heart. Babies' cells have been found in healing tissue in the abdominal scars from belly birth.[11] I love that my baby's cells live in me and my cells live in my baby. I also love the exchange of cells I have with my mother. We are interconnected in so many beautiful ways.

Patrescence similarly happens through a change in hormones, including testosterone, estrogen, oxytocin, prolactin, and glucocorticoids, as well as the development of cognitive brain circuitry.[12] Patrescence starts as soon as a father has contact with their baby and continues in the first few months of infancy. The introduction of the baby causes a release of oxytocin in the father's brain and this is essential to create changes in the brain to augment special abilities for parenting. The vast changes in fathers' brains happen through active involvement in childcare in what we call a "dose-dependent relationship." The more time the father spends with the baby, the more oxytocin they will have and the more their brain will change.[13]

More brain changes in these early days help fathers' and partners' parenting skills long-term. In the early days, when many fathers and non-birthing parents may find it challenging to bond with a baby, know that being with your baby by holding, feeding, bathing, and changing their diaper is the bonding. It is a quiet beginning on the outside, and a dramatic beginning in the brain, toward building a profound relationship of play, interaction, and connectedness. In the first three months of infancy, oxytocin increases in fathers, testosterone lowers, and brain structures change. The more time a father spends with their baby, the more oxytocin is present, the more testosterone is lowered, and the more the male parenting brain develops. Similar to matrescence, the brain areas that change in men are also related to emotional bonding and nurturing babies.[14]

One study looked at brain changes in primary caregiving homosexual fathers in families with no maternal involvement. These fathers showed changes to their brains that were more similar to primary caregiving mothers than to secondary caregiving fathers.[15] This research supports the concept that brain changes are different in primary and secondary caregivers regardless of sex or gender, with more pronounced brain changes and abilities for primary caregivers. It also suggests that contact and time with their baby in the early days will change the brains and parenting abilities of queer parents, adoptive parents, and parents through surrogacy—more evidence to support substantial parental leave for all people who become parents.

Matrescence and Infant Loss

When we experience pregnancy loss or infant loss, our brains have undergone some or all of the profound changes toward being parents, specifically for the mother or pregnant person. The babies we have lost remain part of us forever. The experience changes our brains, changes our bodies, and the babies we lose leave behind their cells. Furthermore, the cells from the babies we lose can transfer from our bodies through the umbilical cord into the future babies we carry, so the babies we birth also contain cells from babies we may have lost. When you begin your transformation into a parent and experience loss, you enter a liminal space in which you are mentally a parent who doesn't have their baby yet, and who is also grieving. Or you may have started the transformation and decide not to be pregnant again. We don't have any research on this brain state. We don't have a word to define it. We don't have specific support or resources that are well known. All of this is needed to nurture us on our journey. I see you. You're a mother. You're a parent. You've changed. And your baby isn't here yet. Or you are not going to have a baby and you've changed. We know that being in this space unsupported and unrecognized can bring on post-traumatic stress, anxiety, and depression.[16] It's essential to recognize this, and we must advocate for more reverence and support.

PARENTING SUPERPOWERS

Your parenting superpowers arise from your new parent brain circuitry that wires you toward nurture; it is called the "caregiving network." Your new brain circuits and abilities include sensitivity to your baby's communication, enhanced empathy to understand and respond to your baby's emotions with nurture, enhanced threat detection skills to keep your baby safe, and motivating, calming, and rewarding feelings by interacting with your baby.[17] Let's dig in to them now.

Sensitivity to Your Baby's Communication

Crying is very important communication for babies and essential to their survival. Babies cry when they need comfort, stress regulation, or have a physical need from their parents. As a new parent, you develop an enhanced ability to hear crying and the drive to run to your crying baby. Crying is the baby's survival brain saying, "I need help now," and your parent brain is adapted to hear this important signal, to go to your baby and respond. Your and your baby's brains have evolved to be connected by their crying. Reliably responding to your baby's cries shapes their emotional brain.

Matrescence specializes the auditory cortex, our primary brain area for hearing, through oxytocin signaling. Amazingly, mothers who have given birth develop a new specialized ability to hear their baby's cries and can identify their own baby's cry over other babies'.[18] Many mothers or primary caregivers experience hearing phantom baby cries, hearing their baby cry at a time when they are not. This commonly happens in the shower. You finally get to take a shower, step in, start washing your hair, and boom, you hear your baby crying. You run out of the shower, only to find your baby fast asleep, comfy and safe. This phenomenon is likely a reflection of how tuned in the parent brain is to the sound of cries.

Many mothers and primary caregivers find that they are more sensitive to their baby's cries than are fathers or secondary caregivers. Many a mother or primary caregiver, myself included, has woken in the night to the sound of their crying baby and the sight of their partner fast asleep. It can be frustrating, but it's necessary to understand that it takes several weeks to months for secondary caregivers' parent brains to develop.[19] However, even after this occurs, there are still differences between primary and secondary caregivers. While all parents respond more than do nonparents to infant cries, the sensitivity of fathers, and likely secondary caregivers, to crying is different than that of mothers or birthing people and likely primary caregivers.[20] Biological fathers do not show the same sensitivity to infant cries as biological mothers do; however, they too can identify their own baby's cry over those of other babies.[21] This is likely an effect of the amount of time secondary caregivers spend with the baby. We'd expect that all primary caregiving parents and caregivers would develop strong abilities to hear infant cries, including biological parents, adoptive parents, and parents through surrogacy. As we see, all parents' brains change when they nurture babies.[22]

Enhanced Empathy—Ability to Understand and Respond to Your Baby's Emotions with Nurture

Parent brains develop enhanced abilities for empathy. This includes an enhanced ability for theory of mind, which is the ability to understand other people's minds and emotions with enhanced empathy, an ability to understand or feel the same emotions as another person.[23] Enhanced theory of mind allows us to respond to our babies' communication effectively and provide a reliable external brain for our babies. The more we develop theory of mind, the more we are sensitive and nurturing to our babies.[24]

Infant crying activates in parents brain areas called the insula and the prefrontal cortex. The insula is involved in emotional and cognitive empathy, so we feel and understand our baby's feelings when they cry. The prefrontal cortex is involved in regulating emotions like frustration that can arise when babies cry. In this way, our parent brains simultaneously feel and understand our babies' pain and help us regulate ourselves so we can help our babies. When we can regulate our emotions more effectively, we can be more sensitive parents and provide more nurture.

As parents, our brain networks for empathy are enhanced. When our babies feel an emotion, our brain mirrors their emotional state in the insula, so we feel a representation of their feeling in our body as well as understand what the feeling is like based on our previous experience. If our baby is in pain, we embody a state that represents that pain in our brain and body. If our baby feels joy, we embody a state that represents joy in our brain and body. This skill equips us to support our baby's emotions.

The ability to consistently respond to your baby's emotions with nurture is hard work and can take up a lot of your energy and attention. Interpreting your baby's emotions, empathy, and providing emotional support make up a lot of the work of parenting. Your ability to understand your baby's mind is amazing, but also exhausting, and often not recognized or celebrated. I can think of all of the times my baby would babble something that no one could understand, and I would translate: "He is asking for his red cup that he left behind the couch," or "He is telling you about when he went on the slide today." Or my baby would get upset and I'd be the only one to understand: "He is upset because he doesn't like that you put your arms on the table." Often I could sense or predict my baby's emotions before he expressed them.

The ability to anticipate our babies' needs can also feel like mental math, and this can be exhausting. As primary caregivers our minds are constantly calculating and tallying numbers of diapers, food, exposure to allergens, finances, time since a bath, appointments, schedules, laundry, clothing sizing. The abilities we gain and the work we do in this domain are often unseen and unappreciated, and it is hard, consistent work that needs to come to light.

Enhanced Threat Detection

The parent brain develops circuitry to anticipate and protect infants from threats. This is a wide network that includes the amygdala. Enhanced threat detection helps us keep our babies safe.[25] Our parent brains are constantly scanning the environment, predicting where threats might occur and directing our babies to safety. I would always imagine the accidents that could happen to my baby. If we were near a pool, I'd imagine him falling in. On a balcony, I'd imagine him falling off. On a playground, I'd imagine him tripping and falling off the equipment. These thoughts are scary, and they guide us to take precautions to keep our babies safe. When the thoughts come up, I thank them for their knowledge, and adjust my attention or the environment to mediate the risks.

Feelings of Motivation, Reward, and Calm by Interacting with Your Baby

When we become parents, our brains become specially wired to feel motivation, reward, and calm from being with our babies. These changes happen in our dopamine system, the system that is activated by anything we find intensely enjoyable, like good food (my favorite is dark chocolate), intimacy, music, or movement. When we become parents, our babies become a primary source of intensely good rewarding feelings.[26] The changes also happen as oxytocin exerts a calming effect in our amygdala.[27] This is why many parents feel calmest and safest when they are with their babies. Before you are a parent you might look at a baby and think, "Oh, cute, but I don't need to hold them." When you have your own baby, you might look at your baby and think, "I need to devour this baby and never stop looking at them and cuddling them." The reward and calm we get from being with our babies drives us to keep our babies close and delight in them. This creates a beautiful feedback system in which, because our baby is rewarding and calming, we are driven to be close to them, and being close to them releases more oxytocin and dopamine, leading to more nurturing. I know that taking care of a baby is hard work, but we also can simultaneously feel an overwhelming joy in holding, smiling, and being with our little ones. For a long time, anxious parents have been separated from their babies as a solution to anxiety. We now know that keeping parents together with their babies, with additional support if needed, can help ease anxiety for many.

Embracing and leaning into these new abilities will develop your strengths for nurturing and supporting your infant's developing brain. These special abilities are the foundation of your intuition as a parent, what your gut, brain, and body tell you about what your baby needs. The more you listen to your intuition, the louder you will hear it and the easier it will be to nurture and parent. Whenever you have feelings to respond as much as possible to your baby's communication, feel deep empathy for your baby, want to hold your baby all day or protect your baby—lean in. This is your parenting intuition. It brings you calm and reward. You can never respond too much, feel too much empathy, hold your baby too much, or be too protective. These experiences are exactly what your brain has been changed to do. Think of your baby as the guru that's teaching and developing your parent brain. We do the best for our brain development—and our baby's—when we stay close and connect as much as we feel called to do so. The more we can listen to this intuition, and ignore anything that gets in the way, the easier it will be to nurture the developing infant brain. You can unlearn myth 7, *Having a baby impairs your brain function*, and replace it with the knowledge: <u>Having a baby changes your brain to give you nurturing superpowers</u>.

PARENTAL BRAIN INHIBITORS

Your parenting brain represents a shift in biology and drive that wires you for nurture, closeness, and shared emotions with your baby. However, you probably also have lots of unexamined ideas about infants and parenting from the way you were parented, the stories you've heard about babies from your family and society, and advice from friends, family, and so-called experts that can inhibit your parent brain from trusting its instincts. When these ideas are examined, you can get better at differentiating them from your parent brain—your intuition—allowing you to work with your parent brain rather than against it.

The Way You Were Nurtured

In chapter 3 we learned that the way you were parented has influenced your biology to influence how much you will innately nurture. You carry epigenetic markers in your brain from the way you and your ancestors were parented that will influence your parenting brain circuits and your innate nurturing. If we received high nurture as babies, our parenting brains will be influenced to give our baby lots of nurture. If we received low nurture as babies, our brains will be influenced to give our baby lower nurture. Of course, many of us are somewhere along the spectrum from high to low nurturing. Understanding where we are on this spectrum can help us develop our parenting brain. If we received lower nurture or didn't see examples of nurture in our life, we might need to see more and learn more as we become parents. If you haven't seen or really experienced nurture, invite a nurturing person like a postpartum doula or grandmother or best friend to spend time with you and your baby. You will learn a lot! Any experience of nurture can be a source of knowledge for how we nurture our babies. My grandmother always kept a tracing of my feet in her purse so she could buy shoes for me if she saw something I might need. Looking back on this, it showed me that she was always thinking of me and I was important to her. I draw inspiration from this for my child.

Stories About Babies

The stories our culture and our family tell about infants and parenting, and the stories in our heads about infants and parenting, have a huge impact on our parenting brain circuits. It is important to get curious about what stories are in your brain right now. Often the "funny," repeated stories in families are deeply traumatic—and telling. A client's grandmother once told us the story of the "good old days," when immediately after a mother birthed her baby, the baby was taken to the nursery and the adults had a party in the hospital room with champagne, smoking, and music. In response to our dropping jaws, she reassured us that it was okay because the mom could get an update about her baby just by picking up the phone. More jaw drops. According to this grandmother's story, an adults-only party immediately after birth was way more fun and way better for parents than what I was planning with my client, which was a quiet time to meet the baby and start breastfeeding. When these stories about infants and parenting go unexamined, a parent might be influenced to suppress their parent brain that says "Hold your baby" by repeating this story that says "It's best for parents and babies to be separated at birth." Examining it through the lens of infant and parent neurobiology, a parent can put this story aside and listen to their intuition at birth.

Another client's mom told her that she was the easiest baby—a "good baby." According to her mom, as an infant, my client spent the whole day in her playpen, never being held, and would watch TV with her mom or play alone all the time. The expectation implicit in this story is that if they are "good," babies should be able to be alone, unheld, for hours a day. My client's mom told my client that she turned out fine. The mother in this family, my client, had severe anxiety and insomnia, and was diagnosed with borderline personality disorder; she did not agree that she was fine. Ending the cycle of mental health struggles in her family was her top priority. If this notion of a "good baby" goes unexamined, a parent might suppress their parenting brain and ignore their baby's cues in order to fulfill the expectations that good babies stay alone all day. When we look at it in the context of accurate infant and parent neurobiology, however, a parent can put this story aside and tune in to what their parenting brain is telling them.

These kinds of stories are common. It is important to deeply investigate the stories in your family and friend groups about babies to examine how they may impact you. We are fish swimming in a culture of low nurture, unaware that there is another way. Older generations, and many of our peers, often don't want to investigate their experiences. As with the anecdote I share above, many future parents share that they hear the common refrain "I turned out fine." As in, "My mother never held me, and I turned out fine," or "We let our baby cry all day, and they turned out fine." "Fine" in this context means that the baby lived. Not that they thrived, not that they had healthy mental lives or healthy relationships or physical health. We can do a lot better than fine; our babies can thrive. To the parents I work with, I often say, "Your elders and your friends who are low nurturers are absolutely doing their best with the information they have." When we understand the benefits of nurture, however, we can do things differently.

The common stories about babies in our society influence us all. They include: Holding babies too much is spoiling; babies are tyrants; you should not respond to all of your baby's cries; babies need to learn emotional independence; babies need to stop signaling for help when the sun goes down; babies need to learn to control their behavior; parents are weak if they hold their baby all the time. All of these expectations are not possible for babies, as we understand that baby brains cannot accomplish a single thing on this list. All of these stories go against our instincts in our parenting brains and what babies need to develop their emotional brains. These stories have all been made up to separate parents and babies. They gaslight us as parents and they deprive babies of the nurturing experiences they need to thrive. Even when we know they are incorrect, these stories can shake us up.[28]

I like to help parents sort through such stories with the question "Whose voice is that?" For example, if you are told you are spoiling your baby by holding them for naps, ask, "Whose voice is that?" In this instance the voice is a long-gone doctor from over a hundred years ago, and the idea is based on absolutely nothing—no research, no data, just the opinion of one guy. Now listen to your own voice inside that says, *"Holding for naps is what my baby needs, and it feels good to me."*

NURTURE CAN HEAL OUR TRANSFORMING PARENTING BRAINS

Whatever the parenting norms you inherit, or the stories about infants you hear in your family and culture, you can choose a nurturing path. You can start a new healing, nurturing cycle of parenting. When you do so, you not only build your baby's brain for resilience and good mental health, but you also have the opportunity to heal yourself.

One phenomenon that might help us heal is the intense neuroplastic changes that occur in parenthood. The brain areas that dramatically change in parenthood overlap with the emotional brain areas that develop in infancy. When we become parents, we experience significant changes in our amygdala, hippocampus, and prefrontal cortex, among other complex networks involved in emotional intelligence, like the insula.[29] I find that parents are motivated to change more than at any other time in adult life. We are motivated to be healthier and rewire ourselves to benefit our babies. Figure 10 shows the brain areas that will change in you more when you nurture your baby more. When you're engaged in nurture, imagine this image, all of your emotional brain areas bathing in a nurture bath toward transformation and healing. If we are low nurturers, we miss out on this opportunity to change our brains—and it can lead to mental health struggles.

Might we get special access in parenthood to rewire our emotional brains that developed in infancy? We can repeat what happened to us— the way we were programmed to parent. Or we can change by consciously nurturing and taking advantage of this adult neuroplasticity that occurs as we become parents. When we immerse our developing parenting brains in oxytocin from nurture and create conscious changes, we can dramatically reshape our amygdala, hippocampus, prefrontal cortex, and insula toward mental health. With lower nurture, there is lower oxytocin, an absence of conscious changes, and a lost opportunity to reshape mental health.

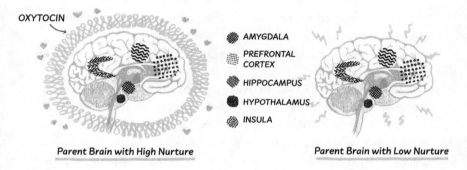

Parent Brain with High Nurture	*Parent Brain with Low Nurture*

Figure 10.

With oxytocin that comes from nurture, the parent brain has neuroplasticity to rewire toward resilience brain areas that were formed in the parent's infancy. Without the oxytocin from nurture, the parent brain misses out on an opportunity to rewire toward health and can become vulnerable to mental health struggles.

We can reparent ourselves, heal our inner babies, and possibly rewire our emotional brains by nurturing our babies in places we were not nurtured. We can teach ourselves, we can be there for ourselves, and we can rewire ourselves. When you are close to your baby, you might tell your inner baby, "I'm holding you." When we respond to emotions in our babies, tell them we're here for them, that their emotions are safe, and that it's safe to feel, we might also learn to talk to ourselves and our inner babies this way. When we form a secure intimate relationship with our babies, it might be the first secure relationship we've ever been in. This can all bring intense healing, especially when we are guided through the process.

Normalizing Ambivalence

While the parent brain transforms, we also experience complicated emotions as we become parents. The emotions of having a new baby are often complex and nuanced. Many caregivers experience strong contradictory feelings, known as ambivalence. Maybe you feel excited about having your baby and also sad that you can't just get up and go out for lunch with a friend like you used to. Or you feel deeply in love with your baby and also desperately want someone to come and take them away so you can grieve or sleep or process your feelings. You might feel totally enamored with your baby's every gurgle and also resentful of not getting enough sleep.

Ambivalence can be one of the most surprising parts of pregnancy and parenting and one many caregivers do not feel comfortable sharing with others. Many people feel shame about their conflicting emotions. We are led to believe that pregnancy and parenting are wonderful and joyous. They are. And they can also be deeply sad and lonely. Please know that you can feel lots of big emotions all at the same time. You can feel deep love and deep sorrow at the same time. This is expected in your transformation as a parent.

When not expected or accepted, ambivalence can make parents feel shameful, ungrateful, or uncomfortable. Many new parents feel like they are failing as parents when they have these feelings. It is perfectly healthy and typical for parents to simultaneously have positive emotions about a baby and negative emotions about major changes to their life. Many parents feel gratitude, joy, and excitement simultaneously with anxiety, grief, and loss. Ambivalence is easier for some than for others. Parents may feel anxious about losses, transformations, and unknowns concerning identity, career, freedom, relationships with romantic partners, relationships with family, relationships with friends, hobbies, exercise, health, sleep, or self-care routines. Parents should know and embrace ambivalence as a normal part of becoming a parent and most major life experiences. Share your ambivalent feelings with a therapist or a loved one or with everyone. We need to normalize it.

PROTECTING THE CHANGING PARENT BRAIN

For parents of all genders, the positive brain changes that come from parenthood can also lead to high vigilance, anxiety, distress, worry, and obsessive-compulsive tendencies. This may be especially true if you've ever had mental health issues in the past, or if you had adverse childhood experiences that might be activated by parenting. These feelings do not happen for everyone, and if they do, they typically do not last beyond the first three or four months postpartum. This makes sense as our babies are vulnerable in these months. In these early months it is important to know that our baby is breathing, eating, peeing and pooping, and growing. You do not have to have a postpartum mood disorder or be diagnosed with one to experience these overwhelming feelings. It is important to know that times of big hormonal change are normal times to expect changes to your mood. For mothers and birthing parents, this includes when your milk comes in a few days postpartum, when menstruation starts again, when your baby sleeps through the night and your milk goes down, and when you wean your baby.

Sometimes the changing parent brain can lead to more intense shifts. Parents of all genders can experience postpartum depression, postpartum anxiety, and sometimes postpartum psychosis. Mental health challenges can arise in the weeks and months following birth or at any point in the first three years of infancy, or even after three years. About one in seven mothers and one in ten fathers experience a postpartum mental health challenge. And if one parent has a challenge, the chances of the other parent being affected increase. It is important to monitor for these changes and have a plan for mental health support in case it is needed (see the Resources, starting on page 261). Your feelings may become overwhelming, especially in situations of parenting isolation, and you may find you're experiencing heightened vigilance, anxiety, distress, and obsessive-compulsive tendencies beyond tolerable levels. It is necessary in this case to get help from someone specially trained or experienced in perinatal mental health. There are many emerging therapeutics for postpartum mental health crises, and it is imperative to get help as soon as possible. The sooner you get help, the sooner you will get relief. It's actually wonderful to have help already in place before you need it.

Just like people in all professions, therapists and psychiatrists who treat postpartum mood disorders are variable; it may take time to find one that is the right fit for you. Mental health treatment works best when you feel connected and have a safe relationship with a practitioner, so if the professional you go to see doesn't feel like the right fit, move on and find someone else. Connect with a mental health provider you already know and trust, or look for a referral from a provider that you know and trust.

A great way to find support—and this is true for referrals for pregnancy, birth, and infancy—is to ask a trusted doula in your community. You don't have to hire them to work with you; most doulas are more than happy to send you referrals for free. You can even look one up on the internet and reach out. They don't have to be in your neighborhood, either, though it can be helpful if they live in your general region. Doulas are intimately connected with the perinatal health community and can help you start to link up with options for good mental health treatment. Part of the doula ethos is that there is a doula for everyone; if the one you contact can't help you or fit within your budget, they can find someone who can and does.

Any emotions you may have about how your baby was conceived, history of pregnancy or infancy loss, your birth experience, your baby's sex, your baby's health, and your early postpartum experience can also have a big impact on your mental health. You may perceive your conception journey as easy or relatively difficult. You may have experienced pregnancy loss, infant loss, fertility treatments, surrogacy, and/or adoption. Birth experiences can be perceived on a spectrum of orgasmic to triumphant, difficult to traumatic. The early postpartum experience can be joyous or difficult—sometimes both in the span of an hour. All of these emotions can impact you as a parent. Processing your experiences can be crucial to helping you access nurture for yourself and your baby. We all need to process our birth stories, so that we don't carry and project feelings onto our parenting. Who can you talk to? A therapist? A friend? A birth or body worker? Look for someone for whom listening and supporting your journey is the heart of their work.

Many parents, including me, benefit from regular therapy beginning before conception, during conception, in pregnancy, or in early infancy. Many parents, including me, benefit from group processing of pregnancy, birth, and parenting experiences. The intention and practice of nurturing is difficult work, and it brings up a lot of emotions. Our babies bring up emotions about our own experience as babies. It is deeply helpful to have the support of a professional or community you trust and feel safe with.

Parent brain changes are well supported by therapy, medication when needed, social support, relationships, and communicating the experiences of early parenting. Remember that it's a time of neuroplasticity unlike any since adolescence, and this means that you're actually in great condition to be receptive to therapy. Parent groups, in person or virtual, lactation support if you choose to body feed, a grandparent, a friend, a caring yoga teacher, your local doula (even if you didn't use one for birth), acupuncture, nurture-centered accounts on social media—there are so many avenues for seeking and finding resources. Many parents find relief within a few weeks or months of good treatment, and some newer treatments can work even faster than that.

Perhaps the most important message here is that while you get treatment, or your partner does, plan for someone to continue to be your infant's external brain as you work to get yours in better shape. This can be grandparents, other family members, friends, a postpartum doula, or another caregiver. Moreover, the baby's presence continues to provide cues to develop your parent brain, even if you are experiencing a postpartum mood disorder. If you want your baby close while you get treatment and it is possible to do so, with or without another caregiver present, it is important for your healing to keep your baby close to you. After my pregnancy, birth, and NICU experience, with multiple traumas, I was in shock and on the verge of going into deep depression. Keeping my baby close day and night, as well as breastfeeding, was my medicine. It bathed my brain in a nurture bath, an oxytocin cascade—and gave me the safety signals I needed to heal. I was taking care of my mental health by being close to my baby. Connection to others is an important piece of mental health. Healing is not individualistic; it's interconnected.

Just as infants and adolescents need and deserve support through the massive brain changes they experience, so too do you, as a parent. Your feelings are valid, your needs are valid, and you deserve to be held, nurtured, and partnered through this experience. Low-nurture cultures are not well set up for this—in fact, it's not common for folks to understand the changes that take place and how significant the transformation—but by leaning into nurture parenting, we can change that. Knowing that these changes happen and are normal can take away some distress you may feel as you make the transition into parenthood, whether for the first or fifth time, but I also encourage you to make a plan to seek the support you need to thrive. I created a postpartum mental health plan for you to fill out on page 261.

I know from personal experience and from working with lots of parents that this isn't necessarily a quick or linear process of transformation. Most of us experience a significant in-between or liminal state postpartum—a time where you are not quite the *you* of before children, but not yet your new form. You are still learning and growing. Remember that adolescence was a multiyear process that involved awkwardness, emotional and physical change, and a shifting identity. It is the same for matrescence and patrescence. For some, this liminal time lasts just a few months, but for many of us, it can be up to three to four years or beyond. As we change, we may grieve who we were and not yet understand who we will be. We are saying goodbye and we are becoming.

Becoming a parent, whether for the first or the seventh time, is a metamorphosis. I want to honor the mucky, muddy in-between state that is so often unappreciated in our low-nurture culture. Like a caterpillar to a chrysalis to a butterfly, we will emerge on the other side transformed and new, with new emotions, abilities, and strengths.

Most of us expect to have a few sleepless nights, less time for ourselves, and lots of time cuddling a baby. The reality is that becoming a parent is the birth of a baby *and* the birth of a parent. You and your baby are undergoing major developmental changes. When we really understand and embody the changes that make us parents, we benefit, our babies benefit, and we might even heal our own emotional systems in the process.

PART II

Chapter 5

HOW TO NURTURE

Nurture is at once an obvious and elusive concept. Most of us enter parenthood with intentions of nurturing, but don't know exactly what it looks like. What are the practices, feelings, thoughts, behaviors, and intentions that create a nurturing relationship? What does an environment that nourishes you and your baby's brain include or exclude? It's easy to be uncertain about the answers to these questions, because for the last hundred years or so many things have been considered to be nurturing that are in fact not. Many of us grew up in households that were in some ways nurturing but that also included physical punishments like spanking or isolation in the form of time-outs. Few of us grew up in families that understood how to parent with emotional intelligence or awareness of stress states and safety states.

The popular parenting practices of today normalize and encourage plenty of practices that are not nurturing to the infant brain and stress system, among them "teaching" independence, sleep training, lack of shared sleep, dismissing stress, dismissing emotions, lack of physical closeness, lack of close feeding, lack of presence, lack of respect, and overuse of baby containers like swaddles, swings, walkers, saucers, jumpers, and floor seats. Nurturing can be confusing to parents because low-nurture culture has policed and condemned nurturing in many ways. The message has been to hug our babies, but not too much, not too long, and not all the time, so as not to "baby" or "spoil" a baby. This is confusing in light of our parental brains developing to hear, respond to, and empathize with our babies and the reality of our babies' brains having intense needs for our touch, presence, and attention.

Beyond our individual families and cultural norms, we need evidence-based guidance for what makes a relationship nurturing for our babies and their brains. The last thirty years of neuroscience research ends this confusion, releases all restrictions, and sets us free to nurture—as much as we and our babies need, unconditionally, and with confidence that we are building lifelong health for the whole family. Consider this and the chapters that follow a compass to guide you toward nurture as your North Star.

Two core concepts that are foundational to nurture are what I call *nurturing presence* and *nurtured empathy*. Together, these concepts form the essence of how we nurture. If you center nurturing presence and nurtured empathy practices in parenting your infant, you'll be well on your way to helping your baby's brain bathe in nurturing hormones and neurotransmitters, growing their emotional brain, and supporting neuroplasticity and healing in your parent brain. You don't need to be naturally equipped with these capacities; they are intentions that you can practice and learn in the relationship with your baby.

NURTURING PRESENCE

The practice of nurturing presence is a shift in mindset from thinking of babies as objects to be managed to thinking of them as human beings who exist in relationships. Rather than trying to change or form them, we need unconditional acceptance for their beings, who they already are, right now.

Babies are born with their whole selves present. They communicate with us from the minute they are born. They are communicating with us at all times. We need to recognize their humanity and genuine need to exist in a relationship with us and our external brain, from their first breath throughout all of infancy up to three years old, and beyond. We lend infants our brain in all of their brain states, and our presence in all of these states matters. From birth through all of infancy babies are focused on one important thing—to get your nurturing presence to join them *in relationship*. They are constantly and relentlessly doing what they need to do to activate your nurturing presence. It's vital in states of connection, stress, and sleep, states that I'll discuss in greater detail in the chapters that follow. For now, I want to emphasize that nurturing presence is a relationship. Parenting is not so much about what you do but how you are in relationship with your baby.

Relationship matters because in the relationship, parent and baby brain waves synchronize, heartbeats match one another, emotions are shared, brains release nurturing hormones, and brains grow and thrive. In babies this emergent connection physically shapes their explosively developing brain. It influences genetics and epigenetics to reduce or silence mental health genetics or intergenerational trauma and begins new cycles of health.

Psychotherapist Katherine Schafler writes that in our everyday lives we unconsciously ask the people we interact with, both loved ones and strangers, four questions to help us know if we are cherished, as in the case of loved ones, or valued for our shared humanity, as in the case of strangers at the grocery store or on the bus. I saw these questions and immediately felt called to them, as they perfectly illustrate nurturing presence. Inspired by conversations Oprah Winfrey had with authors Toni Morrison and Maya Angelou about children and relationships, the questions are:

1. Do you see me?
2. Do you care that I'm here?
3. Am I enough for you, or do you need me to be better in some way?
4. Can I tell that I'm special to you by the way that you look at me?

As parents, we have a nurturing presence when our baby knows that the answer to all of these questions is a resounding YES. In order for this to be true, think about these questions often, put them on your fridge, and work on answering yes to them daily. You can find them on my website at www.nurture-neuroscience.com.

How do we make our baby feel seen? Really see them? Put everything down, no distractions, no multitasking, clear your mind, and look at them. Take them in with your eyes, your ears, and your being.

How do we show our baby that we care that they are here? Light up when they enter your sight, feel and express the joy you have that they are in your life.

How do we tell them they are enough? Accept them in the present moment regardless of their emotional state; direct your attention to the amazing person your baby is right now.

How can they tell that they are special by the way we look at them? Evoke a feeling of awe inside of yourself, think about the miracle of life, your baby's journey to you, and their special qualities. Then look at them with awe.

Sometimes it is easy and other times it's a challenge, especially when we might wish for our baby to be "better" in some way. Perhaps we wish our baby was happier, or clapped their hands in music class or ate all of their food or had fewer meltdowns or learned to use the toilet faster. We can work on these feelings by remembering that our baby's developing brain benefits when our presence reflects unconditional acceptance.

Babies' stress systems and emotional brains thrive when they know without question that they are someone's best beloved. Remember that babies won't remember what we said or what we did, but they will remember how we made them feel. When people feel seen and cared for enough and special in infancy it transforms every moment of their life thereafter for the better. If they do not experience it, the moments of life can be chronically touched by suffering. Babies need us to communicate a YES to these questions to them at all times—day or night, happy or sad.

Being Versus Doing

One common reason parents struggle with being a nurturing presence is living in a low-nurture culture that celebrates productivity over presence. Most of us have been conditioned to do, and keep doing. We must produce something visible in order to feel accomplished. I know that the list of things we think we "should" do or the ways we "should" look when we have a baby is long: a spotless house, matching clothes, baby classes, a perfect playroom, homemade food, and endless art projects, to name a few. When it comes down to it, though, the only thing that is lasting and matters to our babies is our nurturing presence. Babies need us to be with them. They need us to be parents being more than parents doing. Doing means engaging your brain's motor and cognitive systems to move and think; being means engaging your brain's sensory and emotional systems and living with awareness and consciousness.

Nurturing a baby challenges our very notion of productivity. It's possible to be with a baby all day and night and feel ashamed or frustrated that we haven't "done" anything. In actuality, when we are present with our baby, we do a tremendous amount of brain-building work, but it is invisible work. We are building epigenetics, proteins, and connections in our baby's stress system and emotional brain—a paramount task—but all of the work is inside of our baby's brain, out of sight. When we know that being with our baby is meaningful in its own right, we don't have to worry about doing enough to feel worthy. Of course, doing happens—activities, cleaning, and making things are part of life—but being is a priority for our baby's brain. Doing is something that happens in the background for our baby.

Once I was following my son around in the woods as he meandered from one rock or stick to another, as toddlers do, going only a few steps every twenty minutes or so. I felt myself getting so frustrated, wanting him to hurry up and finish the path so we could do the next thing. I felt intense pressure to be doing. My mind was spiraling into the things I could be doing next. I was thinking about emails I needed to respond to, classes to prepare, dirty laundry piling up high. Then I reminded myself that I was doing something tremendous by being with my son—I was building my child's brain and my brain with my nurturing presence. We didn't need to finish the path, and I didn't need to move on to do anything else—being on the path together was the doing. Our house might get messier and more chaotic. The emails would have to wait a few more hours. If I could be present here and now with my child, I'd be doing a whole lot even though no one could see it.

Sally Provence, a pioneering professor in infant mental health, said, "Don't just do something. Stand there and pay attention. Your child is trying to tell you something."[1] I'm asking you to make a shift, one that I know can feel uncomfortable. Even days-old infants are trying to communicate. They seek relationship with you. The way we learn to hear them is by making sure we have plenty of time to stop the train of doing, producing, and achieving and be with them. It is worth it for your baby's brain and for yours. If you can practice bringing your attention back to being present with your baby, you exercise your adult mind to be more emotionally intelligent, better at self-regulating, more empathetic, and you strengthen those parts of your brain undergoing neuroplasticity as you become a parent.

When your mind says, "I should be writing an email, posting on Instagram, finishing that basement remodel...," you can tell those voices, "No. Sitting here, being together, and existing with my child is doing something. Seeing what happens when we sit quietly together and respond to each other's presence and communication right here, right now, is doing something." Here we can unlearn myth 8, *Being with my baby is doing nothing*, and replace it with: <u>Being with my baby is vital brain-building, circuit-sculpting, cycle-starting activism for my baby's future</u>.

Nurtured Talk

Speaking to your baby increases oxytocin, and more than that, the *way* you speak to your baby significantly affects the stress systems, hormones, and neurotransmitters in their brain.[2] Nurtured verbal communication means talking to our babies as if they understand every word we say, because in many ways they do understand every word we say, especially the safety, stress, and emotion we communicate. Beginning at birth our babies are sensing, feeling, whole people who benefit from their presence being acknowledged as such. I like to include babies as whole persons in all conversations.

One way we do this is by expressing how much we love and adore our baby every day from the day they are born. I like to ask my son to look into my eyes and then I like to say things like, "I am so lucky to be your mama," "You make my heart feel so good," "You are amazing to me," "I love you exactly the way you are," "You light up the room," "You are so kind and loving," "I see how caring you are," "I love you when you are sad or mad or happy," and "Everyone wants to be around you."

We can include our child when we're in conversation with others. For example, "Can I tell your aunt your birth story? Do you remember when Mama held you for the first time? Your body was so relaxed, and it was the best feeling I've ever had in my life." Or, "Hey, baby, I'm going to tell your grandmother about going to the park yesterday. You laughed so much, you had so much fun. But you were sad when you fell down and felt better when Mama gave you a big hug. What did we do? We went on the slide. We had milk on the bench." Once babies become verbal, we can ask questions as we involve them in conversations, asking them how they feel about things. For example, "You were crying yesterday. What happened? How did you feel? Did you feel sad about leaving the park?"

Calling them names will give a baby a scared feeling that's stressful, even if they don't know the words. They may not understand the words "You were an impossible tyrant last night," but they know the emotion you are expressing to them, the feeling of "You are not good enough." The true thing is that we are activated in those moments and we need to deal with what's going on inside of us. When we as caregivers are scared, angry, frustrated, or having negative-feeling emotions, it is important to communicate our stress and emotions without calling our baby names or scaring them. In this case we could say, "You were waking up a lot last night and I was so tired and frustrated." Of course, we will have these emotions, likely very often, and we can learn to have them and have nurturing communication. For example, your baby is throwing things off of a table, something falls and breaks, and you get highly stressed and feel instantly angry. You could focus on blaming your baby ("My baby is impossible") or you could focus on naming your experience ("I am so overwhelmed at the moment"). If we are worried about our baby, we can blame them ("My baby is a pig or a monster") instead of naming our experience ("I am scared that my baby eats more than other babies," or "I am scared by my baby's tantrums"). When we blame, we are out of nurtured communication in our relationship with our baby. When we can recognize and name our emotions, we are in nurtured communication.

If we blame and call our baby a name directly or to someone else, we can always repair: "I said you were a monster, and that is not true. You are not a monster; you are a beautiful baby and I love you. I was feeling scared and I reacted by calling you a name. That was unkind and I will do my best not to do that next time." When we name our experience, we are being self-aware, and giving ourselves the opportunity to regulate ourselves. We can teach our babies this process as well: "I am so overwhelmed right now, I am going to stand up and shake it out to see if that makes me feel better. Now I'm going to take a deep breath. Oh yes, I feel a lot better now."

Being a Source of Emotional Safety

Perhaps it goes without saying that in order to be a nurturing presence for our baby, we must be a source of physical safety, and we also want to be a source of emotional safety. Emotional safety means that our baby feels safe expressing all of their emotions—including their most uncomfortable ones. We provide a relationship in which all of our baby's emotions are met with acceptance and not with rejection (I don't want to see your feelings); shame (there's something wrong with you); ignoring (I don't see you); or fear (I will yell). Accepting our baby's emotions can feel challenging for a number of different reasons. If, as babies, our own emotions felt intolerable for our caregivers, then hearing our baby's cry today might invoke the same fear we experienced as babies when we cried and our caregivers began to panic. As a result, we might respond to our baby's emotions by being overbearing, unable to tolerate any expression of emotion that isn't pleasant. On the other hand, if our cries caused our caregivers to shut down, isolate, or become angry with us, we might respond in kind, withdrawing when we hear our baby's cry.[3] However, we can work toward being comfortable with our baby regardless of their state. We do this by wholeheartedly accepting and supporting the entire range of our baby's stress, to the best of our ability, from high to medium to low. Our baby needs to learn from us that they are loved, accepted, and safe regardless of the level of stress in their brain and body. They need us to be comfortable with their stress so that our presence provides safety while they experience big, uncomfortable emotions. This means we practice being genuinely comfortable with big, messy emotions, stress, and intense joy and play, over and over.

Emotional safety means that babies have freedom to express all of their emotions openly, without shame or judgment. We take an approach of being curious about our baby's stress with no conditions—if they are stressed, they are stressed, no shame or accusing them of "faking," or doubting them. Even when our baby is obviously generating a cry or a scream on purpose, they are communicating something to us, and need an external brain and safe emotional expression. Unconditional acceptance means that if we can't identify the stressor, we still provide acceptance, co-regulation, and support for the stress. Sometimes we will understand the cause and easily be able to access empathy when our baby is stressed, such as if they get physically hurt or are cold or hungry. Other times we will not understand the cause and it is harder to access empathy; perhaps they have been held all day and need more holding, or they want a whole banana that we've already cut, or we simply have no idea why they are stressed. Babies are not monsters or tyrants or manipulators—they are little people having a hard time, and we are their only route to calm.

At the root level, you build your capacity for unconditional acceptance by nurturing yourself and your stress system so that you have more reserves for weathering any (or almost any) emotional storm your baby can make or experience. You want your baby to be able to rest in the feeling of trust that you can handle it most of the time—that you're not going to be scared of them, reject them, or be scary when they feel stress. Here we can unlearn myth 9, *Only pay attention to your baby's stress and emotions when there's a reason for them*, and replace it with: <u>All of your baby's stress and emotions need to feel welcome and safe.</u>

Other Caregivers, Nannies, Babysitters, and Support Systems

Babies do not need to be nurtured and cared for only by their parents, mother, or primary caregiver. Having networks and communities to co-nurture your baby benefits you and your baby. You don't always have complete influence over the caregivers available to you, but it can help to keep nurture in mind when bringing a caregiver into your infant's life. Ideally these are people who understand and support your decision to nurture so they can help in a meaningful way.

The people spending time with your child should be as nurturing as possible and in a close relationship with your child. If your baby is not highly nurtured by a caregiver, remember that they can be nurtured by you and you will make a huge impact in their developing brain.

Some parents ask me, "If my baby is going into daycare, should I hold them less and spend less time with them to prepare them for the separation?" The answer is a definitive no. When our babies are going into daycare, we want all of our time with them to be high-quality nurture. Some parents ask if they should wean their babies from breastfeeding or body feeding before daycare. If it's still working for you, feeding from your body is a wonderful way to nurture your baby whenever you are together in the morning, evening, or at night. Time to unlearn myth 10, *Since my baby will be with a grandparent, a nanny, or at daycare, I should reduce my care at home to prepare them*, and replace it with: <u>Providing my baby with as much nurture as possible when we are together is what they need to build</u>

<u>their brain</u>. Your baby is capable of creating a relationship with other caregivers that is nurturing, safe, and respectful. On page 262, you'll find a guide to discussing your nurture expectations with other caregivers.

When you transfer your baby's care to a new person like a family member, nanny, or daycare, a few things can help make the process more nurturing. First, the presence of the mother or primary caregiver's smell or the smell of the home lowers stress and increases connection and synchrony between your baby and a new caregiver. It is powerful to have your scent present while your baby meets a new caregiver.[4] Your scent is the only part of you that can remain when you are gone. If a caregiver is coming into your home, your scent will be in the house. If your child is going out of the home for care, you can transfer your scent onto your child's clothes by sleeping with the clothes or putting them in your armpit or under your bra. You could also put your scent on a transitional object like a blanket or stuffed animal. It's a good idea to do this for the first two to three weeks while your child is building a relationship with a new person.

Second, our babies take emotional information from us, so if it is possible, spend significant time with the new caregiver and your baby. If they are coming to your home, invite them in as a friend and spend time with them and your baby. Your baby will observe your positive and safe social interactions with the person and learn they are safe. Show your baby that you smile with them, laugh with them, and trust them. After a few sessions like this, your baby will begin to be comfortable being alone with the person. You can leave the room, and when your baby asks for you, they can have access to you, get comfort from you, and then go back to playing with the caregiver. After time, your baby will form a relationship with the caregiver so they go to them when they're feeling stress.

If the care is outside of your home, ask if you can attend the place of care with your baby. Spend time with the new caregiver(s) and your baby, showing your baby that they are a safe person whom you trust. Whenever possible, a slow transition is ideal, where you spend a few days (or as much as you can) at the daycare with your baby while they build their relationship with the new caregiver. Dropping babies off at daycare can be hard for both babies and parents, but with a slow transition of care, babies will be less stressed when they are dropped off as they will have a safe adult to go to with their stress. At some daycares you can stay until your baby is calm and playing. If you can't do this, you can say goodbye to your baby and make sure that the daycare is going to comfort and hold your baby until they feel safe.

NURTURED EMPATHY AND THE END OF
BEHAVIOR-BASED PARENTING

Our babies have an internal world made up of physical sensations, stress, emotions, needs, and thoughts. All of our babies' behavior and communication comes from their internal world. When they throw a toy at you, they might be feeling stress and anger inside. When they melt down as you leave the park, they might be feeling stress and sadness inside. When they do something new like walking, they might be feeling stress and joy inside. Remember that beyond the physical needs like hunger, thirst, sleep, movement, or discomfort, babies almost always are needing connection when they have big feelings. See page 269 for the huge range of feelings we and our babies experience and page 274 for the huge range of needs we and our babies experience. You can find feelings and needs resources on my website and put them up in your home to help grow nurtured empathy as well as your own emotional brain.

Nurtured empathy is an alternative to behavior-based parenting. Instead of punishing or rewarding behaviors with the goal of decreasing or increasing behaviors and ignoring the internal world of emotions and needs, we bring our attention to the baby's internal world with the goal of teaching our baby how to navigate emotions, needs, thoughts, and behaviors. We teach them how to be a feeling, needing human with flexible behavior. The process also provides nurtured presence, as we are seeing their internal world, we are curious about their experience, and we provide guidance and protection. The goal is that throughout infancy and childhood, nurtured empathy builds our child's brain toward self-awareness of internal states, self-regulation of internal states, and empathy for others' internal states, and thereby toward managing their emotions and to ultimately manage their own behavior so they do not harm others or themselves. Nurtured empathy teaches babies that there is an internal world behind their behavior and they can interact with their internal world to regulate their stress and emotions to influence behavior. When our babies have big emotions that lead to behaviors, they are communicating to us. Nurtured empathy is how we communicate back to make our babies feel seen, heard, safe, and connected to us.

Nurtured empathy is not what to do; it's how to be. It is the practice of keeping the baby in mind and tuning in to their inner world—it's a posture of curiosity about what's going on for them on the inside. And it is linking their inner world to behavior. It is also about being curious about your mental states and understanding your behavior is influenced by your internal world.[5]

Nurtured empathy is called parental reflective functioning by researchers. Studies show that with practice, parents get better at it. It leads to much higher sensitivity in parenting, which allows parents to be more nurturing, and has huge benefits to the developing infant stress system and the parent brain.[6] It can be incredibly helpful for us to practice observing and wondering about our baby's internal world—their stress, emotions, needs, and thoughts—so we can show up to support them in a nurturing way. This practice is like meditation: When our attention wanders to our emotions or our baby's behavior, we bring it back to "What is happening inside my baby right now?" and "What is happening inside of me right now?"[7]

Nurtured empathy is regulating to babies because you lend them your thinking brain to organize and name their bodily sensations and emotions with their behavior and needs. To practice nurtured empathy, we link the behavior (what the baby is doing) with the underlying feeling (what the baby is experiencing internally) with the need (what the baby might need to regulate their internal feeling). When we name what is happening internally, it connects the thinking brain with the emotional brain to build circuits for regulation. When we meet the need underlying the feeling, we are getting to the root of stress and dysregulation and responding to our baby's communication.

Let's look at an example. A mother and her baby enter a playgroup. Baby clings to Mom's leg, cries, and will not go play. If Mom does not use nurtured empathy and instead focuses on the behavior, she might act to change the behavior by removing her baby from her leg and putting them with the other babies, or saying, "If you stay on my leg there will be a punishment, but if you go play you get a reward." By doing this, Mom is not listening to communication from the baby's survival brain and will augment the baby's stress (feeling) and the clinging and crying (behavior), because the baby needs to be close to their mother to feel safe (need). If the mother uses nurtured empathy, she thinks, "What is going on inside my baby's mind right now, and what is going on inside my mind right now?" She reflects, "My baby is feeling stress and fear (feeling), is clinging to me and crying (behavior), and wants to be close to me (need). This is making me anxious (feeling) that there is something wrong with my baby, so I want to change the behavior and make my baby play (behavior). I know my baby's behavior is because of my baby's mental state and my behavior is because of my mental state. This reduces my anxiety. I can support their need to be close right now, and trust that when they feel safe they will explore." So the mother gets to eye level with her baby and says, "I see you are staying close to me (behavior). I wonder if you're feeling scared (feeling) and need to be close to me right now (need). I will hold you until you feel safe to play. I'm going to take a few deep breaths, so I feel relaxed, too." The baby stays with her mother for ten minutes and then feels safe to play. The clinging behavior changes when the stress goes down and the need is met.

In contrast, behavior-based parenting focuses on modifying, controlling, rewarding, and punishing how babies behave. For example, a parent thinks, "He threw the toy because he is behaving badly and not listening to me," and tries to change the behavior: "If you throw the toy, I'll take away all of your toys." A nurtured empathy approach links behavior to the internal states of feelings and needs. In this example, "He threw the toy (behavior). I'm wondering if he's angry about sharing his toys (feeling) and needs to feel calm with a hug (need). When he is calm we will talk about how to express anger in the future without harming others or himself."

Behavior-based parenting also views behavior as purposeful or manipulative in babies, which looks something like, "He hit me on purpose, and he needs to learn that no one wants to be around him when he's like that." With a nurtured empathy approach, this becomes, "He hit me (behavior). I wonder if he's exhausted (feeling) and needing a rest (need). When he's calm, we will talk about how hitting is unkind and how to express exhaustion without being unkind." A behavior-based approach to crying would be, "She is crying to manipulate me," and trying to change the behavior. "If you don't stop crying, I'll leave you alone until you stop crying." A nurtured empathy approach would link behavior to internal states and needs. "She is crying (behavior). I'm curious if she is scared (feeling) and needs comfort (need)."

Babies don't behave the way they do in order to manipulate or give others a hard time. Rather, their behaviors express stress, emotions, or needs, including developmentally appropriate needs like testing boundaries or asking for attention. They are having a hard time. When we cultivate nurtured empathy—the ability to connect with another person's internal world—we can go to the root of the behavior to name the emotion, which we can regulate; and the need, which is where we can help.

Instead of "Stop whining or I'll put you in your room alone," we might say, "Hmm. I'm wondering if you're feeling upset about something. Let me try to see if I can understand what you're needing so I can help you feel better. Are you hungry? Wanting a hug? Needing some time to jump around and get the wiggles out?" Instead of "He hit me on purpose," we might block the hit with our hands, if possible, and say, "It hurts my body when you hit. Are you feeling frustrated that your brother took your toy? Are you needing a moment with me to recover?" Show curiosity about the feeling or need beneath the behavior and focus on connection—bringing your baby in close to help you both figure out how to meet a need or feel and release an emotion. If the behavior needs to be changed, guiding behavior once the baby is calm will help them choose different behaviors when they feel similar emotions (more on guiding behavior in chapter 7). You will need to have these conversations and support the changes many times until they are learned.

When you learn to observe your baby's internal world you can meet their needs, co-regulate, play, and support exploration. Knowing that, you can connect and support the stress and emotions underlying your children's behavior and communication. Nurtured empathy brings safety, sensitivity, and security to babies, all of the signals that create the nurture bath in the brain. Our babies' internal worlds and our own internal worlds are interrelated. Nurtured empathy is the practice of sharing an emotional brain state connection with someone. When we offer our babies nurtured empathy, we're teaching them to feel comfortable connecting with and sharing an emotional state with another person. That skill will stay with them for the rest of their lives.

When you practice nurtured empathy with your baby, you also give your new parent brain the opportunity to use its neuroplasticity to grow. This skill improves your ability to parent and interact with all people for the rest of your life. It is a powerful opportunity to bolster your mental health and your relationships. This practice rewires your parent stress system, including the amygdala, prefrontal cortex, and hippocampus. It also rewires a vital area of your brain for empathy, the insula, which develops stronger awareness about how your baby feels inside. And it rewires for enhanced empathy, so you are better able to understand how other people feel.

Practicing Nurtured Empathy

Here, we'll look at some of the practical steps involved in nurtured empathy. When you provide empathy like this it helps your baby connect their behavior to a feeling, understand what they are feeling, and that you can handle their stress and emotions and they are safe with you. This wires the stress system and emotional systems in a nurture bath to grow resilient. This is something you might do intuitively, and something you can notice and practice. Be patient with yourself as you learn and practice.

1. Get behind your baby's eyes. Your baby has an internal world; be curious about how they experience a situation. Imagine: What is this like for them? How are they perceiving this moment? How might they feel? When was a time you felt this way? Can you understand the feeling or feel it in your own body? Most of us typically need to practice a lot to do this—and some babies are particularly hard to read. It's not a race; you have your whole lives to get to know each other. Focus on curiosity more than trying to know exactly how they feel or what they're experiencing at every moment.

2. Empathize by reflecting their behavior, how they might be feeling, and their need. This is called marked mirroring. You can do this by:
   a. Showing them how they might be feeling with an exaggerated facial expression—think a cartoony version of happy, sad, angry.
   b. Naming the behavior(s) you see, the emotion(s) your baby might be feeling, and the need(s) they might have—use your emotions and needs lists from pages 269 and 274.
   c. Showing them a reassuring face and telling them that you're here for them.

3. Meet the need. Provide your nurturing presence, co-regulation, play, exploration, sleep, feeding, or otherwise for your baby.[8]

Here are some examples of how this might look in practice, including how to link behavior to feelings and needs:

You walk out of the room and your baby immediately starts crying.

1. Get behind your baby's eyes. Your baby saw you leave, feels sad and afraid that you left the room. They are needing closeness right now.

2. Mirror to your baby. Say, "I left the room and you started to cry (behavior). You are so sad and afraid (feeling) and you're needing

me close (need)," with a big, exaggerated pout. Say, "I am here for you," with a smile.

3. Meet the need. Pick up your baby and hold them close until they are regulated.

Your baby looks into your eyes and smiles.

1. Get behind your baby's eyes. Your baby is calm and alert and initiates communication.
2. Mirror to your baby. Say, "Your eyes are so bright (behavior). You look so playful (feeling) right now," with wide eyes and an exaggerated smile. "What do you want to say (need)?"
3. Meet the need. Respond to your baby's sounds, words, pointing, clapping, and gestures. Give them space to respond back to you. More on baby communication in chapter 6.

You walk into the park and there are lots of kids playing. Your baby holds tightly on to your leg.

1. Get behind your baby's eyes. Your baby is feeling shy. They need to stay close to you to feel safe.
2. Mirror to your baby. Say, "You're not ready to play at the park yet (behavior)," with a timid expression. "You're feeling shy (feeling) and needing to stay close (need). I'm here. You'll know when you're ready," with a smile.
3. Meet the need. Get down on the ground or on a bench or pick your baby up so you're close and at eye level until they feel ready to explore the park.

Your baby jumps out of your arms wanting to crawl.

1. Get behind your baby's eyes. Your baby is calm and alert and needing exploration.

2. Mirror to your baby. Say, "You're jumping out of my arms (behavior). You're so excited (feeling) to get out and crawl (need) today," with a big smile.
3. Meet the need. Provide space for your baby to explore.

After a few minutes they cry and reach for you.

1. Get behind your baby's eyes. Your baby is now feeling stress and needing your mature brain for co-regulation.
2. Mirror to your baby. Say, "You're reaching for me (behavior). Are you worried (feeling)? Let's have a hug (need)," with a concerned look. "I'm here for you," with a reassuring look.
3. Meet the need. Provide the closeness and co-regulation they need.

Your baby wakes up screaming.

1. Get behind your baby's eyes. Your baby woke up and is alarmed and fearful.
2. Mirror to your baby. Say, "You are screaming so loud (behavior). You're afraid (feeling)," with wide eyes. "You're needing a big hug from me (need)," with a soft look.
3. Meet the need: Give your baby a big chest-to-chest hug and rock them back to sleep.

Practicing nurtured empathy takes effort and we won't always have the capacity to do the work. If you don't have any energy for it, think about just being physically there. If you can't empathize and mirror, just be there—pick up your baby and hold them chest-to-chest and tell them, "I'm here for you."

As parents and caregivers, we also have an internal world of physical sensations, stresses, emotions, and thoughts, and all of our communication and behavior as parents comes from our internal world. A vital part of nurtured empathy is to practice with yourself as well. Your behavior also comes from your underlying emotions and needs. This develops the practice and models it to your children. When you do something like yell (behavior), get behind your own eyes and be curious about the emotions happening—"I yelled (behavior) because I'm overwhelmed and stressed (feeling)." Then get curious about your needs—"I need a minute to breathe right now; today I need movement and some time on my own to fill my nurture reservoir (needs)." More on this in chapter 9.

WHEN NURTURED EMPATHY IS HARD

Cultivating nurtured empathy can be particularly challenging if you did not experience it in your childhood. There are two primary ways that stress is handled without nurture, which you might have experienced as a child. The first is to banish, shame, and reject it. Many of us were told things like this by our parents and caregivers: "Stop it." "Calm down." "Enough." "Be happy." "Get out of this mood." "I'll come back when you're happy." "No one likes you when you're like this." What babies hear in these phrases is, "My parent(s) can't handle my stress. My stress makes my parent(s) uncomfortable, scared, or scary. My parent(s) don't want to be around me when I'm stressed." Many of us have been dismissed with a "shhhhhh" or isolated or yelled at or shamed or called names or rejected when we felt stress as a baby and child.

When parents respond to our stress this way, they are refusing to lend us their adult brain to lower our stress curve and bring us to safety. Research shows that it *never* lowers the stress curve. Instead, the baby's stress stays high, and it shapes their brain simultaneously toward stress reactivity and alternative survival mechanisms in lieu of not having access to their adult's brain. When it does not feel safe to show stress, babies learn it is unsafe to be in their body and pay attention to sensations from the body, inasmuch as it is not safe to feel stress because they will not get help to stop stress. Babies then learn to tune out body sensations and internalize the stress by suppressing, repressing, distracting, dissociating, overthinking, or shutting down as a survival mechanism, an alternative to feeling their stress and receiving co-regulation. It teaches babies to ignore the feelings in their body, and to get out of their body or tune out of their body to avoid feeling. It teaches babies not to seek out others to regulate stress—the exact opposite of what is healthy. Or babies learn to externalize stress by acting out or being aggressive. They learn that feeling their stress isn't safe or accepted. This is one of the roots of poor mental health.[9]

Actively going against this message for our babies is so powerful. When our babies are stressed we say, "I'm here for you," "I see you're upset," and we co-regulate the stress. When we nurture we *always* lower the stress curve and bring babies to safety. We want babies, children, adolescents, adults, and parents to seek out others to regulate stress.

The second way stress is handled without nurture is by gaslighting. You're probably familiar with this term; briefly, it means your sanity is questioned over something that you know to be true. In this case a baby will communicate their stress and an adult will say, "Stop reacting that way—nothing is happening, you're fine." Many of us were gaslit; we were told, "You're fine," when we did not feel fine, perhaps feeling panic, rage, or pain. I see this often in babies who have fallen down and start to cry. Their caregivers say, "You're fine, stop crying now," or "Shake it off, you're not bleeding." This communicates to the baby that their stressful or painful experience is not valid, important, or real. It links an internal feeling of stress with the meaning that everything is fine. This is the beginning of teaching people not to trust their intuition, instincts, and what the feelings in their body are telling them. This can wire the brain to interpret high stress, pain, or sensing a threat as "being fine," and it can lead to negative outcomes. When we sense a threat and feel stress, we want to mobilize to get away from the stressor, not suppress, dissociate, freeze, or talk ourselves into being fine with the feeling.

When we nurture, we see our babies feeling stress and we get curious. "How is this for you?" we might ask. "What's going on for you and how can I help?" And we let our babies tell us about their internal experience.

Not being invited to safely express our internal world with our caregivers is one reason many of us have mental health difficulties and need to relearn emotional safety to heal our mental health. Many of us were taught that we are accepted and loved when we have low stress or low emotional needs and are rejected or silenced when we show stress or have needs. When we do this work to support all our baby's emotions, we are also offering our inner baby those same open arms of nurtured presence and empathy.

GIVE YOURSELF GRACE

We as parents or caregivers cannot have a nurtured presence or be accurately attuned at all times. These are practices and mental exercises that take a lot of effort. I like to think of it as an intention rather than a rule; when you have the intention to have a nurtured presence as much as possible, you do your best, which is what your baby needs. You can never do better than your best. Be gentle with yourself at times when you need a rest or are not able to provide this type of presence. Infants benefit from engaging with your nurturing presence regularly and reliably to shape their brain. This does not mean 100 percent of the time.

If you have unresolved early life trauma, or have never seen an example of a nurtured presence, or felt attuned to as a child, cultivating presence and attunement may be harder for you, but it is still possible. It is helpful to invite someone into your home who easily connects with babies, like a family member, friend, postpartum doula, or nanny. Modeling goes a long way; in fact, we need it to know how to parent. If you find it painful or difficult to be present with your baby, a type of therapy known as parent-infant psychotherapy works with parents and babies to develop a nurturing presence that can be incredibly helpful.[10]

Nurtured presence and empathy are a strong foundation for your relationship with your baby, but I'm not suggesting you maintain this twenty-four hours a day, seven days a week. Taking breaks, doing other things when your baby is occupied, sleeping, or being with someone else, losing it and not doing it right are all part of it. Spacing out on your phone or with the television on is totally normal and expected. So don't focus on perfection; focus on growing into these practices bit by bit. Every time we nurture matters.

Chapter 6

WHEN YOUR BABY IS CALM AND ALERT: NURTURING THROUGH CONNECTION

I experienced postpartum depression for the entire first year of my baby's life. I was sleep-deprived, numb, unable to feel joy or connection, and her every cry felt like nails on a chalkboard in my body. I was obsessed with scrolling social media in search of something that would make me feel good. I read sleep blogs, gentle parenting posts, and books trying to "fix" whatever was wrong. One day I saw you post something about the power of nurtured connection and how to practice it. I was sitting on the couch and decided to put my phone down, take a few deep breaths, and put on my favorite song. I felt my body start to move with the music. It felt good. I sat down on the floor and looked at my adorable fifteen-month-old baby. And I just waited. We looked into each other's eyes. Suddenly she started babbling, and as I listened, I realized she wasn't just making nonsense sounds, she was communicating with me! We chatted back and forth for a while, smiling and connecting. It was the closest I'd ever felt with my daughter and the happiest I'd felt in over a year.

With daily practice, I could feel everything shifting. She showed me she liked to turn the pages of a book, how much she liked to mimic me, and how good it felt to hug and cuddle. I could see that she was communicating all the time and that it made her so happy when I picked up on her subtle cues. I'll never get that first year back, but I know that our relationship is so strong now and that I'm going to make connection the first thing I try in every circumstance going forward.

—Rose P.

With Rose's story in mind, imagine the following scenarios: Your baby is in their high chair next to you at the dinner table and they point their spoon toward you, as if asking you to take a bite. Your eighteen-month-old puts up her arms for you to pick her up. Your four-month-old is on the floor doing tummy time and he looks up and smiles at you. You're sitting together and your baby reaches out to grab your nose. Your toddler shows you something they found on the ground. Your newborn looks into your eyes while you change her diaper. Your two-year-old says, "Watch me!" You hear babbles and coos from your baby as you walk. In all of these moments your baby is asking for connection. Their coos, reaching, eye contact, words, and body language make a bid for your attention and your presence.

Connection is deeply nurturing for you and for your baby's brain. This way of being together is fundamental to building the capacity for regulation and resilience in your baby's stress system, like the hippocampus, and building parts of their thinking brain. Connection does this by growing inhibitory neural connections from the thinking brain to the amygdala that contribute to circuits for self-regulation and faster stress recovery. In other words, connection and communication literally build circuitry to regulate stress—within the stress system and in a vital self-regulation circuit in your baby's thinking brain that directly quiets the amygdala and shuts off stress. Nurtured connection simultaneously builds your baby's oxytocin system to boost their social interactions, empathy, lifelong relationships, and their own nurtured parenting.[1]

Nurtured connection only emerges in states of quiet alert—an alert, aware, safe, and low-stress brain state (this is different, as you'll see in chapter 7, from nurturing your baby when they're in a stress state) for both you and your baby. In the quiet alert state, babies' eyes are bright and shiny, focused on you; their breathing is regular and their bodies relaxed. Their movements and posture are organized, not out of control, agitated, or withdrawing. In this state, infants will initiate and guide connection and exploration by making eye contact, smiling, and vocalizing with you. They are reaching out for attention and connection.[2] See figure 11.

To connect, everyone needs to be in a regulated safety state. If you're not in a safety state, use the tools in chapter 9 to support your own regulation and calm. If your baby is not in a quiet alert safety state, it is not a good time to connect with them. They first need your help to be calm and alert. They might need support to calm their stress system (see chapter 7) or rest (see chapter 8).

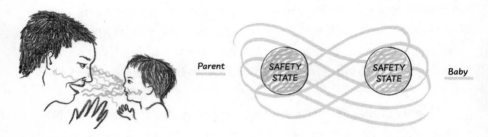

Figure 11.

In safety states, infant and parent brains form connections to support resilience.

Nurtured connection gives babies the repeated experiences of being connected while sharing positive emotional brain states. Remember that a safe emotional connection with other human beings creates the brain circuitry that allows babies to feel safe when connecting emotionally with others for the rest of their lives, and that not having this experience in infancy can lead to discomfort while emotionally connecting with others, while simultaneously needing these connections to be well. It requires working with discomfort to connect with people safely. If you have difficulty connecting with others, this practice with your baby can be an experience for your inner baby and can create new healing connections in your parent brain.

This is not something that babies get from any other activity. Parents often tell me that they connect all day long with their babies—they'll say, "We went to the zoo," "We went to the park," "We had music class," "We had baby gym class," "She played near me while I cooked all morning," or "I sat next to him while he played in the mud." All of this might be great for you and your baby, but they are not necessarily a source of connection unless you make the effort to connect. It takes effort and practice to get into a connected state—it's something you have to do. While it's possible to sit behind your toddler in a music class, this is not a nurtured connection. You might speak to your baby all day, but if they aren't part of the conversation, that's not nurtured connection either. You have to enter their world, be present and engaged. Nurtured connection requires eye contact, touch, interaction, and participation from parent and baby.

Many of us are not used to long, connected emotional exchanges, with eye contact, where you are open to whatever the other person communicates and you respond, and you connect for minutes, don't look away after the connection, don't run away to do something else, and have no control over the situation at all. Whenever I think about nurtured connection I think about my struggle with it. I vividly remember a moment when, sitting on my couch with my six-month-old infant, I was just trying to ignore my mind going in circles about this or that task I had to accomplish so that I could really be present and connect in this conscious, aware conversation.

Despite how challenging you may find this practice, it's so beneficial for you and your baby's brain. Every caregiver can prioritize connection—the point of connection is quality, not quantity.

BABY CHATS

At the heart of connection and relationship is a process that researchers call "serve and return"; I call it "baby chats." It starts when you and your baby are regulated and alert and look at one another. You give your baby time and watch them until they "serve" by reaching out for connection and interaction with eye contact, smiles, sounds, gestures, or touch. You "return" by responding in kind—with eye contact, smiles, sounds, gestures, and touch. Perhaps your baby squeals and you say, "You have a beautiful voice. You're feeling happy! I'm right here, let's chat," and your baby babbles back. You continue to go back and forth, taking turns. These chats are intense for babies, and they often need breaks where they look away for a moment. It's important to wait while babies take a break, as their brains are processing so much, and then to notice when they come back to continue the conversation. True connection—as opposed to forcing your baby to pay attention when they're not in the mood—comes from this back-and-forth, like a good conversation (see figure 11).

When you practice baby chats with your baby, something incredible happens: Your brain waves synchronize. This is called *biobehavioral synchrony*. Specifically, during social interactions, we can measure synchronous theta brain waves in the right brain of parents or caregivers and babies. The right brain, including the stress system's amygdala, hypothalamus, and hippocampus and the thinking brain's orbitofrontal cortex, is highly active in processing stress, emotions, and social cues. Theta waves indicate that babies are learning and wiring this part of their brain in nurtured states of connection toward stress regulation. This synchrony is a necessary ingredient of the nurtured brain bath, fundamental to building the ability for stress regulation that underlies lifelong health in babies. When your brain waves synchronize with your baby's, you're almost like one working brain.[3]

We can also have nurtured connection through play, where we follow our baby's lead. Play is a way that infants express feelings and learn. We can serve and return with them in play by following their cues, just like we do for feeding and sleep. We can notice how our baby invites us to play. Do they serve by holding up a toy, pointing to a book, or putting something in your hands? You can return by commenting on the toy, reading the book, moving the toy in your hands. Then see what your baby serves next, and return that, too. In all nurtured connection it helps to be curious about what your baby might be feeling and thinking.

You won't always read your baby's cues correctly, of course. In baby chats and play, parents and babies follow a pattern of synchrony, rupture, and repair. In synchrony we are in matching states with brain waves connected. In ruptures we "mismatch" and enter different brain states, which is nothing to worry about—in fact, it's actually a good thing. Mismatches help you learn your baby's cues and communication. In repair, you have the opportunity to fix the rupture or mismatch when you pick up the next cue and become synchronous again.

Imagine a father holding his baby on his lap face-to-face. They smile at one another. Their brains are synchronized. The baby makes a surprised face, and the father mimics the face and says in a singsong voice, "Oh, you look surprised. What happened?" The baby smiles and then looks away, a sign that she needs a break. The father doesn't see this cue and tries to make eye contact with his baby again, even though she is looking away on purpose. It is a rupture, a mismatched state. Their brain synchrony is disrupted, and the baby screams, communicating, "I'm looking away, I need a break right now." The father notes the mismatch and gives her a rest. When the baby looks back at her dad with wide eyes, she's saying she's ready. Her father returns the gaze. There is repair and brain waves are synchronized again.

In face-to-face interaction, babies and parents have synchrony about one-third of the time; the rest of the time they are slightly mismatched or fully mismatched. When engaged we mismatch briefly, and then return to being matched.[4] This is why lots of communication is important for both the infant brain and the parent brain. When you're engaging with your baby and you feel a mismatch, like you don't know what they are communicating, sit back and relax and wait to see what your baby will do next. You will connect again, which will be a repair.

Matches, mismatches, and repairs are part of the process of building the infant brain. The goal is to be present with your baby and interact in ways that encourage synchrony. When you have nurtured connections with your baby you release oxytocin, and so does your baby. Higher oxytocin levels lead to more synchrony, so it is a positive feedback loop.

Babies don't need any other toy or game or class. This is it. If you need to choose between sitting face-to-face with your baby and having a little chat and a baby class—choose the time for baby chats. If you're a working parent, get a chat in before and after work and on your time off. If you're a stay-at-home parent, get in some chats throughout the day when your baby is in the mood and invites you in. Here we unlearn myth 11, *You need to buy things for your baby's brain development*, and replace it with: <u>Your presence is the key to your baby's brain development</u>.

ENTERING YOUR BABY'S WORLD: CONNECTING THROUGH THE SENSES

Babies connect and communicate through the senses. This is true for adults, too, which is why spending time in nature, getting a massage or a hug, eating a delicious, fragrant meal, and listening to soothing sounds can all be such healing and regulating experiences for us. But much of the time we adults have turned off and tuned out sensory input in our modern, technology-driven world. It benefits us to reconnect to our senses, and for your baby, sensory input is everything. Babies love multisensory stimulation, and any combination of sensory input is a safety signal; it doesn't have to be everything I discuss below. If one or more is not accessible to you, your unique capacities and abilities for sensory connection are right for your baby.[5]

Your baby's favorite toy is you: your face, your voice, your smell, your touch, and the movement of your body—everything from your heartbeat to the rhythm of your breath to the way you walk and talk. Unlearn myth 12, *I need swings, seats, and containers to take care of my baby*, and also, *My baby needs lots of classes and socialization to thrive*. Replace both with: <u>The sensory experience from my body is the only thing my baby needs</u>. When they're on you, near you, and in utero the world is full of color and wonder. They're receiving a stream of sensory input that helps them feel safe, releases a nurture bath, and stimulates their safety states—which leads to creativity, play, and exploration. They're in a sensory void if they're stuck in a swing or swaddled in a crib all alone.

So the best way to check if you're truly connecting is by entering their world through the senses. Sensory input from your baby is also stimulating and nourishing for your parent brain. Let's take a look at ways to support sensory input for your infant.

Understanding Scent

Your body odor is an incredibly salient safety signal to your baby's brain. It instantly releases an oxytocin cascade and buffers stress.[6] In the womb, babies learn that their mother or pregnant person's scent is a safe, nurturing signal. After giving birth a mother or pregnant person's body odor amplifies in preparation for baby to smell it. When the baby is born, they will seek out the familiar scent on the mother or birthing person's areolas and armpits. The mother or birthing person's scent continues to be a strong safety signal throughout infancy all the way up to adulthood. In animal models, maternal scent activates adult brain circuitry that is protective from anxiety and depression, even when experience in infancy is stressful and there is maltreatment. For parents and caregivers who did not birth the baby, their smell is learned to be safe to baby through experience. When their father or nonbirthing parents spend time holding the baby skin-to-skin after birth or throughout infancy, babies learn that the new person's scents are safety signals.[7]

While babies get safety and nurture signals in their brains by smelling familiar caregivers, it also works the other way around—when parents and caregivers smell their baby, especially their head, their brains get a safety signal that leads to oxytocin and dopamine release to nurture and develop their parent brains.[8] This is one reason why skin-to-skin contact at birth and beyond is beneficial for parents, too. Reject or limit the swaddle, the hats, the gloves, the bassinets, and anything else that bundles up or isolates your baby from the sensory input of your smell. Embrace skin-to-skin contact, baby carriers, and lots of holding.

This goes for artificial scents found in deodorants, shampoo, soaps, cosmetics, laundry detergent, perfume, and room sprays, too. Your baby's safety signal is your natural body odors or chemosignals—just you. Artificial scents, deodorants, and antiperspirants change or reduce your baby's ability to smell you. It's ideal to use unscented shampoo, conditioner, and styling products—nothing with perfumes or artificial smells. Only your natural smell is needed to create a nurture bath for your baby.

If possible, I recommend taking a break from using deodorants and antiperspirants when your baby is young to give them access to your smell. Keeping your armpit hair, or removing it less frequently, also promotes your baby's access to your scent. Wash with unscented, natural soap as needed. Yes, you will smell different. You will have a body odor you're probably not used to. It's worth it to your baby, who is seeking your scent. If you need to wear deodorant, avoid antiperspirants, and choose a deodorant with clean and natural ingredients and minimal scent, and use the same scents every day. A deodorant will be present with your natural scent, but antiperspirants block your scent from leaving your body.

If you love a certain scented product or antiperspirant that makes you happy, I recommend taking a harm reduction approach where you use it from time to time but don't make it a constant presence in your (or your baby's) life. In the first six to twelve months, especially, and for all of infancy, if possible, your baby will get great benefits from smelling the real you.

Artificial scents and air pollution can also be harmful to your parent brain and your baby's developing brain. Artificial scents impact the stress system, especially the hippocampus, and the emotional brain, and can lead to symptoms of depression and anxiety.[9] Removing scents from personal products and your home is nurturing to all of the brains in your house. Adding a HEPA filter to your home helps to reduce artificial scents and air pollution. The best we can do is reduce these factors. We can't eliminate them entirely. In the lab our saying was, "The solution to pollution is dilution," so doing your best to reduce is the goal!

Connecting Through Taste and Feeding

Every feed, by breast, chest, tube, cup, or bottle, is an opportunity for nurturing connection through taste. Beyond that, when babies are fed skin-to-skin on a parent or caregiver's body with a nurtured presence, they receive all of the senses that grow their brains to be resilient—taste, touch, the smell of a caregiver, eye contact, and gentle movement from being in your arms. Babies and parents show beautiful brain-building synchrony when babies are breast, body, or bottle fed with closeness, eye contact, and sensitivity.[10] See figure 12.

Figure 12.

Feeding babies with nurture and synchrony.

The most nurturing way to feed babies is when they are hungry and show hunger cues. Here we unlearn myth 13, *I should feed my baby on a schedule*, which is a mismatch between their cues and when you feed them, and replace it with: <u>I should feed my baby when their body is experiencing physiological signals of hunger and showing hunger cues</u>. Your baby's body is hungry when it is hungry, and your baby is the only person who knows when that is. Learning your baby's hunger cues is a great way to get to know them. My preferred way to tell when a newborn baby is hungry is to gently stroke their cheek; if they turn toward your touch with an open mouth, they are likely hungry. Figure 13 is a chart of common hunger cues; over time your parent brain will learn your baby's unique, early cues. It may take some time, but you will know when they are hungry.

Early	• Smacking or licking lips • Opening and closing mouth • Sucking on lips, tongue, hands, fingers, toes, toys, or clothing
Active	• Rooting around on the chest of whoever is carrying them • Trying to position for nursing, either by lying back or pulling on your clothes • Fidgeting or squirming around a lot • Hitting you on the arm or chest repeatedly • Fussing or breathing fast
Late (calm baby before feeding)	• Moving head frantically from side to side • Crying

Figure 13.
Typical infant hunger cues.[11]

Another feature of connected feeding is to go at your baby's pace. This teaches your baby that they have agency in the world and that the world is not happening to them. If using a bottle, learn paced feeding so you are reading your baby's cues, and your baby can actively drink and take breaks. If breastfeeding or body feeding, read your baby's cues as you feed so your baby can take a break and look away or look at you, and return to feeding when ready. These practices create space in feeding for serve and return to occur.

For connection to happen, it helps to regulate yourself during feedings. Feeding can be triggering or stressful in a number of ways—if your toddler is climbing all over you, for example, or your four-month-old is going through a growth spurt and nursing nonstop. So, take care of you. Give yourself some safety signals and oxytocin release. Try taking a deep breath into your belly, relaxing your shoulders, jaw, and pelvic floor, and looking at your baby. Pause to delight in your baby, speak kind words to them and to yourself.

Know that you will not and cannot have a nurtured presence for every feed. Feedings while looking at your phone, watching TV, or talking to someone will happen and are what you need at that time. Try to also have feeds where you hold your baby's hand, cuddle them, kiss them, talk to them, and connect. You only need to aim to do your best. Your best is revolutionary—never forget it!

If you breastfeed or feed from your body, I encourage you to do it for as long as it works for you and your baby. Feeding from your body for all three years of infancy and beyond is an incredible opportunity for nurture, as long as everyone in the feeding relationship is benefiting. It continues to build your baby's stress system, immune system, and their mouth palate (which is also vital to the developing stress system and brain development). Plus, it provides you with the benefits of oxytocin for every single feed. It is comfort, nourishment, development, health, and closeness. Comfort is not extra, unnecessary, or spoiling; it is vital to building your baby's brain. There is no downside to breastfeeding or body feeding for all of infancy and beyond. Time to unlearn myth 14, *Breastfeeding or body feeding past six or twelve or twenty-four or thirty-six months is extra, spoiling, or for no reason.* Replace it with: <u>Breastfeeding or body feeding at six or twelve or twenty-four or thirty-six months is brain-building and nurturing</u>.

When babies are old enough to eat solid foods, make eating solids a time for nurturing connection, too. At the table you can regulate yourself as best as possible and create positive social experiences as your baby learns to eat. Sit with your baby, talk, and do "cheers" with a cup. When you use mealtimes as an opportunity to connect, you create associations between eating, safety, and connection.

Connecting Through the Senses During Pregnancy

We used to think that infants had no information about the world before they were born, but we now know that they learn a great deal in utero. In the womb infants learn if the world is safe or stressful by the emotions experienced by the mother or pregnant person, and what foods are safe based on the diet of the mother or pregnant person. They learn to prefer the scent of their mother or pregnant person and that it is a safety signal. They develop a preference for the comforting, familiar sound of their parents' voices. Here are some great ways to use the senses to connect with your baby during pregnancy:

1. Your Voice and Music

Auditory bonding, or bonding through sound, begins early in the womb. Through-out eighteen to twenty-five weeks of gestation your baby develops the ability to hear your voice as they begin to learn voices, accents, emotions, and words from the speech they are exposed to. Babies are always listening, and when they are born, they have learned to prefer to listen to the voices they hear the most. At birth a baby will turn toward their parents' voices compared to strangers' voices. This is one way your baby already knows you before they are born. Babies have a great memory for sounds they hear in the womb, which are soothing when they are born. This is a great way to begin your relationship with your baby.[12] Here are some ways to do it:

1. Talk to your baby daily. Tell them how you feel about them and how you are doing. "Hi, baby, I am so excited to meet you. I love you so much and I can't wait to hug and kiss you. I am feeling so tired today, my body is doing so much work to grow you. I can feel you kicking and every kick brings me so much joy."
2. Have your partner talk, read a book, or read a meditation daily, to familiarize your baby with their voice.
3. In surrogacy and adoption, if you are able, record your voice for the pregnant person to play for your baby, and/or visit the baby and talk to them as much as you can.
4. Read a simple baby book to your baby in the womb. They will be able to recognize the book and pay attention when they are born.[13]
5. Sing lullabies to your baby—when they are born the familiar songs will help to soothe them when they are crying, and make them feel safe. Pick a simple lullaby, or ask your parents what songs were sung to you

as a baby. You can nurture your inner baby and your baby with the song. Songs sung by parents are more effective to calm a baby than a recorded song. It doesn't matter if you aren't used to singing; your baby loves your voice no matter what.

6. Play the same relaxing song during a daily breathing practice. Your baby will learn to associate this song with being in a safety state, and when they are born you can use it at naptimes and bedtimes and during times of stress. When you breathe, relax, or meditate in pregnancy, it puts you and your baby into a safety state and your baby gets the benefits, too.

2. Develop Your Touch Relationship with Your Baby

Beginning at twenty-one weeks' gestation, babies respond to touch through the belly with a regulating response. You can start to interact and play with your baby through touch. Some ways to interact:

1. Parents can touch the baby through the belly while talking. Your baby will reach out and touch back. Even if you don't feel it, we see with ultrasounds that babies touch back.[14]
2. Parents can respond to the baby when the baby kicks. When your baby kicks, you can press into the belly in a similar pattern. This is a really cool way to play and communicate.

3. Share a Love of Taste

Tastes sampled in the womb create preferences for babies when they are born. If you have the ability, taste as many foods as you can while pregnant. Make sure to really enjoy your favorites. This will signal to your baby's brain that these flavors are safe, and they will be more likely to try them again when they start to eat.[15]

Sight and Sound

Your voice and your face are important safety signals for your baby. In the womb they learn the voices of their mother or birthing person, their father or nonbirthing parents, as well as other people whose voices are heard frequently.[16] If possible it is a wonderful idea to speak to your baby in surrogacy or adoption, or play a recording of your voice. If you don't have this opportunity, babies who are adopted and born by surrogacy learn your voice after birth. Our tone of voice, or prosody, is what signals safety or danger to our babies and to others.

When we are calm our voices have a singsong tone; this tells our baby we are in a safe and relaxed state and signals them to feel safe and release oxytocin. When our voices have a monotone or flat tone, a high-pitched tone, or a loud and booming tone, it signals to the baby that we are sensing a threat and to their amygdala to detect a threat and launch a stress response. Throughout infancy the voices of loved ones, when calm and regulated, signal safety and cause the release of oxytocin in a baby's brain. When stressed, they can signal danger to a baby and cause the release of cortisol in a baby's brain. It is helpful to use your voice when you can't touch your baby when they need you, like in the car, or when you're in another room. What we say and how we say things to our babies matter. So does providing repair when we signal threats to our babies' brains.[17]

Babies love your voice, including your singing voice. Even if you sing off-key, your baby loves it so much more than a recorded song. So speaking and singing to your baby when you are in a relaxed state will release oxytocin into their brain to provide a nurture bath. I love to sing show tunes to my son, and you can sing anything you want. If you can, inquire about the songs that were sung to you as a baby; your brain has implicit memory for these songs, and when you sing them they can help to calm you and your baby. Singing is helpful to influence your baby to stay or return to a safety state. When your baby is stressed and out of reach, like in the car or in another room, you can use your voice first and say, "I hear you crying. I am here for you. I will be right there," and sing until you can get to them.[18]

Along with sound, your responsive face is a visual safety signal for your baby. When a baby is trying to engage in a chat and their parent or caregiver is unresponsive, it is incredibly stressful. The Still Face experiment shows us how harmful this unresponsiveness can be. When parents respond to infant communication with a still face showing no expression, babies get more and more stressed over time; they might scream, reach out, cry, and arch their backs, indicating high stress. When the parent resumes communicating, babies' stress recedes. There will be many times where it is not possible to engage with our babies when they are ready. In these moments we can tell our baby, "I see you are looking at me and want to have a chat! I need to finish what I'm doing here and I will come to you."[19]

Letting your baby hear your voice and see your face helps you and your baby receive oxytocin, dopamine, and endorphins to nurture both of your brains. You also grow your parent brain to detect your baby's emotions, understand your baby's communication, empathize, and feel good.

Embracing Touch and Movement

The infant brain thrives from closeness and touch; what's more, it expects it. They depend on it for survival and safety. Touch by holding, hugging, kissing, co-bathing, infant massage, and babywearing releases oxytocin and dopamine in our babies and in us. When babies are held, their cortisol release is buffered, effectively keeping them in a nurture bath. The more touch, the more nurture, and the more growth of a resilient stress system. Ideally you want to touch your baby on their skin—another good reason to avoid gloves, socks, swaddles—and keep your baby naked (with a diaper) as much as possible.[20]

The most direct application of neuroscience studies shows us to keep our babies close and provide lots of nurturing touch. In animal models, pups who receive the most touch—the most licking, grooming, nursing, and cuddling from their mothers—grow the most resilience in every part of the stress brain. In human studies, the same results have been found in babies who receive more touch and closeness. These babies grow stress systems and emotional systems wired for lifelong health and wellness.

Combined with touch, movement, like walking or singing and dancing gently while carrying your baby, induces a calming circuit in the infant brain.[21]

Forget the adage "Holding too much will spoil your baby"—with enthusiasm! Hold your baby as much as you want. There is no such thing as too much holding. For some parents, this is a powerful statement. The messaging that says we can hold too much is insidious. You can hold your baby as much as you want. Never, ever hold back on giving your infant unlimited affection and affectionate touch. Your baby needs you to hold them as much as they require, and I want you to feel really good doing exactly that.

Babies in the in-arm phase, which means from birth to the time of crawling, need and benefit from being held most of the time. Some babies will need and benefit from being held nearly 100 percent of the time. I know this can be shocking—I've worked with many first-time parents who were completely unprepared for this reality. Some babies can spend more time out of arms but no matter where your baby falls on the spectrum, all babies benefit from a lot of holding and nurturing touch in the in-arm phase and beyond. Holding ideally is not done by only one parent or caregiver, or even two. The amount of touch and care babies' brains ask for is a twenty-four-hour-a-day job, and that can be overwhelming for one or two people to do. Include all parents and loved ones in holding your baby.

Once babies get out of the in-arm phase, when they start exploring by crawling and walking, their drive for movement and exploration will increase, and this will reduce their need for constant contact. However, they continue to have intense needs for nurtured touch and a desire to connect and be close with you. Often they will go out and explore and move, and need to return to you for you to co-regulate them, and then go back to exploring when they are ready. A generous mindset shift is the key to surrendering to the tremendous need for touch by infants. Our babies need us, and we are growing their brains to health with our touch. All of the cuddles, the holding, and the affectionate touch are critically building a baby's stress system and emotional system and are a gift that lasts a lifetime. Time to unlearn myth 15, *Holding a baby is doing nothing*, and replace it with: <u>Holding a baby is seriously hard and</u>

<u>brain-building work</u>. Hours or days or weeks of holding a baby shapes their stress system and sensitizes your parent brain. It is also helpful to remember that this phase passes, and once it is over your baby will be very busy exploring.

It is common for parents and caregivers to feel "touched out," overwhelmed from the amount of touch. For some babies, a stroller, swing, drive in the car, or attention from another caregiver can give parents a break from touch. One of the best helpers for holding a baby is babywearing. Any type of safely worn baby carrier will give your baby the contact they need and allow you to go for a walk, stretch, tidy up, or use your hands, all while simultaneously building your parent brain.[22] Babywearing is for infants from zero to three years and beyond. There are many carriers for older infants. This is a helpful tool for all of infancy (see page 262 for babywearing resources). Another key support is being able to ask for help from another parent or caregiver so your baby continues to have contact and the primary caregiver has time for a shower, movement, socializing, or anything else they need.

Connecting at Your First Meeting: The Baby Hello

The idea of a "golden hour"—the hour after giving birth—is gaining more traction in hospitals and birthing centers. While this is a good thing—it means that more medical professionals are supporting birthing parents in having skin-to-skin touch and zero separation immediately following birth—it also unfortunately creates a rather limited view of meeting your baby. For one thing, calling it a "golden" hour can often feel misleading, since for many birthing parents, the hour after giving birth is not exactly a tranquil, serene time. Some parents do feel this way, but not all do. You may be having tears sewn, your abdomen closed after belly birth, be birthing your placenta, have contractions that are still quieting down, legs shaking, nurses running in and out, and feeling exhausted and drained rather than golden. The "hour" descriptor is also rather limited. If you give birth via surgery or need to be separated from your baby after birth for health reasons, it can feel like you missed out on something important. Adoptive, surrogate, or foster parents may feel left out of this experience altogether. And while some parents feel overwhelming joy and love immediately when they meet their baby, other parents take days or weeks to fall in love, and they worry that they've failed if that first hour didn't feel blissful. In other words, the idea of a golden hour immediately following birth puts too much pressure on that one moment—and then we miss the opportunities we have to do this beautiful, nurturing bonding whenever and wherever we meet our baby.

The truth is that the first time you meet your baby *and the six weeks following*, whether immediately after birth, in the NICU, at the end of an adoption process, or when you recover from a postpartum health or mood issue, or even partway through their infancy if you haven't had this experience before, is a special, sensitive time, whenever and however it happens. All parents deserve tools to support that meeting. For all these reasons, I find it more productive to think of the first time you meet your baby as the "baby hello." Babies have a special way of saying hello. It's slow. It takes time. And it happens through the senses.

To say hello to a baby, first take off your shirt (or open your shirt or robe). Then take off your baby's clothes except for their diaper, lay their naked body on your naked chest, and cover them with a blanket. If this is overwhelming, start smaller, with your baby's cheek on the skin of your chest, and work up to more. Your chest is a one-of-a-kind special home for your baby. Both babies and parents have special nerves in their chest called CT-afferent nerves. These sensitive nerves respond only to pleasurable touch and release oxytocin and dopamine into the baby and parent brains, which puts both baby and parents into nurtured safety states. Take off your baby's hat and smell their head, which will lead to a release of oxytocin and dopamine in your parent brain—a direct hit of parent brain transformation.

In this skin-to-skin position on your chest, your baby receives the complete sensory experience that your body provides. Their newborn or baby brain is expecting this experience. Your smell, your voice, your breathing, your movement, your touch are all safety signals for your baby, which release nurturing hormones like oxytocin and dopamine into their brain. Their emotional brain begins to be shaped. Your baby's stress is buffered by you as their amygdala is silenced. Your chest regulates your baby's body temperature through the special CT-afferent nerves.[23] In skin-to-skin with a lactating mother or parent, your baby's body receives cues to start feeding when they are ready and the parent's oxytocin and prolactin rise to produce milk and develop the parenting brain. The baby may enter a deep and restful sleep. Everything nurturing happens for babies in this multisensory and vital skin-to-skin position.

When you meet your baby, they see your face at a distance of about six to eight inches, the exact amount of space between their eyes and your eyes when you cradle them in your arms. Most of us have an instinct to hold a baby on our left side over our hearts. In this position they can take in emotional information, which is highly expressed on the left side of your face, and they hear your heartbeat.[24] They synchronize their breath to yours and their heartbeat to yours. You regulate their temperature, oxygen levels, and glucose levels. They hear your voice, which they prefer and recognize if they have been hearing it throughout pregnancy, or which they've begun learning. They smell you and begin to learn your scent or are nurtured by the scent of the mother or birthing person. They feel your touch and your hugs and kisses. They feel your feelings. Your brains and bodies synchronize into one connected being.

Speak softly to them so they can hear your voice; hug and kiss them so they can feel you. If it's available, you can feed them. Make faces for them to imitate, and imitate their faces and sounds back to them. This is the beginning of baby chats.

In this skin-to-skin position, you also receive the sensory experience that your baby provides. Your parent brain is expecting this experience. Your baby's touch, smell, and sounds are a safety signal to your brain. The CT-afferent nerves in your chest send signals to your brain to reduce stress hormones and release oxytocin and dopamine into your brain to make you feel calm, connected, and in love. These hormones transform your parent brain and increase your confidence as a parent. Your amygdala activity is reduced to promote lower anxiety and fear. Baby in skin-to-skin also helps recovery if you have just birthed, by stimulating the uterus.

Ideally, you'd lie in contact with your baby like this for at least sixty to ninety minutes at the first meeting, up to hours or days, followed by multiple daily sixty- to ninety-minute sessions throughout the first six weeks of knowing them. This is known as "kangaroo care" and has been well studied to have brain-nurturing benefits.[25] If this is not feasible for you, just do skin-to-skin whenever and for however long you can. Remember that any nurturing we do benefits our babies and us.

The current default for many parents and in many hospital births is to wrap the baby up in a tight swaddle like a burrito, invite the whole family in, and pass the baby around like a hot potato. When newborns are home, most are swaddled constantly, with a pacifier, sound machine, and lots of time in a movement machine or a bassinet, swing, or stroller. These are not nurturing practices. It is not respectful to the baby's or parents' brains. In this way neither baby nor parent is getting a nurture bath. We need a dramatic shift. Please unlearn myth 16, *Newborn babies are happy with a swaddle, hat, pacifier, and bassinet*, and replace it with: <u>Newborns are happy on someone's skin, chest-to-chest, covered by a blanket—no swaddle, hat, pacifier, or bassinet needed</u>. See figure 14.

Figure 14.

A baby hello; this is the default place for babies when you meet them and at least the first six weeks that follow.

Skin-to-skin, sensory closeness is not just a nice thing to do for bonding—it's vitally important for your baby's brain and stress system. These must be protected. It builds your baby's social-emotional brain, promotes growth, decreases pain, and changes DNA expression via epigenetics.[26] Being close to a caregiver and being touched regulates all of the survival brain functions; it boosts physical health; stabilizes heart rate, breathing, blood glucose, blood oxygen, body temperature; builds the immune system; improves sleep; promotes breastfeeding or chestfeeding success and weight gain; decreases pain perception; decreases crying episodes and duration; and activates infant speech motor areas and imitation of sounds. It boosts mental health by lowering stress and anxiety for the baby and parent(s), enriches infant-parent interactions, increases baby smiling, promotes bonding, increases parent confidence, and has effects twenty years later.[27]

Tips for the baby hello:

- In many vaginal births, you can put your baby on your chest immediately. All of the examinations that happen post-birth can be done with your baby on your chest. This is the default care by midwives. With obstetric care you or your partner must state clearly your preference, often many times, to influence the staff to provide this care. You can delay a vitamin K shot and erythromycin eye drops for one hour or so after birth, to allow for an undisturbed skin-to-skin as well as for looking into your baby's clear eyes as you meet them.

- In many belly births you can also put baby on your chest immediately. You can absolutely ask for examinations to be done on your chest in this case as well. You might be able to hold your baby skin-to-skin for sixty minutes and delay vitamin K and erythromycin as well. However, if there are medical considerations for the baby or the birthing person, you might not be able to hold your baby. In this case it is ideal if the other parent (or partner or family member or doula, most ideal if it is someone whose voice is familiar to baby) stays with the baby and talks to them in low tones, touches them, and holds them skin-to-skin as soon as is medically possible.

- If your baby is taken to the NICU, remember that with few exceptions all babies benefit from skin-to-skin there as well—including premature babies and babies with medical concerns. This is a medical best practice, and ideally is done in all NICUs. However, it is often not done, and you may have to state your preference very strongly to get as much skin-to-skin time as possible.[28]

- There are wonderful stretchy wraps that parents can bring to the hospital, and that some hospitals provide, that enable you to wrap your baby in skin-to-skin as you recover so that they are secure on your body. It is perfectly fine to use the swaddle and bassinet, as parents do need breaks, but always remember that the bassinet is ideally only a temporary place for baby, while skin-to-skin is the ideal default place. If you are comfortable, you can sleep on an angle with your baby on your chest in the hospital—some babies will only sleep in this position (see appendix, page 262, for safe sleep resources).

- Know that physical, sexual, and relational trauma can and do make skin-to-skin difficult for many of us. If it is not comfortable, you might work up to it, starting with small amounts and increasing if it becomes more comfortable. If you are not comfortable with small amounts, think of who in your life might be. Other people in your life might be more comfortable and support your family by holding your baby skin-to-skin.

- If your baby is older, and you didn't do a lot of skin-to-skin in the newborn or infant time, you can do it now. Repair is always possible. Older babies benefit from skin-to-skin, and so does your parent brain.

A CONNECTION PRACTICE

Connecting with your baby might be the first time you are fully present with another person, which can be both challenging and healing to your emotional brain and transformative to your developing parent brain. This isn't to suggest that you spend the whole day connecting with your infant, but rather that you commit to supporting the relationship, just like you would any relationship, by checking in, spending quality undistracted time together, and building the connection between you. I suggest taking ten- to twenty-minute sessions throughout your day to intentionally be in relationship with your baby.

Nurtured connection means being present, engaged, and responsive with your baby. You're paying attention to the present moment, not thinking of tomorrow or what to make for dinner. Much like meditation practices, you draw your attention back to the present whenever you feel it slipping away. No distractions, no phones, no television on in the background. You notice your senses—what you hear, feel, smell, taste, and see. And you're curious about your baby's senses—what do they hear, feel, smell, taste, and see? You and your baby are in a dance, a conversation with your bodies—a back-and-forth between you. They communicate with you and you with them. Your stress is regulated in your body, so you are calm and able to give your full attention to your baby. You have an open body posture, with your whole body facing toward your baby; your eyes are bright and at the same level as your baby, and you look at your baby. You are prepared for eye contact when your baby offers it, calmly directing your attention to your baby to take in all of the communication they send out from their survival brain. Using words, sounds, and body movements, you respond to your baby's communication and exploration. You enter a back-and-forth dance of communication or comfort.

In practice, this might look like sitting face-to-face on the couch with your newborn, your knees bent, and their body propped up on the incline of your thighs. You take a few moments to gaze at one another. What do you see? Take all of them in with your eyes. Their little nose. Their lips. Their hands and feet. How does your baby smell? What sounds do you hear? Their breath? Yours? Little gurgles and burps? How does your baby feel to the touch? Soft? Fuzzy? Warm? Don't rush. You have all the time in the world for this. You don't have anywhere else to be, and nothing to do but be together, sensing and taking each other in.

For an older, wigglier infant it might look like setting your phone down, getting on the floor so that you're at eye level with your baby, and directing all your attention toward them. A colleague of mine finds that bath time is a good time for this. Her two-year-old son, Oliver, likes to fill a cup with water and pour it out over and over again and kick his feet and swim around in the water, and she finds this relaxing to observe. So she sits next to the tub and watches with her full presence: talking with Oliver, touching his hair, telling him she loves him, listening to the sloshing of the water, noticing his focus and engagement as he fills and pours, and singing silly songs with him.

You may already have the skill of nurturing connection, and if so, then this will come easily to you. Or if you are like me, it may be something you struggle to do. Maybe just the thought of not doing something makes you want to tackle your to-do list instead or turn on the television. That's okay—despite many social media posts making it seem like the moment you see your baby you'll know exactly how to connect with them and will happily fill your days staring into their eyes, it's actually very common for parents to need to practice nurturing connection. It does take effort and concentration. It will come easier with time—and even once you've got it down, some days it will be easier than others. With time and intention, you can continue to cultivate your presence so you can better participate in a relationship with your baby. Jon Kabat-Zinn says, "We don't practice mindfulness to get good at mindfulness, we practice it to get good at life." The same goes for a nurtured connection with your baby. It might always be a struggle to practice it, but we don't practice it to get good at it, we practice it to grow our baby's brain and our parent brain.

Applying Nurtured Presence and Nurtured Empathy to States of Connection

Let's look at some practical ways you can work on applying nurturing presence and nurtured empathy, the cornerstones of nurture, to connecting with your baby. It's okay if it's a little awkward at first or if you only remember after the fact to bring your nurtured presence to an interaction with your baby or use nurtured empathy to understand them better. Be gentle with yourself as you practice.

I recommend trying to find ways to make this time together enjoyable for you both. There are endless ways to practice nurturing connection, so think about what might work best for you. If you don't enjoy bath time or find sitting on the couch to be too sedentary, you can always put on your favorite music and hold your baby close while you dance and sway, or sit outside in the grass together, or do tummy time together, or go to a café together. The "what" and "where" don't matter as much as the "who" and "how"—you and baby, chest-to-chest or face-to-face, in a calm and regulated state, entering each other's world while everything else filters out.

Nurtured Presence for Connection

With your presence communicate the answer to your baby's unconscious questions:

Do you see me?

Take a breath and look at your baby—they are bursting with excitement to connect with you.

Do you care that I'm here?

Take a minute, care that they are there—radiate the awe and joy you are feeling with your baby.

Am I enough for you, or do you need me to be better in some way?

Show radical acceptance for this state, right now. Your baby is bursting with more-than-enough-ness right now. They don't need to say or do or perform anything to be enough.

Can I tell that I'm special to you by the way that you look at me?

Look at them with love and acceptance.

Nurtured Empathy for Connection

1. Get behind your baby's eyes. Be curious about how your baby experiences this connection.

   > What is this like for them? Being with you is the most important thing in the world.
   >
   > How are they perceiving this moment? As the best time of their life.
   >
   > How might they feel? Excited, joyful, expressive, loving, playful.
   >
   > When was a time you felt this way? When was the last time you felt deep connection?
   >
   > Can you understand the feeling or feel it in your own body? Love, openness, joy.

2. Empathize by reflecting their behavior, how they might be feeling and their needs. You can do this by:

   a. Showing them how they might be feeling with an exaggerated facial expression—a huge smile and bright eyes.

   b. Naming the behavior(s) you see, the emotion(s) your baby might be feeling, and the need(s) they might have—say, "You are looking at me (behavior). I wonder if you're feeling happy (feeling) and want to talk to me (need)." Or, "You shared your toy with me (behavior). That must feel so good inside to be kind (feeling). Let's keep playing (need)."

   c. Showing them a reassuring face and telling them that you're here for them. "I am here for the fun baby."

3. Meet the need. Provide your nurturing connection—go back and forth with serve and return; give your baby breaks to look away and notice when they come back.

Imagine that every time you have a nurtured connection with your baby, you are wiring powerful circuits in their brain that will fire at all the best times of their life, like when making friends, falling in love, and feeling deep connections, as well as at all of the challenging times in their life, like during breakups, hardship, loss, and disappointments. The circuits will support resilience, safety states, sociability, thinking, and problem solving.

Chapter 7

WHEN YOUR BABY IS CRYING, CLINGING, WITHDRAWN, OR MELTING DOWN: NURTURING STRESS

For the first nine months of my baby's life I was very worried that something was wrong with him or wrong with me. I was constantly exhausted, anxious, scared, and confused. None of my friends' babies were like mine. My baby cried a lot. He usually woke up crying in a bad mood. For sleep, my baby needed to be held, in a baby carrier and sometimes in a stroller. If my baby was put down alone at any time, he would instantly let out an intense, piercing cry. My friends were going to coffee shops and baby classes with their relaxed babies, but I couldn't dream of doing anything like that. They all thought I was being uptight. But getting into the car seat was a nightmare, and that was once we got out the door. A friend gave me a baby book as a solution, but my baby did not "eat, play, sleep" like the book said—and it sent me further into uncertainty. I thought I wasn't a good mother because I couldn't follow these simple rules. Or that there was something wrong with my baby because he couldn't follow.

One day I was sitting on the toilet, hiding in the bathroom from my cranky, clingy baby, and I saw your post about normal infant behavior and how that applies to my unique baby, as well as the changes in my intuitive parent brain. I learned to tune in to my instincts, which were to respond to my baby's distress, hold him constantly and help him to feed and sleep on cue, however irregular and unpredictable. I understood that schedules and sleep training would not fundamentally change my baby, who didn't have problems, but had high needs for regulation and a highly sensitive stress system. I learned to ask my partner, mother, and a nanny to help so I could have time for myself too. In the end I did not change anything about my parenting, but I did drastically change how I saw my baby and myself as a mom. I went from seeing a baby who might have something wrong to a baby who was expressing deep, important needs. I went from a mother who was questioning every move to a mother with bold confidence and deep strength.

—*Elena S.*

From a neuroscience perspective, the way to support infants when they are stressed—in pain, in need, frustrated, sad, lonely, uncomfortable, disappointed, withdrawn, crying, clinging, or having a tantrum or a meltdown—is clear and simple: Your infant needs to borrow your calm, regulated brain to help them regulate and come back into a safety state. All infant stress is communication; they are telling us that their stress systems are overwhelmed and they feel unsafe and dysregulated. Their cortisol is high, their oxytocin is low, and they sense a threat. They need us to provide oxytocin to help them feel calm and safe. As illustrated in figure 15, when infants are in a stress state, they need us to reliably and consistently be in a safety state, present with them, and curious about what they need in order to come back into safety and regulation. Or as Carly Grubb, founder of Little Sparklers and The Beyond Sleep Training Project, puts it, "Your child needs you to respond. Every time. Day or night. It's that simple, and it's that hard."[1]

Nurturing your infant's stress is often one of the most challenging aspects of parenting. Infants feel stress and big emotions often. You can unlearn myth 17, *Babies' stress and emotions don't matter and can be ignored*, and replace it with reality: <u>Babies feel transformational stress and a huge range of emotions that influence how their brains and bodies develop</u>. They feel stress deeply and intensely, and unlike many of us adults, they hold nothing back. In the three years of infancy, your baby will likely need to borrow your mature brain to recover from stress every single

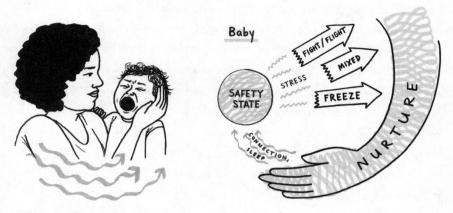

Figure 15.

When babies are in a stress state, they need you to be in a safety state, nurture them back to a safety state, and growing their emotional brain. Nurtured connection (chapter 6) and sleep (chapter 8) grow babies' emotional brains in safety states.

day, and most nights. Babies are born with the healthy pattern of being free to feel stress, express themselves completely, and seek out a regulating caregiver for co-regulation. Their brains are wired to seek their reliably nurturing caregivers when they don't feel safe or regulated, whether that arises from a need for closeness or for kissing a boo-boo or trying a new experience. They've not learned to hide, divert, distract, or suppress stress the way many (or most) of us did through low-nurture parenting.

We want to help our babies keep this healthy freedom of feeling and expressing themselves so that they know that feelings are safe, temporary, and provide important information about needs. We want our babies to depend on us to provide a nurture bath, lower their stress curve, and transform their brains. Another parenting myth about infant stress is, *If we respond to our crying, clinging babies, we teach them that that behavior is good, so they learn to cry and cling more.* This is inaccurate. Let's unlearn myth 18 and replace it with: <u>When we respond to crying and clinging, babies cry less and we build the infant brain to be more independent</u>

later. When parents are more responsive, babies cry less and often for shorter durations.[2] More responsiveness to stress leads to a resilient stress system, which supports social development, secure attachment, language development, cognitive development, fewer behavioral issues, less aggression, and more parent confidence and less parent anxiety.[3] Helping babies move from a stress state to a safety state profoundly builds the vital brain regions in the stress response—the amygdala, hypothalamus, hippocampus, and prefrontal cortex, and thereby the rest of the emotional brain—neurotransmitter systems, gut health, and cognitive systems (see figures 6, 7, and 8).

Just like with nurturing connection, we nurture our babies' resilient stress systems through listening to them, being curious about what they are communicating with their behavior, learning their unique temperament, sensitivities, and preferences, and offering our nurtured presence for co-regulation and connecting through the senses.

I've worked with many parents for whom the idea that lending your adult brain to your baby regulates and calms them brings on shame or self-blame when their baby cries. Some parents assume their baby's cries mean they aren't making their baby feel safe enough. I want to be clear that nurturing stress does not mean that if you are calm or responding "correctly," your baby will automatically be calm or never cry (or the opposite—that if your baby is stressed, it's your fault because you aren't calm enough). I like to use the metaphor of a bridge to explain how this works. In your baby's brain there is not yet a bridge between threat and safety states. They cannot get from point A to point B without you. You add that missing part with your adult brain. When you are calm in a safety state, your oxytocin is boosted and you're able to increase oxytocin in your baby; when you soothe your baby in that state, you're creating a pathway for their brain to move from a threat state to a safe and calm state—you're being the bridge for them. Your calm state helps encourage their bodies to release oxytocin and over time stop the stress so their bodies can return to a relaxed safe state. This part is important: *Only your baby can walk over that bridge. You are the responsive, attuned witness to the process.* How reactive to stress they are, how intensely they feel stress, and how long it takes them to come back into a state of safety is a product of their temperament, genes, and other factors, such as if they are hungry or tired at that moment. Your nurture is the bridge, but your baby's own nervous system determines when and how they'll walk over.

It's not going to be predictable and you can't control it; sometimes the journey from a stressed threat state to a regulated safety state will be fast, and sometimes it will take a long time. You don't have to stop your baby's stress—that's not your job—but you (or another caregiver) do have to be there to be the bridge so that they can cross it when they're ready.

So the question for us nurturing caregivers is: How can I support and regulate my infant during times of stress so that they have experiences of being partnered through their stress and have someone there to help them make sense of it? Or to use the language of neuroscience: How can I increase oxytocin and decrease cortisol when my child is stressed? For many of us, it also encourages us to ask: How can I support and regulate *myself* in order to be a nurturing, calm presence for my child during times of stress?

YOUR BABY'S STRESS RESPONSE

Here's how the stress curve works. Your baby's brain senses something that feels scary or threatening, such as being put down, being alone, hunger or thirst, shyness, discomfort or pain, tiredness, loud sounds, or something you might not be able to figure out. Their amygdala sounds the alarm—"There is a threat"—and their hypothalamus is activated and releases stress hormones to transform the brain and body to deal with the threat. The stress curve goes up and they go into an active alert state. Their survival brain activates behaviors like clinging and crying in order to find you and keep you close so you can help with the threat and help return them to a safety state, bringing their stress curve down, back into a state of quiet alert (see figure 6).[4] These cascading and involuntary physiological changes that influence the brain, body, and behavior are the stress response; they're also known as the fight, flight, or freeze response. Some babies tend to have a fight-or-flight response, others a freeze response, and some have combination fight-flight-freeze responses.

When babies are in an active alert state, they show early stress cues. In a fight-or-flight response, common early stress cues are whimpering or whining, lower-intensity crying, clinging, repetitive movements, or running around. These behaviors indicate feelings of fear, upset, irritation, frustration, crankiness, agitation, or annoyance. The early cues of a freeze response are hiding behind you, withdrawing from social interaction or play, staring, and low movement. These behaviors indicate feelings of fear or sadness. The early cues of a combination response are a mix of fight-or-flight and freeze behaviors, with feelings of anxiety, worry, or hypervigilance. In all of the states we might see irregular breathing, no eye contact, an active face and body, and sensitivity to internal stimuli like hunger or discomfort and external stimuli like sounds, bright lights, or too many people. If we are able to respond to those early cues indicating an active alert state, with nurtured presence and empathy, we can usually lower their stress curve relatively quickly and return them to a quiet alert state where they want to engage or explore.[5]

When babies are in a crying state, they show later stress cues. In a fight-or-flight response, later stress cues are usually screaming, loud crying, irregular breathing, face turning red, body posture like an arched back or flailing, asymmetrical arm and leg movements, hands in fists, spinning, repetitive movements, head shaking from side to side, biting, hitting, and kicking. These behaviors indicate feelings of fear, frustration, and anger. The later stress cues of the freeze response include more intense hiding, withdrawal, curling up in a ball, lying down, or unresponsiveness. These behaviors indicate feelings of fear and despair. The later stress cues of combination responses are a mix of late cues of fight-or-flight and freeze, with feelings of anxiety, worry, or hypervigilance. Your baby's need for co-regulation is urgent. These cues are signs that their fight-or-flight or freeze nervous system response is in high activation.[6] Figure 16 shows the common early and late stress cues.

In fight-or-flight in the highest level of stress the body can handle, babies can vomit, have diarrhea, lose all postural control, thrash around, hit, bite, and kick, indicating that their brains and bodies are flooded with stress, fear, and rage. After flooding, their nervous systems can progress into a collapse or freeze state, which may look like staring,

Early Stress Cues	
Fight-or-Flight	Whimpering or whining, lower-intensity crying, clinging, repetitive movements, or running away
Freeze	Hiding behind you, withdrawing from social interaction or play, staring, and low movement
Combination	Mixed fight, flight, and freeze cues

Late Stress Cues	
Fight-or-Flight	Screaming, loud crying, irregular breathing, face turning red, losing body posture like an arched back or flailing, asymmetrical arm and leg movements, hands in fists, spinning, repetitive movements, head shaking from side to side, biting, hitting, and kicking
Freeze	More intense hiding, withdrawal, curling up in a ball, lying down, or unresponsiveness
Combination	Mixed fight, flight, and freeze cues

Figure 16.

repetitive movements, lying down, drowsiness, or sleep. In freeze at this high level babies look tired and sleepy. In both states these behaviors indicate feelings of exhaustion and sleepiness. Combination states at this level can also progress to the highest levels of freeze.[7]

Stress responses occur on a spectrum, so every baby's stress experience will be different. Some babies have obvious early cues, while others don't—they just go straight to the higher stress state. Some babies will only have minor stress that you can buffer easily just by being with them, and others will have explosive stress that requires more soothing and support. Your baby has a unique temperament, and one aspect of that temperament is stress reactivity.[8] Take a look at figure 17: On one end of the spectrum are infants with low stress reactivity. This is about 40 percent of babies. They don't feel a lot of stress and cry rarely; they have regular schedules, positive emotions or moods, settled sleep, and lower needs for co-regulation. About 50 percent of babies fall in the middle of the spectrum between low and high reactivity. Ten percent of babies are on the other end of the spectrum, with high stress reactivity. These babies feel stress very often, and their stress is high-intensity: They cry a lot, have negative emotions or moods, need constant co-regulation, touch, or movement. They have irregular routines, are difficult to calm to sleep, and have unsettled sleep patterns. They can be very sensitive to sound, light, clothing or blankets, food textures, and more. It is harder to buffer the stress of these babies. They need a lot of support, and even with a reliably responsive external brain to soothe them, they feel stress often and deeply.[9] Since they make up a low percentage of the population, many parents with highly reactive babies don't know another baby like theirs, so please know it is normal.

When we nurture babies on any part of the spectrum, we change their epigenetics toward lower stress reactivity. Temperament is influenced by genetics and epigenetics that act in the stress system or sensory systems. We can't train our baby to have a different temperament— for example, to be less reactive to stress—but when we nurture our baby's stress, we help them develop lower stress reactivity as they grow up because we are wiring their stress system, regardless of where they start on the spectrum. (The opposite is also true. When we ignore our baby's stress, they can develop a stress system with higher reactivity than where they start on the spectrum.) I think of it as nurturing the stress from past generations, to heal our ancestors' experience in our babies. My mother nurtured my highly reactive stress system in infancy, which could have been from the epigenetic markers from previous generations, and that influenced me to be in the middle range of stress reactivity after

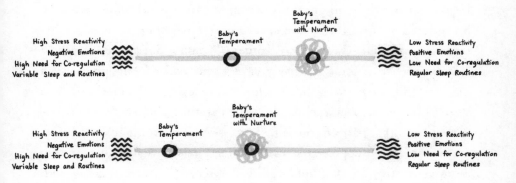

Figure 17.

Stress reactivity is a feature of temperament and occurs on a spectrum. Nurture helps develop lower stress reactivity in babies, regardless of their baseline temperament. The baby on the top is born with lower stress reactivity than the baby on the bottom, and nurture moves both babies toward a lower stress reactivity.

infancy. Then I nurtured my baby's stress, and now his stress system is less reactive than mine—and his baby's stress system might be less reactive than his, and so on.

It doesn't mean anything is wrong with your baby if they are reactive to stress—it's their biological makeup. We can have wholehearted acceptance for this. They're babies whose genetic and epigenetic inheritance creates a more reactive stress system and perhaps higher sensitivity to the environment. They have a higher need for you to nurture their stress in order for them to flourish.[10] It may be more challenging to help a high-needs baby come back into a safety state, but you don't have to worry that their brain is bathing in toxic levels of stress just because they feel stress often and intensely; we know that we make a transformative difference to their brain and stress system when we show up consistently and are present with their stress physically and emotionally. Your nurtured presence is putting oxytocin in their brain and body and buffering negative effects of their stress.

Stress isn't inherently bad. In fact, the experience of becoming stressed and then having a calm, responsive caregiver lower your stress curve helps your baby's brain grow resilience; but infants need their stress to be buffered by a nurturing presence. An external brain is necessary. As trauma expert Dr. Gabor Maté argues, "Trauma doesn't have to be a war experience or some atrocity you've witnessed. It is enough that as a kid, you had parents who didn't help you process your bad feelings. You were alone and so overwhelmed by your painful reality that you disconnected from that part of yourself."[11] Stresses only become toxic if babies are repeatedly unsupported, denied, shamed, rejected or if a caregiver is a source of stress by withholding their presence. Nurture is being with and supporting stress, and lowering the stress curve as needed. Consistent, reliable experiences of being supported and partnered through stress build the brain and buffer our infants from the effects of toxic stress, no matter how often and how sensitively your baby feels stress.

Imagine your child's stress system as a ship at sea. Stress is when a storm hits. If there's no lighthouse on the shore to guide the ship home, or the light that is present is disorienting and flashing on and off, or guides them farther out into the storm or onto some dangerous rocks, their ship gets wrecked or lost, and their brain gets changed by the stress toward reactivity and the mental health vulnerabilities that come along with that. But if when a storm hits there is a clear and bright light guiding them home to safety, a light that says, "I'm here. I'm listening. You need help. Come this way. How can I support you?," you help your baby's brain grow resilient from stress.

The best way to nurture your baby's unique temperament is by observing them and getting to know their stress response patterns and their safety response patterns. It's helpful to learn your baby's cues for basic needs, learn their early stress cues (if they have them), and learn what calms your baby so that you can respond to their stress cues as early as possible. We are not trying to stop babies from becoming stressed from life's events, but we want to support them to *return* to safety states and minimize the experience of very high and very long periods of stress states when they're alone.

Nurturing Learning and Exploration

Babies have a strong drive for exploration, especially when they've had all their needs for sleep, food, and connection met and they're in a calm, quiet, alert state (babies cannot learn or explore when they are experiencing fear). It's necessary to give them opportunities to explore and move when their brains are seeking exploration. We don't want to avoid this learning state by doing everything for our baby. If you are hovering and taking every obstacle away, like never letting them try a spoon or a cup or never struggling with lifting their head during tummy time, sitting up on their own, or taking their first steps, it can cause stress for your baby as it hinders their exploration, motor, and cognitive development and can prevent them from building perseverance, confidence, intrinsic motivation, and resilience in their stress system.[12]

Sometimes when babies are learning, playing, or exploring in a calm, quiet alert state they can enter a low-stress active alert state, showing some frustration, anger, and hesitation. They are physically engaged and motivated and they're trying to do something challenging or new that activates low-level stress, like the frustrating but rewarding struggle to roll over for the first time, or the determined attempt to bring their hands to their mouth, get a puzzle piece in the right place, or put on their own shoes. In this learning state, their bodies are indeed releasing stress hormones like cortisol, but they are releasing rewarding dopamine at the same time, because learning and exploration are pleasurable and exciting! If you are close while they are learning, you are also adding oxytocin, which buffers the effects of the stress and might help them stay in the learning zone. So you want to encourage these learning states by being close but not hovering or interrupting, staying curious about your baby's internal experience, doing marked mirroring as needed, and being ready to regulate them if and when their state escalates to a higher crying level of stress.

It might look something like this: You put your baby down on a blanket on the floor for some playtime and they start trying to grab their feet or bring a toy to their mouth. They're happy and babbling at first, but then as they try and fail, they begin grunting and breathing hard. You work to resist any urge you have to immediately step in. You can chat with them: "You're working so hard to grab your feet!" "I'm right here if you need me." They will signal to you when their stress rises and they need to be close again—usually with disorganized movements or posture and loud cries. In response, you give them your nurtured presence by picking them up, giving them a hug, and maybe saying something like, "I'm here for you." Once they feel regulated again, they may want to play more.

Babies who can crawl and walk may seek exploration by crawling away from you, climbing on the couch, throwing their toys, dressing and undressing themselves, picking up rocks and sticks to examine, and exploring other babies. In instances of emergency, absolutely run to your baby and get them out of harm's way, but in instances where they are engaged and learning—maybe they've encountered an obstacle or they can't quite get their shoes on or their hands got messy, or they fall down—try to resist the urge to intervene. Instead, be present and curious: "How was that for you?" "You're working so hard to carry that toy over to the bench!" "Hmmm, I wonder how you're going to fix that?" "What are you going to do next?" When your baby's state moves from learning to stress, they will signal you: They may run back to you, have a tantrum, throw things in an out-of-control way, stand off by themselves, or become aggressive toward other kids. Whether they come back to you on their own or they signal that they need you to come to them, when that stress curve rises, you are what we call their "safe haven"—your role is to comfort, regulate, and organize their feelings—in other words, lend your baby your mature brain. When we do so our babies go out and explore again feeling regulated and curious.[13]

Some babies are only comfortable when they're being held by an adult, so if you find that your baby rarely wants to explore out of arms, especially in the early months before crawling, don't worry. This is completely normal and expected baby behavior. Every baby is different. Nurturing learning and exploration means paying attention to your baby's communication so that you can be their safe anchor in the way that they need it. You do not need to teach your young baby to tolerate long periods of time away from you. You are the ultimate safety signal to them.

Nurtured Stress Practices

When babies do reach a stress state, we can bring them back into safety first and foremost with our nurtured presence to co-regulate them. You being there is important. The lack of an adult response to an infant's early cues is sensed as another, bigger threat to the amygdala, which signals to the hypothalamus to release more stress hormones into the brain and body. Even when we do respond to our baby's early cues, they can escalate their stress; but your presence even if stress rises is always a powerful safety signal. It's also a good idea to check in with their basic needs: Do they need food, water, or sleep? Are they in pain or uncomfortable? Are they getting enough movement and play?

Approach your baby's need for your presence by following their cues. Young babies often want to be held chest-to-chest immediately. They will put up their arms and be comfortable with being held. As babies get older, in the range of twelve to eighteen-plus months, they might want space before being held. This is what we would think of as a tantrum. The first part of a tantrum is often stress with the emotion anger, where your baby might push you away, or hit or kick—this is communication that they don't want to be touched. You can sit next to them, yourself regulated or in the process of regulating, and provide nurtured empathy: "You're crying so hard (behavior). I see you're so angry right now (feeling) and you don't want me to touch you (need). I've been angry too and I know how that feels. It feels really big at first and then gets smaller. I will be here when you are ready for a hug." The second part of the tantrum is often stress with the emotion sadness, where an infant will want contact and put up their arms or seek you out for a hug.

Proximity and connection are soothing to your baby. When they are ready to be held, you can offer chest-to-chest holding, including skin-to-skin if that works for you and feels needed. Physical touch gives both you and your baby a release of nurturing hormones oxytocin and dopamine, as well as endorphins. Breastfeed or body feed if that is available to you. Breastfeeding was my superpower in bringing my son from stress states to safety states, all the way up to three years old. In my experience, powerful co-regulation is an underrated benefit of breastfeeding or body feeding for all of infancy. Nursing gives babies an incredibly pleasant feeling, like an internal massage. Milk is calming and rewarding and quickly releases oxytocin and dopamine in both baby and parent. Nurture all of the senses; babies are calmed by multisensory experience. You can try different combinations of touching, singing, speaking, moving, facial expressions, and emotional connection. Marked mirroring—reflecting your infant's stress in your facial expression followed by a reassuring facial expression—is deeply regulating.

If your presence alone is not enough to bring your baby over the bridge or back to shore to a safe, calm state—and this can be especially true for infants with more reactive nervous systems, or for older infants, especially if you are the person causing them stress because you're holding a safety or other boundary—here are some things to try to lower their stress curve. I think of these as "change the energy" approaches:

- Move. Movement can be regulating for babies and parents. Walking while holding a stressed baby initiates a calming circuit in the infant brain.[14] Many parents enjoy using a baby carrier to keep baby close, to calm stress, and also to have their arms available for other tasks if needed. Moving in a figure-eight motion can be calming, as can swaying back and forth. Rocking is rhythmic and calming to the infant brain. You can rock your baby in your arms or while sitting in a rocking chair, or bounce on an exercise ball.
- Sing. Singing and your voice are calming to the infant brain. Knowing a repetitive song, or a few, that will calm you and your

baby can be very regulating. Even singing or chanting a word or phrase in low tones like "I'm right here" or your baby's name is soothing. Sounds that match a baby's rhythm of fussing or crying, but not the volume or intensity, help a baby feel seen in their stress. My mother's strategy to calm a baby is to hold, walk, and rock while singing in a low tone, *Aww aww bay bee aww aww aww aww,* and repeating this over and over.

- Pick them up and move into a different room, preferably somewhere dark and quiet, without lots of noise, people, or stimulation. Hold and/or feed in this new place.

- Initiate something silly or playful: a dance party, silly faces, peekaboo. This is not meant to avoid a stressful feeling, but instead to interrupt an agitated child's stress response if it's ongoing and doesn't seem to be calming down.

- Back off from the stressor, if possible or needed. If a diaper change is getting really stressful or getting shoes on to go out the door is becoming a battle, it's okay to take a break if you can. Take a breath, laugh together a little, connect to get the oxytocin flowing, and then try again.

- "Get them outside or get them wet" is a helpful saying about calming a stressed baby. Going outside is a great way to change the energy. Fresh air and greenery can be calming for both parent and baby, but wherever you live, going outside changes the energy from the stressful state you were all stuck in in the house. You can continue your holding, movement, and singing outdoors. Water is also soothing for most babies—you can even get into the bath or shower with your baby during times of crying or clinging, which can be calming for you both, as can feeding in the bathtub.

Be wary of any suggestions to calm your infant in rigid and prescribed methods, particularly advice like only patting their back, not making eye contact, only speaking to them (rather than holding them) while they cry, picking them up and putting them down over and over again, and holding them but not speaking or moving. Popular ways to "instantly" quiet a baby like combinations of shushing in their ear at loud volumes, tight swaddling, and pacifiers are more likely putting your baby in an instant freeze stress response rather than slowly calming them into a safety state. Instead, be with your baby. Be in the relationship with them. Try some of my suggestions and do what comes naturally to you. Your baby will tell you what feels soothing to him or her.

As you work to learn your baby's stress states and safety states, keep these words in your mind: "Can I be more flexible right now?" If you are trying to feed your baby, sing to them, or walk with them and they are not responding, think about shifting to something else. If you say to your stressed baby, "You seem frustrated right now. Do you need a hug?," and it only makes them more upset, shift to something else—go outside or sit quietly next to your child and take a few deep breaths. You will likely not remember this immediately, but when you're in a moment and what you're repeating is not working, eventually you might think, "Let's try something else!" Often, being flexible is the answer.

Remember that all stress is communication. It tells you something about your baby's inner world and their experience of the outer world. Stress can't be avoided. There are times when your baby has to get in their car seat, despite vociferous protest. There are times when you need to put them down when they would much rather be held. They will fall. They will be frustrated. This is part of life. But if they have a nurturing presence, a well-regulated, empathetic caregiver nearby who can be an anchor of calm for them when things feel chaotic, overwhelming, painful, or frustrating, infants can grow from stress. In all stages of distress, our babies need us to be a witness to their feelings, a source of co-regulation, and curious about how to meet their needs.

Periods of a Higher Need for Co-regulation

All infants go through periods where they seem to need endless amounts of closeness, support, and co-regulation. These are phases that involve massive shifts in brain development related to things like perceptual changes, cognitive changes, emotional changes, separation anxiety, and motor development, such as crawling, talking, or walking. You may see their need for support surge during the first three or four months of life, at six months, nine months, twelve months, eighteen months, twenty-four months, thirty months, or when any major life changes happen. However, instead of watching the calendar, I advise practicing radical acceptance for your baby's emotional needs. When they need you, they need you. When they need you more, they need you more. Whenever my baby was going through one of these times, which usually last two to four weeks, I would remind myself that the phase would pass and I had to ask for help to take extra care of myself. When you understand that you are their external emotional brain, an undeveloped brain part, you can grow to understand that whenever your baby's stress system is activated is when they need your nurtured presence to support the growth of their brain.

Your baby's stress and need for closeness declines over time, though the process is not necessarily linear. Infants are babies for the entire three years of life. Sometimes it's surprising when a talking, walking baby has the emotional needs of a newborn, but their brain is still growing for all of infancy. At two years old, my son had the highest stress and highest needs of his whole infancy. He needed to be held constantly, he breastfed a lot, and he had intense feelings of anger, sadness, and disappointment. It was a turbulent emotional time for us. Other babies have their highest needs at other times. Some babies have high needs for co-regulation all throughout infancy. We can't predict or know when our baby will have high needs. All we can do is listen to the survival brain and be the external brain for them when they need us.

WHAT ABOUT BEHAVIOR? USING NURTURED EMPATHY TO GUIDE BEHAVIOR

Nurturing stress and supporting emotions does not mean permissive parenting, wherein you ignore behavior that is dangerous, antisocial, or unhealthy. Always love your baby by nurturing the stress state, and simultaneously you can guide their behavior when it's dangerous, antisocial, or unhealthy. Guiding behavior helps our babies feel protected, safe, and social. All behavior has an underlying emotion, and when we use nurtured empathy to teach our babies self-awareness of their emotions, needs, and behavior, we can guide them toward safe, social, and healthy behavior.

Our babies must be in a safe, calm state in order to learn, and the learning is usually a very slow process that requires our patience and understanding. When you try to teach your baby not to bite when they're screaming and crying, or your toddler not to run out into the street by yelling at them, you're just wasting your time and stressing yourself and them out more. Remember that they are just starting to wire their thinking brain in infancy and that you can't engage the thinking brain in stress states. Their survival brain, which senses threat, is a much stronger influence at this age. They need to feel calm, in a safety state, before you can appeal to their thinking brain, and even so, this is much more likely to be effective as your infant grows into toddlerhood. A nurtured approach to changing behavior is responsive, happens over time, honors your baby's emotions, and always has their stress response in mind.

In order to help your baby keep the healthy expression of their feelings they were born with but also teach them what behavior is safe, social, and healthy, first hold a boundary if needed, such as pulling your nipple out of their mouth if they're biting you, or physically stopping them from hitting someone, or turning off a screen after a specific amount of time, or taking something dangerous away. For crawling and walking infants it might be physically stopping something dangerous like throwing rocks or climbing too high. You might be the cause of stress when you hold a boundary, and that's okay because your job is keeping your baby healthy and safe. Don't avoid saying no to unhealthy or dangerous things to avoid stress—you are both capable of experiencing stress and returning to safety.

Then, check in with their stress state. If needed, lower their stress curve with nurtured presence and other soothing. Meet their needs. They might be biting because they're teething or hungry or feeling lonely, or perhaps they are feeling the need to bite and you can give them chewy food or a teether or toy to bite. They may be hitting because they're tired or feeling out of control and needing co-regulation or perhaps having a need to move with a hitting motion, and you can direct them to use their arms to hit a pillow or take them outside to hit the ground with a stick. Toddlers may be testing boundaries and exploring their independence—usually this behavior of throwing rocks or climbing too high suggests a need for throwing, climbing, or general curiosity, so you can offer them a safe alternative to move or explore. It also might suggest a need for attention and connection.

Once they are calm, review the experience and teach a new behavior. Think of it like the infant version of storytelling and narrative medicine that is helpful for us as adults to make sense of our lives and experiences. With your full presence and eye contact, if available, say, "You really wanted to pull the dog's tail (behavior). You were curious (feeling) and wanting to explore the dog (need). When you have that feeling, this is how we hold our hand out for the dog to sniff (link feeling with new behavior). It is important to be kind and gentle to all living things, people, animals, and plants (a rule or guideline to learn). Let's practice: Imagine you're feeling curious about a dog. Show me, how do you hold out your hand? (create new brain circuits linking the feeling to the new behavior)."

Or, "You were screaming very loud (behavior). You were feeling silly and playful (feeling) and wanting to have fun (need). It's kind to use a lower volume voice when you play, even if you're so excited. Instead of screaming when you're excited, how about you run or jump or sing a song or something else that feels good? (link feeling with new behavior). Screaming can hurt people's ears and it's important to be kind and gentle with our friends (new rule or guideline to follow). Let's practice: Imagine you're feeling so excited. Can you show me how you can jump up and down? (create new brain circuits linking the feeling to the new behavior)."

Or, "You hit me very hard (behavior). You were feeling angry (feeling) and needing to express it (need). When we are angry we can hit a pillow, or stomp our feet, or something else that feels good (link feeling with new behavior). We all have big feelings, and it's important to express them, and it's important not to hurt others with our body or our words when we have them (a rule or guideline to follow). Let's practice: Imagine you're feeling angry. Can you show me how you stomp your feet? (create new brain circuits linking the feeling to the new behavior)." Don't expect them to learn what you're teaching them until you repeat it many times, sometimes hundreds of times—and probably not until they're older and their prefrontal cortex is developed. Remember, they are always listening and learning even if you don't see them do the new behavior right away.

When we use nurtured empathy to teach new behavior, we are teaching babies to express their feelings with safe behaviors that don't harm themselves or others, physically or emotionally. They learn, "My anger is safe. It tells me something about how I feel and what I need. When I'm angry I'm not going to hurt myself or someone else with my anger." You're teaching them a healthy way to feel their feelings and then not act reactively. This is something we all have to work on (see chapter 9 for adult practices), but our babies don't have to wait and then unlearn harmful ways to be with their feelings. They can learn it now.

Reviewing the experience is a good habit to practice with your baby from birth even when you're not trying to teach them a new behavior. In that case it might sound something like: "You were so sad that your banana broke apart. You got a big hug while you felt sad and now you are feeling calm. Your big feelings will always have an end. I will always be here for you. I love you when you feel all of your feelings. I love you when you're upset, happy, angry, or sad." If you do this, you might be surprised how emotionally literate your baby is when they start talking. I've had many parents share that their two- or three-year-olds tell them when they're feeling mad, shy, frustrated, scared, lonely, happy, and more!

You can also review with yourself: "That tantrum felt overwhelming and I thought that it would go on forever, but it didn't. My baby will always return to calm, and I am building their brain by being there. This is important work."

Boundaries and rules for safety and health are important, but they require a thinking brain to master, so I encourage you to be patient with your baby as they learn. It's also developmentally appropriate for them to want to push, test, and question boundaries as they explore the world. They want to know how flexible a boundary or rule is. Expect to teach these lessons hundreds of times before their brains are ready to understand and process this information.

When Babies Cry for Hours

It's not unusual for young babies to cry for long periods of time, sometimes for up to five hours a day or more, especially in the first weeks after birth up to three to four months. If this is your experience, it is important to investigate any causes of crying. If you suspect your newborn has feeding or digestive difficulties, an International Board Certified Lactation Consultant (IBCLC) can help to investigate further. If you had a fast labor, a long labor with hours of pushing, a typical labor, a belly birth, or if your baby had an oral restriction released, they might benefit from some support from a pediatric chiropractor, osteopath, craniosacral therapist, or physical therapist. You may also want to have your baby checked for skin irritations, physical discomfort, pain or illness, sensory processing issues, or other sources of sensitivities. Sometimes, though, there is not a specific reason for the crying, meaning it's likely a developmental stage their brains will grow out of. Dr. James McKenna hypothesizes that prolonged crying in babies could be due to an area of their survival brain that is unable to stop the crying until the survival brain grows out of this phase.[15]

If your baby is crying for hours—for some babies it could be weeks or months—know that you are nurturing your baby even if they don't stop crying. When your baby is in your arms and you are co-regulating, you are buffering their brain from stress and providing oxytocin.[16] This is completely different from your baby crying out of your arms, where they will experience high cortisol and no oxytocin. Time to unlearn myth 19, *There's no difference if I hold my crying baby; they're crying anyway*, and replace it with the reality: <u>Holding my crying baby provides a nurture bath to their brain regardless of how long they cry</u>.

If this is your experience, getting additional help wherever possible is almost essential. It is a monumental task for parents to be present and co-regulate with a crying baby daily for weeks. Babywearing with walking, outside if available, might help; the touch, movement, and fresh air can help parents and babies to regulate. Invite other family members, friends, or caregivers to visit and hold your baby on different days so the parent or parents can have a break. Always put your baby down in a safe place and walk away if you feel your stress rising high and you need a break.

HOW TO REPAIR WHEN YOU ARE REACTIVE

We are not perfect, and we do not need to be perfect at nurturing our baby's stress. There will be times when we react to our baby's stress in a scary way by yelling at, rejecting, or shaming them. There will be times when we are annoyed or even scared by our baby's stress response, likely because it brings up our own experiences as an infant. There will be times when we parent the way we were parented, rather than the parenting we want to do. There will be many times when we respond to our baby's stress in a way we can't control and in ways that aren't aligned with our values or goals as a parent. I know that these times can be scary for you and your baby. They can make you feel deep regret.

Have compassion for yourself when this happens. You were having a hard time when you responded this way. It's usually a sign that you had a need at that time—for more sleep, more alone time, more support, more food, more fun—in order to support your infant's stress, just like your baby needs support in a threat or stress state. Responding without nurture from time to time is expected and normal, and completely avoiding it is impossible and not the goal of nurture. When we are not nurturing there is always repair.

In fact, repair is an important skill for our babies to learn. All humans have emotions, and we all react out of anger, frustration, annoyance, or fear at times. We all make mistakes, and we can all repair mistakes. Our babies learn how to repair when we repair. Our relationship with our babies remains connected and nurtured when we repair.

Whenever you react in a way you don't like, take some time to feel regulated and calm again, and wait until your baby is calm, too. Then connect, review, apologize, and repair:

1. Connect. Go to eye level and make eye contact. Touch your baby. Get the oxytocin flowing.
2. Review what happened. "You were upset, then I got overwhelmed (feeling) and yelled 'STOP' at you (behavior). I needed to take a deep breath before responding (need)."
3. Apologize. "I am sorry for yelling at you. It is okay for me to have feelings, like being overwhelmed, but it is not okay for me to yell at you. Mommies or daddies or people that love you should not yell."
4. Repair. "I will do my best to take some space when I need it, so I can better support you. The next time I feel overwhelmed my plan is to take five deep breaths."

I am often asked about repairing months or years of low nurture and yelling, shaming, ignoring, or otherwise not supporting infant stress. The answer is that we can absolutely provide repair at any time. You can begin to be nurturing at any time in your child's life from age three months to age sixty years. You can start the conversation by saying to your child, "I parented you in a way that I regret (name the way, if possible). I have learned new information and I am sorry I didn't (name it— maybe 'connect with you,' 'see you,' 'listen to you,' 'support your stress,' 'teach you about emotions,' or 'regulate myself'). From now on, I want to be a safe person for you to express your stress and your emotions to.

I am learning. I want to hear what that was like for you and how I can support you." Then do your best to practice nurtured parenting.

The places in the brain where the repair is wired will be different at different ages. If a parent comes to nurture partway through their baby's infancy, their repair will be influencing the season of brain growth in the stress system and emotional brain. If a parent is unaware of nurture for all of their baby's infancy, they can still repair. The stress system and emotional system will be built, but we can always build new connections to integrate with that circuitry. While it can take years of repair and various therapies to make the changes for some babies or children or adults, repair is absolutely possible. I have worked with grandparents who have provided repair for their adult children and changed the course of their adult children's mental health. The lessons in this book are vital in infancy and remain key to relationships throughout life.

IT'S THAT SIMPLE AND THAT HARD

Our babies challenge us to feel and regulate a lot of stress. The big and constant emotions of infancy trigger many parents' threat systems, especially if you did not have a safe, well-regulated caregiver with whom you could express stress, anger, sadness, pain, disappointment, or even happiness in your own infancy and childhood. It can be hard to witness your baby openly express stress and emotion if you didn't have that foundational experience yourself or if you have learned to take on other people's stress and emotions—elements of codependency or enmeshment. If you get on the roller-coaster of stress and emotion with your baby, it's easy to get overwhelmed, burnt out, and have trouble being stable enough inside to co-regulate effectively.

Our babies are nurtured when we can process our own stress, move through it, and regulate ourselves. They are nurtured when we aren't afraid or dismissive of their stressful feelings and experiences and can be present with them to help them move through their stress. They are nurtured when we can give them the freedom to feel their own feelings without joining them in their stress by feeling what they're feeling.

In order to co-regulate and support your baby in times of stress, it helps to differentiate your baby's stress from your feelings. We often need to create a pause between our baby's stress and our response. In-the-moment regulation goes a long way—take a moment, take a breath, and tell yourself, "I'm not stressed; my baby is stressed," or "My baby isn't giving me a hard time; she's having a hard time." You can say these aloud—"You're stressed because I'm changing your diaper," or "You don't want to get dressed right now." It can help you hear that it's your baby having the feeling rather than you.

With practice and support, you can nurture your infant's brain in stress without taking on the stress yourself. Your baby's stress is not your emotion; it's theirs. Try to understand what they are feeling (cognitive empathy) rather than feel what they are feeling (affective empathy). When you can empathize with the experience your baby is having, and separate how you feel, you can be a more powerful external brain for your baby. This will help you not be afraid of your baby's stress. They need to know that you can handle their stress.

In service of this, I practice responding in words with a song or a low tone, as singing and low-tone speaking brings us from a stress state to a safety state.[17] I'll sing or say in a low tone something like, "What is happening?," or "You are upset," or "I am here for you." Breathing is incredibly helpful here; even one deep belly breath—but five to ten are even better—activates your brain to bring you from stress to safety. Another strategy is to empathize out loud: "I see you're crying. You're so sad you spilled your food." "You're upset because he took your toy." "You're mad that I said no more cookies." This helps differentiate your emotions from your baby's.

It helps me to remember that babies have the very human right to express their stress and emotions openly and honestly and that it is healthy for them to do so.

APPLYING NURTURED PRESENCE AND NURTURED EMPATHY TO STRESS STATES

Some days you'll feel totally in the zone and capable of welcoming and supporting whatever your infant throws at you without getting triggered or knocked into anger, frustration, insecurity, shame, and more. Other days—maybe most days—you'll need some help to anchor yourself when your baby is stressed, to remember your baby's feelings are not yours, and that they're a tiny baby who is feeling scared or overwhelmed and who needs you. I offer more in-the-moment and long-term strategies for supporting your parent brain in chapter 9, but here are a few additional tips for nurturing your baby when they are in a stress state.

Nurtured Presence for Stress

Remember, our goal is nurtured presence, without judgment, shame, or condition. With your presence, communicate the answer to your baby's unconscious questions:

Do you see me?

Take a breath and look at your baby—they are having a hard time. Are they tense, crying, reaching for you, out of control? They need help.

Do you care that I'm here?

Show genuine concern for their stress state. Don't make them feel like their stress is an annoyance to you. They are a small human feeling normal human feelings. They will return to a safety state; it's just a matter of time and needing support to get there.

Am I enough for you, or do you need me to be better in some way?

Have radical acceptance for all of their emotions. They are their amazing self at all times, even in stress, and maybe especially in stress with their beautiful uninhibited expression. Don't give the message that they need to calm down for you to accept them. Think to yourself, "This will pass and I can handle this stress."

Can I tell that I'm special to you by the way that you look at me?

See the real them, the infant beneath the stress state. They are so small and so overwhelmed. There is nothing "wrong" with your baby—they are a beautiful, precious little human who is having a hard time.

Nurtured Empathy for Stress

Here is some support for attuning to your baby's needs with nurtured empathy when they're stressed. These will not necessarily occur in chronological order; reality is often a bit messier.

1. Get behind your baby's eyes. Take a pause and a breath to help you calm and differentiate. Your baby, not you, is feeling stressed. Be curious about what is going on for your baby. Sometimes you will know—she's mad because she dropped her toy or he has a hard time with transitions—and other times you won't. If it's not obvious, just be curious. "Hmmm...something is upsetting you. You are having a hard time. You need help."
2. Empathize by reflecting their behavior, how they might be feeling, and their needs with marked mirroring. You can do this by:
   a. Showing them how they might be feeling with an exaggerated facial expression—a big pout of sadness.
   b. Naming the behavior(s) you see, the emotion(s) your baby might be feeling, and the need(s) they might have. Say,

153

"You're crying so much (behavior). I wonder if you're feeling so sad (feeling) and needing a big hug (need)."

c. Showing them a reassuring face and telling them that you're here for them: "I am here with you, baby."

3. Meet the need. Be in the relationship with them. Offer your adult brain to help them calm, and be curious and flexible about what would help them come back to safety. One part of meeting the need is providing your nurturing presence. Sometimes that is all they need. "You fell down and are upset. I'm right here." "You're lonely and wanting to be held. I can't wait to hold you as soon as I finish using the bathroom."

Infancy is a time—for most of us the first time—to learn how to really be there meaningfully for others in times of stress and discomfort. A time to learn how to be present for others in a healing, supportive way when things are hard. It is an opportunity to develop ourselves to be truly compassionate and to learn to empathize with others. As we model this to our babies, they learn these vital human skills as well.

Remember the science—when we provide co-regulation, thousands of times, we are sculpting and building our baby's stress system: their amygdala, their hippocampus, their hypothalamus, and their prefrontal cortex (see figure 7). This deep emotional core is the ultimate gift that can come from infancy and that we all benefit from making the focus of infancy.

Every time you regulate your baby from stress to calm, imagine the epigenetic markers binding to your baby's DNA, forever changing inherited trauma, laying down a regulated stress system, neurotransmitter systems, gut health, and cognition—that will all be solidified in the brain at the end of infancy (see figure 8).

Chapter 8

WHEN YOUR BABY IS DROWSY AND SLEEPING: NURTURING SLEEP

When I was pregnant everyone told me, "Sleep now because you'll never sleep again." This was not funny to me at all. It was terrifying. I need sleep. Right then I became obsessed with controlling baby sleep. I studied sleep training books and social media accounts to learn the sleep training rules, schedules, how to prepare for sleep training, and all of the sleep training methods. As soon as my baby was born, I was focused solely on tracking and controlling my baby's sleep. I never fed her to sleep, and kept her on a tight schedule. I got every sound machine available, and blocked every shred of light from her room. I was doing everything I was supposed to do, but my baby's sleep was unpredictable. She never slept more than thirty minutes in her bassinet, she absolutely hated being swaddled, and she refused to take a pacifier. No matter how perfectly I charted her schedule and controlled her sleep environment, neither of us was getting much sleep. I felt as if we were constantly fighting each other.

Every day I grew more and more frustrated that my baby wasn't doing what the books and accounts said. In utter despair, I tried looking for alternatives and found your account. I learned about normal infant sleep and the nonlinear way it develops. I started to nurse my baby to sleep and when she was upset. I embraced letting her sleep on my chest and next to me in bed. I took off the swaddle and ignored the schedule. The first day I nursed my daughter to sleep she napped for almost two hours! This had never happened before. I could finally have snuggles and connection with my baby without feeling guilt. Sleep became something sweet we did together. I even realized that I had severe postpartum anxiety and I didn't know it until the sleep obsession ended and my anxiety subsided. I lost months of that snuggle time and I will always have guilt. But the rest of my baby's life will be a journey about relationship and acceptance.

—*Mara K.*

Infant sleep may be the most anxiety-inducing aspect about having a baby, which makes sense. You need sleep. You've heard that babies wake frequently in the night or have seen or heard from friends or television and the media how sleep-deprived parents of infants are, and you're worried. It would feel good to have some kind of control over this, to help make sure you're getting the sleep that you need, and that your baby is, too. I certainly identify with those feelings.

Sleep is the most hotly contested topic in most parenting circles, which you'll discover if, like most parents, you find yourself scrolling through social media or searching the internet at 3 a.m. for baby sleep support. As a low-nurture culture, our understanding of infant sleep is largely driven by myths that are not science-based. These prevalent myths include: *Comforting your baby to sleep (with breastfeeding or body feeding, rocking, singing, cuddling) is a bad habit that you will resent; night waking is an unhealthy problem that needs fixing; if you don't train your baby to fall asleep alone and sleep alone, they will never learn; and babies must learn to soothe themselves at night.* None of this is true or based on a shred of evidence. <u>Comforting babies to sleep is nurturing; night waking is healthy and normal; sleep training doesn't change infant sleep or teach sleep; and babies are not able to soothe themselves</u>. In place of good evidence-based information about normal infant sleep and how to support it (and your sleep, too), we get lots of information based on outdated beliefs that do not reflect the reality of the neurobiology of babies. This puts parents in an impossible situation where myths tell them their baby shouldn't be acting like a baby, yet they have a baby who is acting like a baby. This is confusing at best and the makings of anxiety and depression at worst. It must end.

Sleep is as necessary to our health as food, water, and air. During sleep the brain encodes important memories and learning, forms new connections, grows, releases hormones, eliminates waste, heals wounds, regulates the immune system, reduces stress, and sustains life.[1] Sleep makes up a significant portion of infancy—the first three years of a baby's life total almost 26,300 hours, and over half of those, about 16,000 or more hours, are spent sleeping. The hours of naps and nighttime are a precious opportunity to build your baby's stress system and their entire developing brain.

Nurturing your baby during sleep has benefits that are unique from the nurture you do while they are awake. In nurtured sleep you build not only the stress system, but also every other system in the developing infant brain to wire resilience against a long list of mental, neurological, and physical illnesses.[2] All mammals, you and your baby included, fall asleep into healthy restorative sleep in a safety state.[3]

When you and your baby are close together in sleep states or when your baby is sleeping in a carrier, both of your brains are bathed in nurturing hormones and neurotransmitters. This is illustrated in figure 18. When your baby wakes during the night, their brain state may stay in a safety state as you quickly feed or hug them back to sleep, or when they wake in a stress state, your adult brain returns them back into a safety state to fall back to sleep. This is illustrated in figure 19.

As we know, your baby borrows your brain, so your brain being in a safety state is a prerequisite for your baby to feel safe enough to fall asleep. You need to be in a safety state and help your baby get into a safety state in order for sleep to happen. While you and your baby sleep close together, your brain waves have the opportunity to coordinate and synchronize, which enriches your infant's sleep and their brain development for all of the many hours they spend sleeping. Nurturing the infant brain in sleep changes their brain waves toward building a healthy brain. With oxytocin present during sleep states, the quality of sleep changes to influence the development of the stress system and other brain systems. Throughout the night, as you soothe your baby back to sleep when they wake, you're using your safety state—including neurotransmitters like oxytocin—to bring your baby back into a safety state so they can go back to sleep. Nighttime nurture builds the stress system to be resilient and shapes how infants respond to stress after infancy, specifically by lowering cortisol responses following a stressor and faster cortisol recovery.[4]

Parents also benefit from the safety signal of their infant by having restorative sleep, lower stress, lower anxiety, and higher oxytocin.[5] When you are close to your baby, your parent brain sleeps differently than when you are separated from your baby. Sleeping close further matures your developing parent brain to help you be more nurturing in your waking life.[6]

When you nurture your infant's sleep you are teaching your baby that sleep is a place of safety and rest. They will continue to have this association for life. This is vital because sleep is essential to mental and physical health at all stages of life. When babies learn that sleep is a place of isolation, stress, or fear, they can continue to have this association for life.

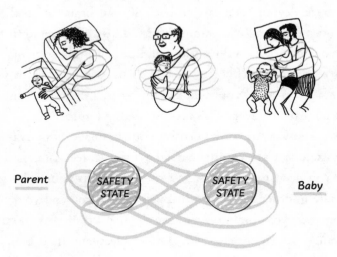

Figure 18.

While parent and baby sleep, they are both in a safety state and their brain waves coordinate, infant sleep is enriched, and parent sleep is influenced to be more responsive. This synchrony bathes the infant and parent brains in oxytocin to develop resilience and wellness.

Figure 19.

When a baby has a night waking and is in a stress state, the parent, in a safety state, uses nurture to bring them back to a safety state. When in a safety state, nurtured connection (chapter 6) and sleep (chapter 8) grow babies' emotional brains.

WHAT ABOUT "SLEEP TRAINING"?

Sleep training is the unfounded process of "training" your infant to "sleep independently"—to fall asleep alone, sleep alone through the night and the duration of naps, without getting support from you to go to sleep or back to sleep. It takes various forms, but the most common end goal is to be able to put your infant in their crib, in their own room, and walk out, leaving them alone to fall asleep, usually around 7 p.m., until you come back to get them in the morning, usually around 7 a.m. Sleep training promotes the idea that infant sleep should be predictable and on schedule. Naps should be at exact times of the day and for specific amounts of time, bedtime is at the exact same time each evening, and sleep location is identical for every sleep.

It does sound nice, doesn't it? Sleep training sells the idea that sleep is something parents can (and should) control. If you just follow the rules (strict "wake windows," not "giving in" to your baby's cries) and buy the right products (swaddles, sleep suits, sound machines, sleep training courses and coaching), your baby will sleep in a predictable and controllable way. That is very appealing when so much of parenting feels beyond our control. Research does show that sleep training infants, for the subset of babies that stop signaling, is beneficial for parents to get more uninterrupted sleep at night.[7] Unfortunately, this leaves out a very important person: the baby.

In reality, sleep training is not neuroscience-supported or evidence-based. It's not trauma informed, it's not nervous system informed, and it's not mental health informed. It is based on absolutely no evidence of efficacy or safety for the infant brain. It is simply practice-based, meaning it is done because others have done it before. It's not even particularly effective: One study of over two hundred infants found that sleep training only stopped nighttime signaling completely in 14 percent of babies who were sleep trained at home.[8] Many parents find (and sleep training admits this) that they have to "retrain" their infants multiple times, after illness, teething, travel, or any other event in which an infant gets support to feel safe and relaxed throughout the night. Babies are not learning to sleep; they are learning to stop signaling, and their need for co-regulation is so strong that they signal again if their parents respond again. It's also a totally unregulated and quite lucrative field.

There are various methods for achieving the sleep training goal of "independent sleep," but they all involve some amount of letting your infant cry until they "learn" that they have to go to sleep on their own, that you are not going to soothe them to sleep. Some approaches encourage you to let your baby cry while you sit in the room but don't pick them up or hold them; others teach you to leave the room altogether for timed intervals, returning not to hold your baby, but to touch them or talk to them before leaving again. You are out of the relationship with your baby in all cases, providing no care, or providing only nonresponsive care. Eye contact is discouraged. The most extreme approach teaches you to simply leave the room for twelve hours and let your baby cry until they stop. Many approaches will tell you that it's okay for your baby to throw up, have diarrhea, aggressively shake or bang their head, pound their mattress, chew their crib, or scream, among other signs of distress. They'll acknowledge that this will be hard for you to hear, but claim that you need to do this for your infant's health because sleep is so important.

We don't have as much research as I'd like to tell us the effect of sleep training on infant brains and stress systems; we've yet to see a properly conducted study on this. What we do have is research that tells us that sleep training in no measurable way stops night waking, or changes infant sleep in duration or quality of sleep architecture.[9] So what happens when babies are sleep trained?

Many mental health professionals, myself included, hypothesize that what really happens when we leave our infants alone to cry is that they respond to a nonresponsive presence (in the example of staying in the room) or the threat of isolation (in the case of leaving the room) first with a fight-or-flight stress response: Most babies will cry hysterically, vomit, have diarrhea, and thrash around, a stress response that can go on for minutes or hours. When no one comes or no one responds to co-regulate the baby, their response to the threat changes to one of freeze and dissociation, which also looks like falling asleep. After the sleep training process—which can continue for days, weeks, or months— it's hypothesized that babies go straight to the freeze-dissociation-sleep response cued by the environment they were trained in. Some babies develop other ways to cope with their stress like chewing their cribs until no paint is left, repetitively rubbing their heads, or repetitively rubbing or chewing a stuffed animal or blanket or pacifier. In other words, while some babies are indeed quiet in their cribs after they're sleep trained, we know that nothing has actually changed in their development, so those babies are still waking, and still in stress, but they know that no one is coming to co-regulate them, so they stop bothering to signal for help. This process uses babies' innate survival mechanism to shut down if no one is around to help. Instead of entering sleep through a safety state, they enter through a fearful stress state.

Sleep training puts the infant brain at risk of experiencing high and/or prolonged periods of toxic stress. It puts the infant brain at risk of developing a highly reactive amygdala and hypothalamus, with a diminished ability to regulate stress via lower stop signals in the hippocampus and prefrontal cortex. There is likely a spectrum of how babies are affected by this experience. It's not a deterministic risk, as genetics and experience certainly contribute—genetics might be protective for some babies and increase vulnerability for other babies. Sadly, it's often vulnerable, highly reactive babies who need the most co-regulation—and thus wake the most at night—who are likely to be sleep trained.

Here's what we do know for sure: Infants need us to co-regulate with them during the day. They can't be taught to self-regulate during the day—it's a developmental process that will mature in time—so they certainly are not learning to do it selectively at night. Infants thrive from sensory input from their caregivers: Your body, your movements, your smell, and your sounds are highly regulating and nurturing to your infant. Babies need to borrow our brains to help them feel safe so they can explore, play, and learn. Our parent brains are wired to respond to our babies; we hear and feel their cries more distinctly and we are wired to respond to them. Why would any of this be different at night? Why does sleep training tell parents to turn the sound off on the baby monitor so that parents aren't tempted to respond to their baby's screams during sleep training?

I know that nighttime parenting is hard. I've done it myself every night of my child's life, and I've worked with families from every walk of life who support their babies' sleep. I also know that it's a finite period of time, a season that passes and doesn't return. This period of powerful brain development in your baby and in you won't last forever. It is possible to nurture your infant's sleep and your own, and it's possible to benefit tremendously from the experience. It might be the hardest thing you ever do, and the most rewarding.

Babies cannot be taught to sleep, to fall asleep alone, to wake up less, to self-soothe, or not to need you at night. They know how to sleep—they've been doing it in utero all along—and their ability to self-regulate or self-soothe can only come when their brains are more developed, way past three years old. Babies are born with brains that are entirely capable of sleep; they just sleep differently than adults. While adults generally have long stretches of nighttime sleep, take care of themselves when they have night wakings, and rarely take naps, infants have shorter stretches of sleep, night wakings with needs for feeding, hydration, contact, and co-regulation, and they require naps during the day.

They need your help to support their sleep. This isn't so unheard of—we all benefit from safety signals from loved ones in sleep. People of all ages benefit from sleeping with or near other people or pets. Your baby needs you to understand normal infant sleep so that you can support them to have opportunities to get the sleep their developing brain needs and practical ways to protect both you and your infant's sleep as a fundamental aspect of your health.

If you're reading this and you have previously sleep trained your baby or child, know that repair is always possible. You can start to support your baby's sleep again and repair their relationship with sleep. Start with connection; hold your baby and look into their eyes. Review what happened, something like "I have not been coming to help you when you cry in your bed. I wonder if you are feeling angry, sad, and scared when this happens? I want you to know that when I did that I thought that it was what you needed, but I have new information now." Then apologize: "I am so sorry that I didn't answer your cries. I thought that I was helping you but now I understand that you needed me." Finally repair: "I always want to help you and I am curious about all of your feelings, day and night. I will answer your cries from now on. You can always depend on me." At any stage of your baby or child's life you can begin to use sleep cues for naps and bedtime, sleep close for all or part of the night, connect at bedtime, accompany your child as they fall asleep, be responsive when they wake at night, and welcome them to sleep close to you when they need it.

UNDERSTANDING NORMAL INFANT SLEEP

Two processes govern sleep in our bodies. The first is called *circadian rhythm*, and the second is called *homeostatic sleep drive*, or sleep pressure.[10] Both of these processes are unique in babies. Circadian rhythm is a twenty-four-hour daily rhythm generated by the brain. Many processes in the body work on a daily rhythm, including sleep and wake states, hormone production, body temperature, metabolism, and feeding rhythms.[11] Circadian rhythm is the reason we are alert or sleepy at approximately the same time each day. Circadian rhythms in our body tell us to be in wake states in light phases of the day (from sunrise to sunset) and to be in sleep states in dark phases of the day (from sunset to sunrise). The circadian rhythm is affected by cues called *zeitgebers*, meaning "time givers" in German. These cues include sunlight, temperature, and regular daily activities like eating.

Babies are born with an immature circadian rhythm, so your newborn does not have a clear daytime when they are alert and a clear nighttime when they are sleepy. Circadian rhythm begins to develop around six to eighteen weeks of age.[12] Before this time, babies have wake and sleep states distributed across twenty-four hours—in other words, they don't consolidate all their sleep needs in one nighttime period. After this time, babies develop the pattern of more sleep at night and more wakefulness during the day.

Sleep pressure, the homeostatic sleep drive, is a process in which the need for sleep builds as time awake increases. While we are awake our brains produce sleep-inducing hormones and neurotransmitters that increase our sleep pressure and make us feel sleepy. While we sleep the reverse happens: Our brains produce wake-inducing hormones and neurotransmitters that eventually build enough to wake us up. These processes are also immature in babies.

Adenosine is an example of a sleep-inducing neurotransmitter that builds when we are awake. Adenosine is created as the brain uses energy.

While you sleep, sleep-inducing neurotransmitters like adenosine go down, sleep pressure goes down, and eventually you wake.[13] Adults build sleep pressure throughout the day and consolidate all their sleep at night. Babies build sleep pressure faster than adults and need naps to relieve it throughout the day. In addition, sleep pressure drops throughout the night, which is why it is common for infants to have a longer stretch of sleep in the beginning of the night and more frequent waking in the second half of the night. Cortisol is an example of a hormone that helps wake you up. Adult brains have mature cortisol rhythms where cortisol is highest in the morning and generally decreases throughout the day. Infants, however, don't develop a mature cortisol rhythm until after three years of age, and as a result, infants need to relieve cortisol more often than adults by taking naps throughout the day.[14]

Sleep is a developmental process that emerges in babies like other developmental processes such as walking and talking. In time, their brains and bodies mature enough to support longer stretches of sleep with less need for support through the night. Their circadian rhythms will develop with time, as will their sleep pressure. Just like a three-year-old needs fewer (or no) daytime naps while a newborn might sleep most of the day, as your baby's brain develops, so will the way they sleep. You don't have to do anything to make this happen; it's a normal part of human development.

The states of sleep are:

- Drowsy: Your baby is about to enter sleep, they show tired cues, their body relaxes, they breathe irregularly—you can help your baby to fall asleep in this state with nurture.
- Active asleep or REM sleep: Babies are in a light sleep where it is easy to be woken up, they breathe irregularly, their eyes can flutter, they can make faces and sounds—many babies want to be close to you while sleeping in this state.
- Quiet asleep or NREM sleep: Babies are in a deep sleep where it is hard to be woken up, their breathing is regular, their face is calm,

their limbs are limp—this is a good state to roll away from your sleeping baby if needed or support the state by being close.

The number of hours your baby will sleep in a twenty-four-hour period will depend on your baby. The amount of sleep infants need is highly variable. For newborns, the range of sleep recommended is fourteen to seventeen hours, and eleven to nineteen hours may be appropriate. From four to eleven months, the range of sleep recommended is twelve to fifteen hours, and ten to eighteen hours may be appropriate. From twelve to twenty-four months, eleven to fourteen hours is recommended, and nine to sixteen hours may be appropriate. Finally, from twenty-four months to five years, ten to thirteen hours is recommended, and eight to fourteen hours may be appropriate.[15] These guidelines do not include how much of that sleep is at night and how much is during daytime naps; only the baby's body can tell us that. Notice how much variation there is—a six-to-eight-hour range is a striking difference. It is more challenging to have a baby on the lower end of these sleep needs, and you will need more support. You can unlearn myth 20, *Babies need to sleep from 7 p.m. to 7 a.m., with four hours of napping daily,* and replace it with the reality: <u>There is a huge range of sleep needs for babies, and in a safe, comfortable sleep environment my baby will sleep the amount that their brain needs.</u>

Night Waking

Night waking is a normal feature of infant sleep. When your infant wakes up crying or asking for you in the night, they need to borrow your brain to fall back to sleep; it's that simple and that hard. Infants signal to their caregivers when they wake up in the night and have a need for feeding, hydration, touch, co-regulation of stress, discomfort, loneliness, or fear. Expect your baby to have night wakings until they are two and a half to three years of age. Wakings will likely happen for all of infancy, and it will be a pleasant surprise if they end sooner. Also, don't be surprised if they stop and then come back. Some babies do stop when they are under twelve months old, and many others continue to need help until two and a half to three years. Then some children continue to need help at night up to six to eight-plus years old. The variation is enormous; we cannot teach babies to stop waking, and we need to respond to the survival brain at night at all ages.[16] Night waking is part of normal sleep for adults, too; we just don't usually need the same support infants need to fall back asleep, but many of us do need a different kind of support.[17]

Infants wake up fully rested after a night with many wakings. Night waking does not deprive infants of sleep; it is part of how they sleep. Infant waking, under twelve months, is protective for the infant brain against sudden infant death syndrome (SIDS).[18] There are no risks to night wakings (in the absence of medical issues—see page 169), and babies who have more night wakings have excellent social, emotional, and cognitive development.[19] There is no evidence that night waking leads to any negative outcomes for infants.[20] On the contrary, I often tell my clients with wakeful babies that an upside is they typically grow up to be very smart when their sleep is nurtured.

Infant night waking may occur at the end of every sleep cycle, which in infants occurs every forty-five to sixty minutes; adult sleep cycles are ninety minutes.[21] Newborns typically wake every one to four hours for frequent feeding. After the first three to four months, infants may sleep several sleep cycles or two to six hours without signaling, sometimes even six to ten-plus hours. However, on a typical night it is normal for infants to signal after one to three sleep cycles and need a caregiver one to four or more times a night.[22] Since needs vary drastically across development, night waking also varies. The number of night wakings can go up and down across time. They do not reduce in a linear pattern; however, by the end of infancy they typically stop. Please unlearn myth 21, *Night waking in babies who are three to thirty-six months old is harmful or unnecessary*, and replace it with: <u>Night wakings are part of infant sleep, and babies stop waking at night as their brain develops</u>.

While your infant will grow to have fewer night wakings and longer stretches of sleep over the first three years, they will go through periods of more settled sleep with fewer wakings and more unsettled sleep with more night wakings.[23] Learning a new skill like crawling, walking, or talking and undergoing psychological changes like separation anxiety are times of explosive brain development that can lead to more wakings and more difficulty with sleep.[24]

Your baby will likely have their own unique times of intense development that are accompanied by sleep changes, but you may notice unsettled sleep around four to six months when their sleep architecture changes, nine to twelve months when separation anxiety peaks, and eighteen months and twenty-four months when emotional, cognitive, and motor circuits develop. Supporting infant sleep typically happens for all of infancy, from zero to three years, and after that, the needs plummet in babies who have had nurtured sleep. Please unlearn myth 22, *Babies have sleep regressions and need sleep training to learn to sleep again*, and replace it with the reality: <u>Babies are always progressing. When they have a massive change in brain development they often have more wakings, and when it passes sleep becomes more settled again as the brain develops further</u>.

Sleeping like an adult, with long stretches and less need for support at night, takes time to develop. Temperament, the maturity of sleep circuitry in the brain, and the maturity of stress circuitry in the brain are all factors that impact consolidated sleep. Sleep is on a big spectrum—some babies' night wakings are infrequent, with settled sleep; and other babies' wakings are more frequent, with unsettled sleep—it likely depends on the genetic and epigenetic inheritance in the stress and sleep brain systems. We know that babies with more reactive stress systems typically have more unsettled sleep and babies with less reactive stress systems typically have more settled sleep (see figure 17).[25] However, remember that nothing is true for all babies or people, so knowing your baby is the most important.

It's so important to know what's normal for infant sleep; it allows you to let go of stressful, unrealistic expectations, see through the myths that you can somehow train a baby to sleep like an adult before their brain is mature enough to do so, and find concrete, practical ways to support both you and your baby's sleep during this delicate period of development. It's normal for infants to wake anywhere from one to four or more times a night.[26] It's normal for your baby to want to be close and to need you to soothe them to sleep. This is infancy. It won't last forever.

When to Be Concerned About Night Wakings

While night wakings are normal, there are some red flags to keep in mind. Listen to your intuition, too. If you observe any of the following red flags or have an intuition that your baby's wakings or sleep patterns are not normal, reach out to an appropriate, trusted medical professional (see box on page 170). Here are the most common red flags.

Feeding and Digestion

Frequent or infrequent breastfeeding or body feeding in the newborn period when you are establishing feeding. If your baby is sleeping for very short periods of time and feeding constantly, or if your baby is very sleepy and feeding less than every four hours, it is possible they are not transferring enough milk. See an IBCLC, particularly one knowledgeable about oral restrictions like tongue ties and lip ties, as this is another cause of not getting enough milk. For gas, reflux, digestive discomfort, mucus in stool, or constipation, see an IBCLC or pediatrician. There may be a sensitivity to diet in breast or body milk or to ingredients in formula.

Breathing

Snoring or open-mouth breathing. See an ear, nose, and throat specialist (ENT) or pediatric dentist with a specialty in the upper airway. In the case of tongue tie or lip tie revision, consult an IBCLC or pediatric dentist. Make sure you have oral physiotherapy with a physical therapist and body work with a craniosacral therapist or chiropractor before and after any oral restriction revision.

Physical Discomfort

Trouble turning their neck or feeding on both sides, pain in certain physical positions, including tummy time. This can happen as a result of physical discomfort from breech position in utero, all types of births, or oral restrictions. Seek body work with a craniosacral therapist or chiropractor, an airway-informed IBCLC, and/or an occupational therapist specializing in infants. Restless legs are usually a sign of low iron; this and other deficiencies can be measured by a naturopathic doctor, functional medicine doctor, or pediatrician.

Sensory Processing

Trouble calming down enough to fall asleep, overly sensitive or underresponsive to stimuli like touch, sound, taste, lights, and/or movement; prone to falling or clumsiness; fear of or seeking movement; having trouble handling transitions. See an occupational therapist specializing in infants.

For Sleep, Be Careful Who You Consult

Many pediatricians know nothing or very little about the developing infant stress system or normal infant sleep. In the United States, doctors typically receive twenty-seven minutes of infant sleep education in medical school, and in Canada less than 1 percent of doctors receive any training on infant sleep in medical school.[27] In Australia, health professionals scored less than 50 percent correct on a test about infant sleep.[28] So unless your doctor or medical professional has taken a specific training in biologically normal infant sleep and is supportive of nurturing infant sleep, do not rely on them to help. This goes for any breastfeeding or body feeding, nutrition, sensory processing, or airway issues, too—you deserve to work with someone who is an expert in their field. Be very careful with the people you trust your baby's developing brain with. If any professional suggests stress cascade interventions like separation, isolation, or limiting or restricting your responses to your baby, you can find another professional who will be an appropriate layer of support for your baby, and will support you and your baby's mental health.

You may need to be a fierce advocate when finding the appropriate practitioner. If, for example, someone recommends weaning, starting solid foods, isolation, reducing your responsiveness, or sleep training to "fix" a sleep concern you have, this is a red flag. You want to make sure the professionals you see will support your decision to continue nurturing your infant's sleep while seriously investigating if there is a medical issue behind the sleep concern. Telling you to sleep train when you're concerned about your baby's well-being is negligent, potentially dangerous, and disrespectful to you and your baby. Sleep training will solve exactly none of the medical concerns that can be present. Please unlearn myth 23, *Sleep training is the answer to your night waking concerns*, and replace it with: <u>If you are concerned about your baby's night waking, investigate medical or sensory processing issues</u>.

NURTURED SLEEP

So, what should we expect as we nurture infant sleep? In short, nurtured infant sleep is a regulated caregiver supporting the development of circadian rhythms; learning and noticing your infant's communication of tired cues and providing sleep opportunities when your baby is tired; nurturing your baby to sleep with co-regulation, feeding, cuddling, rocking or carrying at naps, bedtime, and when they have night wakings; sleeping close to your baby; and prioritizing your sleep with support from others. There is an art to infant sleep, but the basics are straightforward.

Regulated Caregiver

Did you ever notice that the naps and nights you want your baby to fall asleep fast are the ones that take way longer than normal? There's a reason for that: Babies depend on their caregivers to signal safety in their bodies in order to fall asleep. If your body is signaling excitement, anticipation, or stress, your baby gets the signal that there is something to be aware of and it's not a good idea to sleep. Maybe you planned a phone call, will be leaving the house, have a big meeting the next day, or are just especially tired and want to be done for the day—whatever it is, your stress goes up in anticipation, and your baby senses it and has more trouble feeling safe and going to sleep. When parents are stressed, babies get the message that it is not safe to go to sleep. I know this is annoying and often inconvenient, but a regulated parent is the baseline foundation for infant sleep.

So as best as you can, get into a safety state before bedtime or nap-time. Be aware of your stress. If you observe it going up, or if you observe it way up high, make sure you can regulate yourself. Many parents have special regulation practices at bedtime and naptimes, such as a breathing or mindfulness practice or using earbuds to listen to a podcast or audiobook, that help them get into the ideal state to help their baby to sleep. It is also an opportunity for parents to rest at the same time as helping their baby sleep. See chapter 9 for a lot more on taking care of you.

Support Circadian Rhythms

Zeitgebers like natural sunlight during the day and darkness and lower temperatures at night help support circadian rhythms as they develop in your newborn and also support sleep throughout infancy to adulthood.[29] Expose your baby (and yourself!) to sunlight in the morning and throughout the day through windows or being outside, and dim the lights (including screens) one to two hours before bedtime in the evening. This includes waking up to natural light, going outside for ten to fifteen minutes first thing in the morning with no sunglasses to give your circadian rhythm the signal of sunlight through your eyes, as well as another ten to fifteen minutes midday, and then setting up dim lighting in the evening. If sunlight is not available during different seasons, light boxes mimic the spectrum of light in the sun, especially the blue light frequencies. Dim lighting can be set up with blinds, lamps, candles, and light-bulbs that do not have blue light frequencies. Cooler temperatures in the evening of 16–20°C, or 60–68°F, facilitate sleep in babies and adults.[30]

Daily routines can also optimize circadian rhythms. Your baby will observe routines in your life like eating meals and snacks at similar times of the day or in a similar order in the day, going outside at similar times of the day, or doing activities at certain times of the day.

Some babies and parents will be sensitive to light and zeitgeber cues, while others will be less sensitive.

Follow Their Cues to Optimize Sleep Pressure

There are seemingly endless infant sleep schedules available online, and I know these can be attractive because they are so clear-cut and straight-forward. The truth is they are based on nothing, and should be ignored. The only person who knows when your baby needs sleep is your baby. Let your baby's rhythm and tired cues be the guide, not a time pulled out of thin air, like a bedtime of 7 p.m. and a wake time of 7 a.m. with set naptimes or wake times or any rigid schedule. Those times might fit well with our modern lives, but babies don't know about that.

Be aware of your infant's tired cues so that you can optimize their sleep pressure by providing opportunities for naps and bedtime when they are tired. I recommend not waking your baby from naps or in the morning (if you don't need to for a specific reason like daycare)—we want their brain to go through all of the sleep cycles it needs to build the brain. Spend time being with your baby and trying to learn their unique cues, signs that they have built up enough sleep pressure and are ready to sleep. See figure 20 for some common tired cues—your baby may or may not show these; they may have their own, and that's cool! Every baby is different, and by being with your baby you will discover their personal sleep cues. Some babies' cues are more difficult to figure out, so cut yourself some slack if you're doing a lot of trial and error fig-uring out their cues. Know that sleep cues can change as they grow up; when we continue to be present with our babies we will notice when they change.

When babies show tired cues, that is the signal to give them an opportunity for sleep, for all naps and bedtime. It's an opportunity that they may or may not take. You will miss cues sometimes and you will get it wrong sometimes. If you miss cues and your baby is overtired, they might be harder to settle. If you get their cues wrong, your baby may not be tired and you'll need to go back to playing until they are. Sometimes a nap or bedtime needs to be tried several times for the timing to be right. I know this can feel messy, but messy is normal. Babies are not robots; they're human. Their sleep needs can fluctuate just like yours. It's okay to be flexible and to be in the relationship with your baby—if they're telling you they're overtired or not tired yet, you can listen and respond.

Early Cues	Red eyebrows
	Avoiding eye contact
	Turning head
	Blank staring
Tired Cues	Yawning
	Eye rubbing
	Pulling on ears
	Pulling on hair
	Fussy mood
	Sucking fingers
	Frowning
	Seeking hugs
	Clumsiness
	Boredom with toys
Late Tired Cues	Intense crying
	Arched back
	Hands in fists
Overtired Cues	Intense crying
	Arched back
	Hyperactive

Figure 20.

Common tired cues for babies.

When you follow your baby's tired cues and allow them to wake up on their own, their brain takes the true amount of sleep that it needs. That often looks like multiple naps of varying lengths, bedtimes that vary in different babies from 6 p.m. to 11 p.m., and morning waking that also varies in different babies from 6 a.m. to 11 a.m.[31] I remember when people asked me how many naps my young baby was taking— I didn't really know. I didn't count. I watched my baby, put him to sleep when he was tired, let him wake on his own, and watched him again. The number of naps or the length of naps wasn't in my awareness. As he grew, naps became more predictable. Under two years old my baby went to sleep around 8 p.m., then naps changed and at two years old his bedtime became 10 p.m. That was when he built up enough sleep pressure after his afternoon nap. This is very common, and when babies have later bedtimes we often want them to go to sleep earlier, but that is for us, not their developing brain. See page 263 for a sample day of sleep for your baby. Keep in mind, there is no adult on Earth who is qualified to tell your unique baby when they should be waking up or napping, or to prescribe nap lengths or bedtime. Your baby's body provides this information. Sleep is vital to their developing brain and it is a fundamental human right; we must give babies the sleep they need. Please unlearn myth 24, *There are set bedtimes, wake times, and naptimes for your baby*, and replace it with: <u>Your baby's brain will tell you when they are tired and will take the amount of sleep that it needs to grow</u>.

Nurture to Sleep (and Back to Sleep)

The best way to put your baby to sleep is whatever way they feel the most safe and calm. Use your superpower of increasing oxytocin with your connection, presence, and co-regulation to help your baby to sleep in a safety state. Many babies feed to sleep by breastfeeding, body feeding, or bottle feeding, and this is a wonderful way to nurture babies to sleep. Some babies like being cuddled, having their back rubbed (usually with some pressure rather than a light touch) or bum patted, or being rocked or carried to sleep. You can always change the way your baby is nurtured to sleep if it is no longer working for you or them, in a nurturing way. Here we unlearn myth 25, *You should use minimum input to help your baby back to sleep*, and replace it with: <u>It is beneficial to provide the most comforting and easiest method to soothe your baby at night</u>. When your baby or child feels safe falling asleep alone they will tell you; you do not need to teach them to fall asleep alone or go back to sleep alone before they are ready.

If your baby wakes up in the night feeling safe, they might go back to sleep on their own or need a brief touch or cuddle. If they wake up with higher stress, they need to borrow your brain for some co-regulation. Many babies wake up to have a drink of milk. In breastfeeding or chestfeeding families it is called breastsleeping or chest sleeping.[32] Bottle-feeding babies also wake to drink milk or water. With my baby, who did regularly wake up two to five times at night up to about two and a half years old, I would breastsleep in a bedsharing setup. I would offer a feed every single time and he would rarely even open his eyes. People would ask me if my baby was sleeping through the night and the answer was yes. To me he slept through the night since birth with few exceptions. He didn't wake up; I would be aware of his stirring, and he would feed while continuing his sleep. I barely woke up most of the time and he almost never woke up. Many families experience this. If you are bottle feeding or pumping, you can prepare all of your supplies right by your bed, with all of the equipment and even a mini fridge so you never have to get out of bed or fully wake up. These options are very different from nights of fully waking up, walking down a hall to a fully awake crying baby, trying to settle a baby into their own space, and repeating over and over again. You can unlearn myth 26, *Stop feeding in the night at three, six, twelve, twenty-four, or thirty-six months*, and replace it with: <u>Babies can be thirsty or hungry in the night throughout infancy, from zero to three years and beyond</u>.

Some babies need more than a feed or a cuddle for some wakings, especially if they are going through a period of massive brain development or have high stress reactivity. There are no rules here—do what your baby needs to feel safe and return to sleep. Being responsive at night is not a bad habit. These practices are nurturing to your baby's brain and nervous system. You are giving your infant a safe, comforting association with sleep that will benefit them for the rest of their life.

Getting Support from a Sleep Specialist

You may find you need more help with infant sleep, especially if you have a high-needs or highly sensitive baby. Some babies resist sleep even when they're very tired. Others will have sleepy cues that are hard to read. Some infants need a more predictable routine and schedule, while others will just fall asleep when they are tired. It's true that there is a lot of bad information out there about sleep, but it's equally true that there are great sleep professionals who can be a wonderful resource for you. Please check my website for sleep specialists who can help with the following infant and family sleep concerns:

- Navigating medical red flags
- Frequent night wakings
- Split nights, or waking in the middle of the night ready to play for an hour (or several) until they're tired again
- Early wakings
- Late bedtimes
- Bedtime or nap struggles
- Long time to fall asleep at bedtime or naptimes
- Changing the way your baby goes to sleep (e.g., from rocking to cuddling or from feeding to cuddling)
- Changing or adding a caregiver who helps your baby to sleep
- Sleep emergencies, such as when a parent is ill or sleep-deprived
- Changing sleep locations, such as from bedsharing to solitary sleep
- Night weaning
- Parents or caregivers who are stressed about infant sleep
- Parents or caregivers who are exhausted and need more sleep

---

Keep Close

While we have yet to fully uncover the potential benefits of close sleep, the few studies we do have show great benefits to building resilience into the developing infant brain. Parenting babies in sleep states leads to a more resilient stress system in childhood and a lower risk of physical and mental health issues.[33]

Infant sleep guidelines from most major governing bodies recommend that infants sleep in the same room as parents or caregivers for naps and bedtime for at least the first six months and ideally up to twelve months of age.[34] This is because the safety signals from caregivers change breathing and sleep patterns to lower the incidence of SIDS in sleep. What these guidelines don't delve into is that in parallel to reducing SIDS, sleeping close to your baby also deeply nurtures their developing brain all through infancy and even after—children four years and older benefit from being close to their parents or siblings for sleep, too.

Infants have a survival instinct to be close to adults and benefit from emotional contagion, mirroring your emotions, and autonomic and motor mimicry, mirroring your physiology; a caregiver's relaxed or sleeping mind and body influence the baby's mind and body—they feel calm; their breathing, heart rate, oxygen, and glucose are all regulated; and their heart rate is higher and less variable.[35]

Infants, at least those twelve months and under, sleep differently in the same room as a caregiver than those who sleep alone. In the same room as a caregiver, infants have more arousals, more time in light sleep states, and less time with shorter episodes of deep sleep states—which builds the brain and is protective from SIDS.[36] The arousals between parents and babies are beautifully connected to support responsiveness: In a study, 40 percent of infants woke plus or minus two seconds after their mother's arousal, and 60 percent of maternal arousals happened plus or minus two seconds following the infant's arousal.[37] Solitary sleep, meaning sleeping alone, changes infant sleep architecture toward a reduction in REM sleep and an increase in NREM sleep and fewer arousals.[38] This is not ideal, because REM sleep is necessary for the brain to consolidate learning and memory and form new connections. Too much time in NREM sleep is a risk factor for SIDS and takes away from time in REM sleep. We see this pattern in animal models, too. Separation of infants from their mothers for sleep shows dramatic changes to patterns of REM sleep. After separation there is an initial increase in REM times and then a dramatic reduction.[39]

In a study of newborn infants immediately after birth, where one group slept skin-to-skin on their biological mother and the other group slept in a bassinet beside her bed, sleep patterns and physiology were altered. Babies sleeping without contact took longer to get into quiet sleep, had less time in quiet sleep, and had heart rate variability consistent with high stress. Babies sleeping touching their mothers entered quiet sleep faster, had more time in quiet sleep, and had more REM sleep and less active sleep, suggesting a lot more time in restorative sleep patterns that build the brain. These changes are specific to the newborn age; as babies get older, adult presence changes their sleep patterns in a different way. Babies sleeping touching their mothers also had heart rates consistent with lower stress.[40]

Another study in newborn preterm infants showed that skin-to-skin contact for sleep showed more organized sleep-wake cyclicity.[41] These healthy sleep cycles are necessary to build fundamental brain circuitry for the stress system, processing learning and memory, and complex brain circuits underlying all brain function.

Just like during the day, sensing the parent or caregiver is a necessary safety signal that bathes the sleeping infant brain in nurturing hormones. When the infant brain sleeps near a parent or caregiver it receives a plethora of sensory safety signals—the smell of the caregiver's pheromones; the sound of the caregiver's breathing; the movements, heartbeat, and touch of their caregiver.[42] Parents touch and look at their babies more when they sleep close.[43] The baby's body interprets this sensory input as safety, which leads to low stress: high oxytocin, high dopamine, and regulated cortisol. Heart rate, breathing, oxygen, glucose, and body temperature are regulated as well.[44]

These conditions are ideal for restorative sleep and building the brain. On the other hand, studies show that when infants sleep separated from parents or caregivers their stress system is more likely to be on, they lack oxytocin, and they can feel fear—conditions that prevent restorative healthy sleep.[45]

Moreover, nurtured sleep via lower stress in infancy can change sleep neurobiology to encourage better sleep for life. We have evidence from animal studies that early stress from maternal separation or maltreatment can increase the risk for insomnia and changes to sleep architecture in adulthood—or as I've phrased it throughout this book, lack of nurture can shape the stress system to be more vulnerable. This research is consistent with numerous anecdotal reports I have heard from adults with insomnia or fears related to sleep who were isolated at night as babies. Therapies like cognitive behavioral therapy for insomnia (CBTI) can help if this is you. One animal study shows that early life stress, a model of maternal maltreatment, disrupts adult sleep, leading to a lifelong decrease in sleep spindles, a pattern important for cortical development and memory, and NREM sleep fragmentation, important for restorative processes in the brain and body.[46] Another animal study shows that the stress model of maternal separation in early life changes the orexin system in the brain, a key signal for waking that is sensitive to stress. In the study, maternal separation in infancy changed adult orexin receptors in the brain, increasing hyperactivity and wakefulness during sleep times consistent with insomnia.[47]

Sleeping close to your baby changes your sleep patterns, your awareness, and your brain waves, too. They shift in order to give you enough restorative sleep even though you are waking to respond to your baby. In a study of bedsharing and solitary-sleeping families, bedsharing mothers had more total sleep. Eighty-four percent of bedsharing moms said they had "good or enough" sleep, compared to sixty-four percent of the solitary-sleeping moms. Due to your changing parent brain in close sleep, you have reduced deep NREM sleep but no change in REM sleep or sleep duration. This means that your deep sleep is reduced to be more aware of your baby and their cues.[48] Moreover, when you sleep close your brain waves synchronize with your baby's.[49] This is beneficial for nurture because when your baby goes into light sleep, so do you, and it is easier for you to wake up, feed, or cuddle your baby and go back to sleep. This effect is highest in breastfeeding or body-feeding parents who sleep close to their baby and has not been observed in other groups to date. The parents I help to sleep close to their babies, regardless of how they feed, have benefits to their sleep when they don't have to fully wake up to help their babies.

FACILITATING CLOSE SLEEP

There are many options for close sleep with your baby, and I encourage you to spend some time exploring what arrangement is best and safest for your family. I advocate for three methods:

Co-sleeping: Keeping the baby close in a crib or bassinet in a parent or caregiver's room, ideally an arm's reach away from the bed.

Bedside sleeping: Keeping the baby close in a crib, sidecar bed, or floor bed that is continuous with the parent or caregiver's bed.

Bedsharing: The baby sleeps close to their parent or caregiver on the same surface of an adult bed that's prepared and maintained for safe infant sleep (see page 262 for safe bedsharing resources).

I recommend sleeping in the same room with your infant up to three years old and beyond if it is working for your family. At the very least for six to twelve months (as well as being in the same room for naps, sleeping or awake, for a minimum of six to twelve months). I recommend motion sleep in a baby carrier, car, or stroller to allow your baby to sleep and allow you to be flexible. Many babies and children communicate to their parents when they are ready to be in their own sleep space—and when they are not ready. There are no rules about this—you can unlearn myth 27, *Babies need to be in their own room at four, six, twelve, twenty-four, or thirty-six months*, and replace it with: <u>Babies tell us when they feel safe enough to sleep alone</u>. When your aunt or the guy at the bank (yes, this really happened to me) tells you you're creating a bad habit and your kid will be in your bed when they're eighteen years old, you can feel confident telling them to back off knowing that studies have found that bedsharing infants are more independent preschoolers, with enriched cognition indicative of a resilient stress system and well-developed thinking brain.[50] Bedsharing buffers stress for infants when there are significant sources of stress in their lives, is preventive to psychiatric problems, and enriches sociability.[51] Our infants thrive when we keep them close for sleep.

Safe Bedsharing

I believe every family should know about safe bedsharing even if you never plan to do so. Why? Because there is an extremely high chance that there will be days or weeks where your baby will sleep nowhere else than on your chest or next to you and you will need a solution for that. Despite the fact that most hospitals and public health professionals terrify new parents about the dangers of bedsharing (some new parents are forced to watch hours-long videos on this topic before they can leave the hospital), about 60 percent of families in the United States and Canada bring a baby under twelve months into their bed.[52]

Many parents come to me after sleeping on a couch or a reclining chair with a newborn baby because they've been told never to bedshare and think it's safer than a bed. It's absolutely not. Parents come to me in a crisis of total sleep deprivation after spending days or weeks staying awake with a baby who won't sleep anywhere but on their chest. Many families have newborn babies who are only able to sleep while lying on or touching a person and they are worried that something is wrong with their baby. Parents often resort to taking turns staying awake holding the baby over twenty-four-hour periods. This is unsustainable for most, and frankly really dangerous. It is not serving parents who need to sleep or babies who have a drive for contact sleep.

Bedsharing is often the only option to provide the whole family sleep. At the same time, safe sleep is the number one priority for infants. There are critical infant sleep safety guidelines to follow for bedsharing and co-sleeping, which are included on page 262.

High and Low Touch Needs Babies

Some babies, especially at very young ages and sometimes for all of infancy, need full body contact with an adult to sleep. This is called "contact sleep," and it is normal. It means their stress system requires the presence of an adult to feel safe enough to enter the vulnerable state of sleep. Their brain needs the nurture bath created by a caregiver to enter rest, and without it stress is too high for sleep.

We call babies who need contact sleep "velcro" or "barnacle" or "joey" or "koala" babies—they need to be attached closely and fully. I was a velcro baby and my own baby was a velcro baby until about ten months old. As a newborn my baby was held for every daytime nap, he slept on our chests in the evening while we had dinner or watched a movie, breastfed while sleeping when we went out for meals, and at night he slept right beside me in a bassinet, or beside me bedsharing, or sometimes on my chest. A friend has a velcro baby who, at thirty months old, still sleeps in full body contact with her. It's the best way for both of them to get enough sleep.

If you find that your baby is a velcro baby, know that there's nothing wrong with giving your baby what they need. By providing constant contact you are nurturing their brain in the way that it needs to be nurtured in order to allow healthy brain wave patterns to build the infant brain, which is a fundamental human right. As your baby and their stress system grow, they often stop needing full contact for all sleep. For some this happens three to four months after birth, for others around one year old, and for high touch needs babies it could go all the way up to three years old and beyond.

Bedsharing or a sidecar bed is probably your best option for a high touch needs infant. While you can't train or teach your baby's brain to stop needing contact for sleep, you can give them opportunities to sleep without contact to see if the ability has developed. If they communicate that they aren't ready (by crying, clinging, or otherwise protesting), go back to close sleep for a while, until you're both ready to try again. Please unlearn myth 28, *Babies need to learn to sleep without contact*, and replace it with: Many babies require contact to feel safe enough to sleep.

There are also babies who, typically after zero to four months, prefer to not be touched for sleep. Some families prepare for bedsharing and contact naps and have babies who prefer their own sleep space. If this is your baby, follow your baby's cues. Instead of bedsharing you can set up a sidecar bed or a crib next to your bed to allow your baby to sense you but not touch you. Anything is possible with babies and nothing is true for all babies. As always, be with your baby, and watch and listen to them to understand what they need.

A Special Time of Day for Connection

Bedtime is a unique, not-to-be-missed opportunity for connection with your baby. When we connect emotionally and physically at bedtime, babies and children have lower stress and more settled sleep.[53] Bedtime connection becomes one of the most treasured memories people can ever have with a loved one. It is a time of slowing down, unlike any other, where you can repair any ruptures from the day, talk about memories you made, talk about new things your baby did, talk about people you love, say good night to loved ones, and connect in shared brain synchrony. Bedtime rituals are so emotional that they become very strong memories of being seen, important and good just as you are. I will forget many things, but my stress system will never forget how my mom made me feel as she supported my sleep and all my wakings as an infant. My memory will never forget how it felt for my mom to read me a book and sing me a song every night as a child or how my grandmother played with my hair as I fell asleep as a child or how it felt at my family cottage to go to sleep listening to the voices of the people I loved. Many adults have shared with me their parents' bedtime rituals, such as a dad tucking the duvet like a mermaid, the scent of lavender, holding hands, reading books, singing songs, adjusting the pillow perfectly under the head. These memories are important for our lifelong emotional well-being. Waking up beside your baby is also a unique time for connection. Cuddles, kisses, and morning chats are a treasured daily experience of deep connection unlike any other. You can unlearn myth 29, *Your baby or child needs to outgrow connection at bedtime in infancy or childhood*, and replace it with: <u>Bedtime is a precious time where nurtured connection and nurtured sleep overlap. Children will tell you when they no longer want to connect at bedtime</u>.

Move, Connect, and Support Stress During the Day

Believe it or not, one topic I always bring up when helping families optimize their sleep is daytime practices. How much does your baby get to move, play, and explore? More specifically, how much is your younger infant getting floor time to practice rolling, kicking, grabbing their feet or hands, staring at light or colors on the ceiling or wall? How much tummy time are they getting? For older babies I ask, How much time do they get to jump, dance, laugh, climb, walk, and run? Carry heavy things around? Swing? Spin? Crawl? Push and pull? For babies of all ages I'm curious if they're getting free time for sensory exploration and time outdoors. The reason is that free movement, free exploration, free play, and time outdoors are great for building sleep pressure and enriching sleep, so adding these into your day can have an influence on naps and nighttime sleep.

Connection and support for stress during the day are very important contributors to your infant's sleep. By making nurtured connection and nurtured stress a part of your baby's day, you support their sleep. Connection and responding to stress during the day reduces night wakings and leads to more settled sleep. Being emotionally connected at bedtime, which is so beneficial to your relationship and nurtured connection, also has benefits for infant sleep.[54]

Support Your Sleep

It is absolutely essential for parents and caregivers to prioritize their own sleep as they support their babies' sleep in infancy. We'd be so much better with longer parental leave, flexible work schedules, and access to quality childcare, to name a few supports. Yet we can protect our sleep while we as parents advocate for these societal changes.

It is possible to support infant sleep with night wakings and night-time care and be relatively rested. Of course there are times when you will be extra tired, especially with newborns and when your baby goes through intense developmental periods, but it is possible. It does require you to make your sleep a priority, which you may never have done before. You may need to make significant changes to your sleep habits. Many parents I work with slept from 12 a.m. to 7 a.m. before having a baby—this will not get you adequate rest while you nurture your baby's sleep. Some steps to take: Make sure you get sunlight every morning, avoid screens for yourself one to two hours before bedtime, and make sure you meet as many of your basic needs as possible for water, nutritious food, fresh air, movement, and connection. Go to sleep early and sleep in when you can to make sure you're in bed for the number of hours of sleep you need. Most adults need seven to nine hours of sleep to be rested, and when you have night wakings, you probably need to be in bed for more hours to get this amount of sleep. Think about putting your inner baby to sleep at the right time—when they are tired. When your baby is a newborn and doesn't have a clear day and night, it helps if you operate this way, too, by sleeping or resting nearly every time your newborn baby sleeps. Think about how many hours of sleep you typically need. For example, if available, if you need eight hours, stay in bed until you sleep for all of those hours. You might need to be in bed for twelve hours to get eight hours of sleep.

If lack of parental leave or flexibility of work hours puts constraints on your sleep, asking for as much help as possible from a partner, family, friends, or a professional is critical. Others can care for your baby for parts of the night or day so you can get more rest. Nurturing infant sleep is not for one person; parents need help to support infant sleep. It is ideal if more than one parent or caregiver can nurture babies to sleep for naps, bedtime, and when they wake up at night. Many families have one parent who parents more at night. This person absolutely needs support so they can get enough sleep. This can look like having someone else take over baby care in the mornings so the person can sleep in, or during the day for naps, or in the evening to go to sleep early, or baby care throughout the day so they can have time to themselves to meet their needs.

I know that many parents like to stay up late—that's when they can get time to themselves. If you do this, try instead to get this time to yourself during the day. Look for help so you can get your needs met during the day without sacrificing your sleep. In order to support your baby's sleep I do recommend going to bed early, at the same time as your baby if possible. There will be time once your child is older for you to stay up after their bedtime. In the years of infancy, putting sleep first is always a good idea.

APPLYING NURTURED PRESENCE AND NURTURED EMPATHY TO SLEEP STATES

When we provide a nurtured presence and empathy to sleep states, we are lending our baby our brain at their most vulnerable time, when they relax into unconscious brain states. Connection is very influential to promote sleep. Some naps and bedtimes will be easygoing and others may be emotional and stressful; when we practice presence and empathy we support whatever our babies experience as they prepare for sleep.

Nurtured Presence for Sleep

With your presence communicate the answer to your baby's unconscious questions:

Do you see me?

Take a breath and get comfortable with your baby—lie down beside them, hold them in your arms or feed them, and look into their eyes. You are there to be with them to feel safe to fall asleep. Are they sleepy, alert, comfortable, uncomfortable? See what they are saying and might be needing—"I feel safe when you're near me." "I am relaxed." "I need you here." "I'm not ready to sleep." "I have energy and I need to move." "I'm needing more connection." "I am so tired I need extra help."

Do you care that I'm here?

Think about how you get to be with your baby during their most vulnerable time of sleep. They feel completely safe with you and can rely on you.

Am I enough for you, or do you need me to be better in some way?

Practice radical acceptance for what they need to fully relax into sleep and stay in sleep. Feeding, rocking, singing, closeness. Your baby is enough while needing any and all of these things.

Can I tell that I'm special to you by the way that you look at me?

Reflect on the day, the amazing things your baby did and learned, and how beautiful they are. Look at them with all of the awe and love you feel.

Nurtured Empathy for Sleep

1. Get behind your baby's eyes. They are sleepy, possibly stressed about separating from you or the fun of the day. They are needing you, in a safety state, to help them relax and accompany them to sleep.

2. Empathize by reflecting their behavior(s), how they might be feeling, and their need(s). You can do this by:

    a. Showing them how they might be feeling with an exaggerated facial expression—a soft smile and closing your eyes, or a pout of sadness.

    b. Naming the behavior(s) you see, the emotion(s) your baby might be feeling, and the need(s) they might have. Say, "You are yawning and have tired eyes (behavior). I wonder if you're feeling sleepy (feeling) and needing to cuddle with me to sleep (need)." Or, "You're crying (behavior). I wonder if you're overwhelmed or afraid (feeling) and needing some rocking and feeding to feel connected, sleepy, and safe (need)."

    c. Showing them a reassuring face and telling them that you're here for them. "I will always be here when you need me to fall asleep."

3. Meet the need: Provide your feeding, closeness, singing, movement, to help your baby feel safe and connected as they fall asleep.

Infant sleep doesn't have to be a battleground. It doesn't have to be your needs for sleep over your baby's need for comfort and soothing, a stressful time of separation, or a power struggle. It can be sweet, connected, supported, and nurtured. Of course there will be nights where it doesn't go smoothly. As well as early mornings, naps, and late nights. You will need support and help. But it's brain-building to soothe your baby to sleep. It's brain-building to love your baby to sleep. It's brain-building to follow their natural rhythms, and yours. You may have to make some changes to your old sleep routine, and you may have to throw out a lot of cultural pressure and some popular books that say you should force independent sleep on your baby, but you owe it to yourself and your baby to do this work. To reclaim gentleness when it comes to sleep. To let it come from within your physiology and bodily needs and not from some external schedule. Imagine every time you share sleep with your baby or comfort your baby to sleep, you are building their brain toward being regulated, connected, joyful, and curious. See page 262 for additional resources.

Chapter 9

HOW TO NURTURE YOUR CHANGING PARENT BRAIN

Think of yourself as having a nurture reservoir inside. When your nurture reservoir is deep and wide and full, you feel comfortable, safe, and able to deal with the stressors of daily life without becoming out of control, depleted, or anxious. When your nurture reservoir is full, you can function without your stress system activating your fight-flight-freeze response. Your stress system is not reactive or in a threat state. You're in an oxytocin cascade.

When your nurture reservoir is deep and wide and full, you feel grounded, flexible, creative, open, curious, present, and well regulated. You can hold boundaries without shutting down. You can be warm and relational without losing yourself or becoming enmeshed. You are in a safety state. In this state you feel calm, relaxed, at peace, and "just right."[1]

When your reservoir is narrow, shallow, or draining (or empty)— maybe because you're tired, hungry, overwhelmed, lonely, or haven't had other needs met—you are more likely to switch into a stress state of fight, flight, or freeze, when things, big or small, go awry. You may experience hyperarousal; a fight-or-flight response (anxiety, anger, feeling overwhelmed, hypervigilance, chaotic); or a freeze response (numb, dissociated, withdrawn, depressed, ashamed, victimized, passive). You may be reactive and impulsive. You may yell or lash out. You may withdraw and avoid. You may take others' behaviors personally. You may say shaming or blaming things or set hard boundaries that push people you love away. You are in a threat state. You're in a cortisol cascade.

As parents, we're helping to build our babies' reservoirs through experience, but we also have our own capacity for regulation and dysregulation—safety and threat states. Infancy is a season that asks a lot of us. Nurtured caregiving requires a lot of emotional and physical energy. It becomes harder to meet your needs for water, food, alone time, social time, sleep, and time to recharge by doing what you love. We also all bring our own stress systems, which were shaped by our experiences in infancy, into parenthood. Your stress system may fall anywhere on the spectrum from resilient to vulnerable, or from regulated to dysregulated, meaning that it may take more or less to drain your reservoir.

As your new parent brain develops, it becomes more wired for nurture. You can support your inner well of energy and the neuroplasticity of your parent brain with practices that help you become more aware of your nurture reservoir. Learning to notice when it's feeling low, and how to fill it, grows your parent brain, too. Over time these practices can even help you deepen and widen your reservoir so that you have more capacity to stay in a safety state (and are less likely to be drained). You can nurture your stress system, and even change your stress system so that you spend more time in a safety state, through practices that rewire your brain for resilience and a more expansive nurture reservoir. This is how you nurture your parent brain so you can nurture your baby.

In essence, the nurture reservoir helps you think more consciously about your state. The practices in this chapter will help you fill and build your nurture reservoir so that you can more often be in a safe, warm, and open state that allows you more capacity to nurture your baby. While you can follow nurturing scripts when you're in any state—mask or repress your anger or feeling of being overwhelmed to respond calmly to your baby's tantrum, or override your depression or numbness to gently soothe your baby back to sleep at night—we nurture best when we are not just saying the "right" words or having the "right" nurturing response but actually speaking and acting from a grounded, flexible, open, and well-regulated place inside. We nurture best when our reservoir is full, in a safety state. A safety state is the optimal state for parenting, regulating our baby's emotions, learning, teaching, patience, empathy, connection, and mental and physical health.[2] Being in a safe state inside is not something we can script, act, or fake, at least not very well. Our babies pick up on our heart rate, microexpressions on our faces, tension in our muscles—all things we cannot fake, that tell them what we must truly be experiencing. To be in safe states we must practice. We can use the neuroplasticity of our parent brains to widen and deepen our nurture reservoirs in the long term, and we can use regulating in-the-moment practices to support safety states as things come up throughout the day.

If while reading those last four chapters you were thinking, "There's no way I could possibly do all this," that's probably a good indication that your nurture reservoir is feeling drained or that it's narrow and shallow and hard to find. You will benefit from practices that will fill you up. Perhaps, like many of my clients, you have concerns about having a baby while you still feel you have your own inner work to do. The good news is that the presence of your baby is a great time to do inner work because of your changing parent brain. Remember that "neurons that fire together wire together, and those that don't won't." All adults can improve their emotional intelligence, improve the ability to be more self-aware, improve self-regulation, improve empathy, and improve social skills. As a parent, you benefit from an extra boost of enhanced neuroplasticity; this will help you make changes in your brain, especially in your brain circuits that support relationships, empathy, and your mental health. You are likely also in a time of enhanced motivation to make changes for yourself because of your baby, more so than you may have been in the past. Time to unlearn myth 30, *You have to have all of your inner work sorted out before becoming a parent*, and replace it with: <u>Becoming a parent is a unique opportunity to learn about your stress system and do inner work within the relationship with your baby</u>.

The research is clear that stress states and safety states are contagious, especially between caregivers and babies.[3] Whether in pregnancy or postpartum, our nervous system informs the environment in which our baby's brain grows. If you feel stressed and chaotic or rigid and controlled, your baby mirrors that state; if you feel safe, calm, and coherent inside, you can mirror regulation to your baby. In other words, you can be a more effective external emotional brain if you are well regulated.

Many of us don't know this, but we have to give our body safety signals to fill our nurture reservoir. This process is commonly known as self-care, but it's more fitting to call it nervous system care. If your nurture reservoir is empty, if your needs are not met, if you have no breaks from nurturing your baby and are nurturing relentlessly, you will likely have a hard time staying in safety states or returning to safety states from stressed states. Safety states, and the ability to return to them, are where your parent brain and your infant's developing brain thrive. If you don't do nervous system care, you will have a harder time nurturing, and you will have a harder time supporting your baby's states of connection, exploration, stress, and sleep. Nurture should not be relentless; you must take breaks and fill your reservoir in order to nurture. Your baby will benefit from you being in safety states more often, and other people in your baby's life can nurture your baby when you are taking time for yourself.

Remember that there is no perfect parent brain. We are all unique and our experiences in life make us so. Wherever you are, the goal is simply to nourish and calm your nervous system, nurture your brain, and become more aware of your emotions. That will be different for everyone. Let's make good use of our changing parent brains by supporting our nervous system and brain to feel safe, connected, open, creative, and nurturing.

GENTLE WAYS TO GROW AND FILL YOUR NURTURE RESERVOIR

I like to approach nervous system care from two angles: long- and short-term. My I CARE practices are geared for building your reservoir over time, and Growing SPACE practices are my suggestions for in-the-moment strategies you can use when you feel your stress system activating. I CARE practices will help you fill your nurture reservoir, while Growing SPACE practices will help you regulate your stress in the moment and bring you back to a safety state. This is illustrated in figure 21.

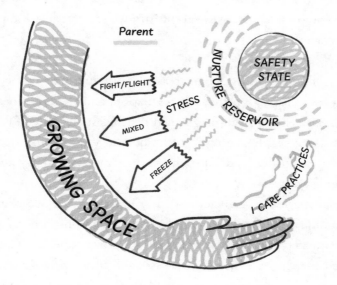

Figure 21.

Filling your nurture reservoir with I CARE practices will help you stay in safety states and grow your parent brain. When you find yourself in a stress state, Growing SPACE practices will help return you to safety states.

Nervous System Care with the I CARE Approach

With regular, repeated practice, over time you can rewire your stress system to be less reactive, so that you feel more at ease, your brain and nervous system are bathed in calming, soothing hormones and neuro-transmitters like oxytocin, and so that you feel more able to connect with and nurture your baby. I've organized the techniques that have been most successful with my clients into the acronym I CARE:

Intuition or Interoception—To nurture your insula, prefrontal cortex, and amygdala

Curious about your physical needs—To nurture your hypothalamus
and hippocampus

Aware of your emotions and emotional needs—To nurture your
amygdala and prefrontal cortex

Regular breathing—To nurture your prefrontal cortex and amygdala

Evoke compassion and awe—To nurture your amygdala and prefrontal cortex

Each technique gently feeds areas of your brain to influence and
grow self-awareness, empathy, self-regulation, and responsiveness. Each
of these areas benefits from heightened neuroplasticity as you become a
parent or caregiver. Engaging in techniques as you become a parent in
the infant years grows and fills your nurture reservoir and your ability
to recover from stress.

I encourage you to engage in a daily practice with one or more of
these techniques that will help you feel your emotions in order to, ultimately, regulate your stress system. This will, over time, help your stress
system recover more easily from stress, and improve your emotional
intelligence, self-awareness, stress regulation, and empathy. Think of it
as building a new map or blueprint inside yourself, one where you give
your inner child (or teenager) all the compassion you need and endless
space for safe emotional expression. One where you feel safe, attuned to,
and accurately mirrored by your caregivers.

Think of these practices as "nurturing *your inner baby*." They nurture new connections among many of the brain areas that developed in
your infancy as well as others that are in networks with your stress system. They rewire your amygdala alarm to reduce your stress activation.
They also strengthen circuits in your prefrontal cortex and hippocampus
stress brake that quiet your amygdala alarm, and they act in the insula
to enhance empathy.[4] See figure 22 for a visual representation of the
changes you can make.

You can start these practices as soon as you come to them. In pregnancy, they will manage your stress to influence the early development

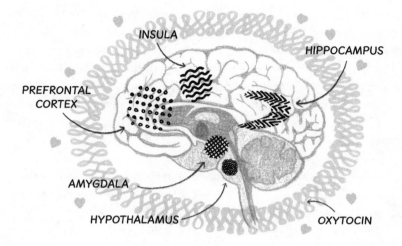

Figure 22.

When you practice I CARE and Growing SPACE you rewire and grow brain areas that were formed in your infancy toward more safety states, more self-awareness, more self-regulation, more empathy, and more nurture for your baby. The areas include the insula, amygdala, hypothalamus, hippocampus, and prefrontal cortex.

of your baby's stress system as well as your stress system when your baby is born.[5] In birth, they can help you manage physical or emotional sensations or pain. In infancy they will help you be in a safety state more often and return to a safety state when you need to regulate yourself and your baby, thousands of times. They will also help expand your capacity to be in a safety state.

Consider I CARE a menu you can choose from; you don't have to do it all. I invite you to sample each option, and then order your meal, or the main way(s) you want to engage with a regulation practice.

Meet Your Stress and Safety States

Just like your baby, the way you experience stress states and the way you regulate to safety states is unique to you. What happens in your mind and body when you are stressed? How does it feel when your stress escalates from low to high?

What thoughts do you have when you're stressed? "Get me out of here, I can't do this" (flight); or "I'm confused and chaotic, the room is spinning" (flight); or "I am furious, I need to yell at someone" (fight); or "I'm completely shut down" (freeze, collapse); or "I'm overthinking this" (flight)? What emotions do you feel? Angry, sad, afraid, numb? What does it feel like in your body—racing heart, tense muscles, numbness? When you have more self-awareness about your own experience of stress, you can use techniques to feel your stress and regulate to recover from the stress to safety states.

The way you experience safety states is also unique to you. What happens in your mind and body when you're in a safety state? Do you have more patience, more awareness, more connection, more fun and laughter, more ability to be calm when your baby is stressed?

There are usually initial signs that you are entering a stress state. You might first feel nervous and upset when entering a fight-or-flight state. You might then escalate to irritated, cranky, annoyed, resentful, frustrated, and angry—and at the highest level to hysterical and rage-filled. When you are entering a freeze state you might feel checked out, withdrawn, have a blank mind, experience difficulty thinking or speaking, sadness, despair—at the highest level you might feel drowsy or sleepy. Sometimes you might experience mixed states of freeze with fight-or- flight with feelings of anxiety, worry, or hypervigilance.

It is helpful to know what causes you stress and how stress manifests in your body. When you recognize your habitual early stress state signs you can regulate yourself back to a safety state relatively easily. Regulation is still possible if you miss those signs; it just takes more effort. One way to track this is to keep a journal to note what experiences are causing a stress response in your body. Then I CARE techniques will help you feel your emotions and engage a plan to regulate your nervous system. See page 262 of the Resources for a stress journal template.

I—Intuition or Interoception

Intuition or interoception is the ability to observe signals from the body like heart rate, muscle tone, hormones, and gut feelings to make fast decisions without conscious reasoning. In the brain it involves the amygdala, insula, and parts of our thinking brain or prefrontal cortex (median orbitofrontal cortex and ventral occipitotemporal regions).[6] Practicing intuition rewires these brain areas; see figure 23.

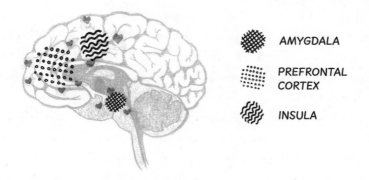

AMYGDALA

PREFRONTAL
CORTEX

INSULA

Figure 23.

Practicing intuition or interoception grows your insula, amygdala, and pre-frontal cortex toward resilience and wellness.

The amygdala is involved in circuits that detect threats. If we can tune in to intuition, we can be more aware of people and experiences in our lives that feel either threatening or nonthreatening. The insula is one of my favorite brain regions. It receives messages of sensation from our body so we have a sense of how our internal organs, systems, and muscles are feeling. Our brains receive information from our body; we need to learn how to listen, and when we practice listening we hear the signals louder. The insula is also involved in empathy, so when we imagine how our baby or another person is feeling we are building our insula, empathy, and intuition. It is also a brain area that is strengthened by a breathing or mindfulness practice.

Often when we're faced with a decision or situation we can turn toward our body's sensations and know, "My body says yes," or "My body says no." Then the next step is to act on our intuition. When my son was young a neighbor wanted to hold him in a pool. My intuition said "HECK NO," but I said okay because I was people pleasing and freezing and I had not learned to listen to myself yet. My intuition continued to say "NO" as the neighbor held my baby, and it took me awhile to finally say, "Can I have my baby back, please?" I will never forget that day because my intuition was screaming at me and I really regret putting my baby and myself in a position that my body sensed as dangerous. I decided at that moment to never ignore my intuition again, and to pay close attention to my freeze response. We need the courage to listen to ourselves and speak up—it doesn't mean we're difficult or controlling; it means we're being authentic and we can be very proud of that. When we feel in our bodies, "This is a no," and do it anyway, we often regret it. It matters only what you think, not anyone else.

Intuition is important to your nervous system care as well. It is important to do the things our bodies say yes to because these things bring us joy and manage stress. For example, a night out with friends or a type of movement. It's important to say no to what our bodies do not want to do. I and many of the parents I've worked with have felt intuition to slow down and not engage in high-intensity exercise or activities, and instead to do slower movements that feel good. I've also worked with parents who have felt intuition to do high-intensity exercise and activities. Everybody is different.

Other situations in which it will be important to listen to our intuition are when we interview caregivers or daycares who will spend lots of time with our baby. When I met the various caregivers who took care of my baby over the years, I chose the people that made my intuition say "Heck yes" and I said "no thank you" when I didn't feel that or felt a no in a different way. When we decide our baby is ready for something new, like solid foods or facing out in a baby carrier, if we see something we are worried about in the environment, our intuition is present. We need to practice using it and practice being led by it.

Practice turning inward when you are faced with a decision. Pay attention and be curious about sensations and feelings in your body. Is my body saying yes or saying no? Try some low-stakes questions to practice:

- First thing in the morning, do I want coffee or tea or water?
- Do I need rest right now?
- Do I want to move my body right now?
- Does that person feel safe?

C-Curious About Your Physical Needs

Your hypothalamus is an area of your brain that constantly monitors your physical needs. If it detects a need, it will send out a stress signal so your body mobilizes to meet the need. If you have a physical need that goes unmet, it will stay in a stress state. Being aware of your basic needs and meeting them prevents a lot of stress and helps you stay in a safety state.[7] As you manage these needs for your baby, imagine you are also managing them for your inner baby. Your hippocampus thrives when you meet your needs, lower your stress, and regularly move your body. When it is thriving, new neurons in your hippocampus grow to survive, grow complexity, and help buffer stress.[8] When you practice curiosity about your physical needs, you signal safety to your hypothalamus and you rewire your hippocampus; see figure 24.

Your basic physical needs include clean water, nourishing food, nature and air, movement, sleep and rest, touch and connection, and safety. We all have access to each of these in varying degrees, but no matter your circumstance, you can make a practice of checking in with yourself: "Have I eaten today?" "Have I moved my body in a way that feels good to me?" "Have I been outside?"

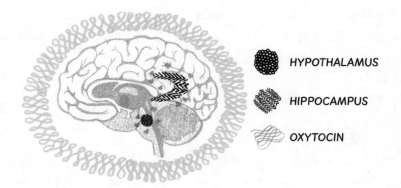

HYPOTHALAMUS

HIPPOCAMPUS

OXYTOCIN

Figure 24.

Meeting your needs sends safety signals to your hypothalamus to reduce stress, while movement and positive emotion grow resilience in your hippocampus.

Clean Water

Over 70 percent of your brain is made up of water, and even slight dehydration can lead to stress, emotional dysregulation, anxiety, headaches, attention issues, fatigue, and sleep issues.[9] Begin with the general guidelines suggesting adults drink eight to twelve eight-ounce glasses of water each day, and over time, try to tune in to your body's cues of thirst. The guidelines are only an average, so you might need more or less than what is recommended. In pregnancy and when producing milk, it is important to drink lots of water, and your thirst cues may be (much!) stronger. If your baby is thirsty, you get them a drink; when your inner baby is thirsty, they also need a drink. You might:

- Start the day by drinking a big glass of water.
- Keep a water bottle with you all day to drink regularly throughout the day.
- Drink through a straw. This little trick helps you consume more than you would just by drinking from a cup. Bonus: A reusable water bottle with a built-in straw is easy to drink from while in labor, holding or rocking a baby, or feeding a baby.
- Drink a big glass of water before every meal or snack.
- Make big pots of herbal tea to drink hot or iced. (Many herbal teas are not recommended for pregnancy, so be sure to check!)
- Add fresh lemon or lime to water.
- Purchase a machine that carbonates water.

Nourishing Food

Your hypothalamus is on the lookout for essential nutrients for your body. You don't necessarily have to change what you are eating, but think about adding in more nourishing and fresh food. Nutrient-dense fresh foods like fruits, vegetables, nuts, seeds, legumes, and complete proteins give your body the signal that there is abundant nutrition, which is a safety signal to your brain. You feed your baby the most nourishing foods possible, and so your inner baby also benefits from nutrition. You might:

- Make a daily smoothie with frozen or fresh foods like berries, spinach, cauliflower, and/or broccoli. Add chia seeds, hemp seeds, flaxseed, nut butter, or avocado. Smoothies can be extra helpful in pregnancy when these foods alone might not be appealing.
- Add a vegetable side dish to your meals. Frozen vegetables can be heated and prepared quickly.
- Add in bone broths and vegetable broths.
- Include brain-healthy foods like walnuts, fish, blueberries, black beans, eggs, leafy greens.

If you are unsure, check in with a naturopathic doctor, nutritionist, or functional medicine doctor for input on your diet.

Nature and Air

Trees, plants, and flowers are instantly stress-reducing to your brain. Being in nature regularly is a physical need and it signals safety to your brain. Looking at nature reduces stress. Trees and plants release compounds that we smell and that directly decrease our stress. Walking in nature reduces brain activity in depressive circuits in our brain, including the hippocampus, to lower stress and decrease depression.[10] Wherever you live, there is always some nature, big or small, accessible to you—whether it's a nature preserve or a dandelion growing out of the sidewalk, or looking out your window at the sky or a bird. You bring your baby to a park for fresh air; why not do it for you, too?!

At the same time, artificial scents and toxins in the air can be a contributing factor to poor mental health, anxiety, and depression. Most of our senses, like sight, taste, and touch, go through a filter in our brain called the thalamus where they are processed before they become part of our experience or memory. Smell is different. Scents go directly into our hippocampus. The hippocampus is involved in memory and mood, which is why scent is highly linked to our memories. It also means that scents can directly influence your mood. Essential oils can be a positive way you can influence your mood with scent; for example, lavender can decrease stress. However, I only recommend them for adults, as they do have medicinal effects that have not been tested in pregnancy or infancy.[11] Artificial scents, such as those in perfumes and cleaners, on the other hand, can negatively influence your mood because they can act to increase stress, anxiety, and depression.[12] Whenever possible, remove all purposeful scents from the home, like room sprays, cleaners, scented laundry detergents, scented cleaning products, and overly scented beauty products. If you live in a city or near fires or pollution, you would benefit from an air filter for your home. Remember that "the solution to pollution is dilution"—you can't control every scent that wafts into (or lives in) your home, but you can help dilute them all with air filters, fans, open windows (if appropriate), and more. Consider:

- Take a detour on your daily walk to pass through a park.
- Visit a park, read in a park.
- Sit in the grass.
- Walk a trail.
- Look at a tree, plant, or flower.
- Bring a plant into your home and spend time looking at it daily.
- Walk barefoot in grass or mud.
- Go into a wooded area, take deep breaths, and relax your body.
- Put a plant on your desk and spend time looking at it daily.
- Set a timer to look out your window regularly at trees and plants or the sky.

Movement

Moving your body directly reduces stress and rewires the stress system. In pregnancy, movement helps shape the stress system in babies when they are in the womb. Exercise acts in the brain through similar mechanisms as antidepressants and is a mood booster (even if you're also taking antidepressants).[13] During exercise organs and muscles in the body release molecules that pass into the brain. Once in the brain the molecules increase an essential nutrient for brain cells called BDNF (brain-derived neurotrophic factor). BDNF is brain food and stimulates brain health. Since all brain cells are affected by BDNF, it improves many brain systems: BDNF is known to improve memory, attention, and stress regulation. BDNF nourishes the growth of new cells in the hippocampus that act as stop signals in the stress system. In addition, BDNF is known to keep cells healthy and significantly reduce the risk of mood disorders.[14] We often think the goals of exercising are losing or maintaining weight or cardiovascular health. We can now put brain health to the top of this list. You make sure your baby moves all day; same goes for you! Some helpful ideas:

- Any amount of movement is good for you; be gentle with yourself and your abilities. Even five to ten minutes of movement is beneficial.
- Take a daily walk, alone or with a friend, or walk with babywearing.
- Take a yoga class online or in person.
- Take your favorite exercise class.
- Do gentle stretching or even just rolling around on the floor in whatever ways feel most comfortable.

Sleep and Rest

As we discussed in chapter 8, when you don't have enough sleep your stress system is much more dysregulated/reactive and your mental health can suffer. When you sleep, a system in your brain gets activated to remove waste in the brain. Sleep leads to lower stress and better attention and cognition. In sleep we consolidate learning and integrate our experience with our past experience.[15] Do your best to give your brain the opportunity for sleep. This means that during the season of infancy sleep might be instead of other activities you enjoy. However, sleep is the bedrock of health; it is non-negotiable. Many parents find that their relationship with sleep improves when they have a baby, which might be shocking to hear as we also know that babies change parent sleep as well. However, for many parents, parenthood is the first time they prioritize their sleep. You make sure your baby has naps and bedtime when they are tired; your inner baby needs this, too! To make this happen:

- Prioritize sleep by going to bed early, when you are tired.
- Go outside to get sun on your eyes when you wake up, and at midday. Keep evenings dark.
- Limit screens and/or blue light two hours before sleep.
- Limit caffeine to before noon.
- Take naps when possible.
- Try yoga nidra for restorative rest, without the pressure to sleep.
- Resting, without sleep, can be restorative. Sit down and put your feet up, close your eyes, and take a few deep breaths.

Touch and Connection

Touch releases oxytocin in your body to buffer stress, and it lowers cortisol.[16] You can hug and cuddle your loved ones to meet this need. Or you can hug yourself. Hugging for at least twenty to thirty seconds, or until your body relaxes, releases oxytocin and lowers stress. You can also seek touch therapies to meet this need, like massage, facials, manicures and pedicures, craniosacral therapy, and acupuncture. Connection through relationships, eye contact, play, and laughter are all needs. We can connect and make eye contact with family, friends, pets, or in therapy. We can meet our needs through play by connecting with something we enjoyed as a child, like games or sports. We can meet our need for laughter with relationships, comedy, or movies. You give an infinite amount of energy to holding, playing, and interacting with your baby; your inner baby needs this, too! To get the benefits:

- Hug someone or yourself at least once daily for twenty to thirty seconds or until you relax. This includes pets.
- If you haven't had touch in a while, schedule a touch therapy like a massage.
- Find laughter—movies, television, stand-up comedy, friends. What made you laugh as a child?
- Find play—friends, sports, dance, singing, games. How did you like to play as a child?
- Find joy—what brings you joy?

Safety

A feeling of safety in your environment is important to regulating your stress system and lowering cortisol. If you feel unsafe in your home or environment, is there anything you can do to make a change? What would make you feel more safe?

When I was pregnant, my apartment did not feel safe to me—one window didn't lock, there was smoke in the air from wildfires, and my dishwasher had melted plastic inside that was creating fumes in the house. It was within my control to advocate for the window and dishwasher to be fixed, and I was able to afford a HEPA filter air purifier. After these changes I felt much safer being pregnant in my environment. Consider:

- Is there anything in your environment that is making you feel unsafe? Can you make any changes?
- Are there people in your life who make you feel unsafe? Can you make any changes? (See page 265 for resources for domestic violence.)

A—Aware of Your Emotions and Emotional Needs

Many, if not most, of us were brought up in emotional deserts. This is not necessarily unique to our parents or caregivers—many of us grew up in low-nurture cultures. Many of us grew up in environments that did not prioritize emotions in schools, parenting approaches, work, politics, or popular culture. Perhaps your caregivers offered comfort when you experienced negative-feeling emotions and joy when you experienced positive-feeling emotions, but in general many of us have very little knowledge about our emotional worlds, feeling emotions, or working with emotions. Society has a tendency to nurture our intelligence quotient (IQ) while leaving our emotional intelligence (EI) unnourished, ignored, and languishing.

As a result, we unconsciously learn that expressing emotion is weak, unnecessary, and unhelpful. We learn that being vulnerable is embarrassing and shameful. We learn to fear our emotions or to ignore, avoid, or repress them. Some of us stop paying attention to our emotions as young babies or children, and instead focus on how others respond to us. We can become more aware of how others are feeling than how we are feeling. Some of us feel our emotions intensely and don't have the skills to process them. You likely grew up with a limited vocabulary to describe your emotions, an absence of knowledge of how most emotions feel in your brain and body, and with no experience sharing your emotions with yourself and others. This is a highly stressful way to live; it can also be incredibly detrimental to your health. If you grew up in a culture, community, or family with your emotions nurtured, you likely enjoy more mental wellness. The good news is that all of us can learn to grow our emotional intelligence, and when we do, we rewire our amygdala and prefrontal cortex; see figure 25.

We've made emotions pretty complex, but in fact emotions are simply information our minds and bodies give us, telling us what we enjoy, fear, dislike, and more. They tell us when someone or something has

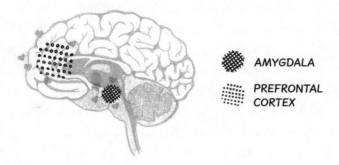

AMYGDALA

PREFRONTAL CORTEX

Figure 25.

Awareness of emotions and needs grows the amygdala and prefrontal cortex toward self-regulation, resilience, and wellness.

crossed a boundary, and when we need more or less of something. They help us know ourselves better.

There are no good or bad emotions. Some emotions *feel* good or comfortable and others *feel* bad or uncomfortable. It's normal to feel them all, sometimes at the same time. No emotion makes you a bad person or should invoke shame, the feeling that you are not good inside. It's healthy and normal to experience negative-feeling emotions like anger, fear, and disappointment. It's even healthier to know how to recognize the emotions, process them, and recover from them without harming yourself or others.

When you work on developing your emotional awareness, you increase your resilience, which you then mirror to your children to help develop their stress systems. When you model and teach emotions to your children, you build a lifetime of stress regulation in them.

The first step to increasing emotional intelligence is to cultivate self-awareness, or the ability to recognize and observe your emotions. You can start by learning an emotional vocabulary. Whenever you have an emotion, either positive- or negative-feeling, look at an emotion list and name what you are feeling out loud. Note how the emotion feels in your body. Expanding your emotional vocabulary and awareness is a tool for self-regulation and emotional intelligence. When you say out loud how you are feeling, you engage your thinking brain to help regulate the stress response in your amygdala. I recommend printing out an emotion list or emotion wheel and placing it on your fridge, desk, and beside your bed (you can find one on page 269 and on my website).

This is helpful because we often think we're expressing emotions but are actually not using any emotional language at all, and this does not help our brain regulate. For example, you might say, "I feel like this is unfair," "I feel like they are being mean," or "I feel like the luckiest person in the world." Despite the fact that the words "I feel" begin these statements, there are no emotions described here.

Let's see how differently it feels to use emotion words. Rather than "I feel like this is unfair," you might say, "I feel insecure and alarmed." Instead of "I feel like they are being mean," you might say, "I feel hurt and disappointed." "I feel like the luckiest person in the world" might sound like "I feel optimistic and empowered." Take a moment to notice how those phrases land in your mind and body.

You might find that you tend to blame others for your emotions, saying something like "I feel like they are a terrible friend" when someone lets you down. When using emotion words, you might find that you actually mean "I feel hurt and nervous about our friendship." With your baby you might say, "My baby is a tyrant," when you mean "I'm feeling depleted and overwhelmed today." Using emotion words clarifies how we feel and helps us understand what we need.

When you express yourself through emotion words, you reshape your stress system by acting on the connection from the amygdala to the thinking brain. When you use positive-feeling emotional words to label your feelings, the fearful areas of your amygdala are quieted.[17] When you use negative-feeling emotional words to label your feelings, you activate your thinking brain to reduce activity in your amygdala fear center.[18] Furthermore, if you *don't* express your negative-feeling emotions, your amygdala can be activated for a prolonged time, which puts your brain and body into an unhealthy stress state.

In nurtured empathy we learned that underlying every behavior is an emotion and behind every emotion is a need. This is true for us just as it is true for our babies. Nurtured empathy is a necessary technique for us as parents, too. Once we can understand our emotions we can link them to the underlying needs and make a plan to meet our needs. When you meet your physical and emotional needs, you reduce stress, you charge your nurture reservoir, and your emotions are better supported. Often in parenthood, the need for rest, play, and connection underlies your anger, sadness, loneliness, or resentment. I recommend printing out a needs list to accompany your emotions list (you can find this on page 274 and on my website). And making a plan to meet your needs (see Emotion and Needs Inquiry for Parents on page 276).

A big part of low-nurture parenting is to ignore, reject, isolate, punish, or shame infants when they feel negative-feeling emotions. When you give infants the message that they are not good inside because they have emotions that feel bad, it plants a root of shame and pain that they can carry for life. Consistently rejecting infants when they have negative-feeling emotions makes them feel like they are wrong inside for life. None of us—babies, teens, adults—can control the emotions we feel, nor can someone else control our emotions. Emotions are sacred. And when we learn to suppress negative-feeling emotions because they are rejected by our caregivers, the health of our minds and bodies suffers. This is by far one of the most emotionally scarring practices of the low-nurture culture. We understand that physical and sexual abuse has long-lasting consequences for lifelong mental and physical health. It turns out that an infancy and childhood without safe emotional expression and support has comparable and sometimes more significant consequences for lifelong mental and physical health.[19] Remember—it is never too late to repair and change our approach with our children, regardless of age. As adults, we can work hard to undo some of the messages we internalized as children.

It's normal for all people, children included, to experience negative-feeling emotions regularly; sadness, guilt, anger, and frustration are part of being human. We can't pretend that they're not. Most of us are in the habit of judging our own emotions and especially the emotions of children and infants. We need to stop making these judgments for ourselves and our children's brain health. We suppress and ignore emotions we call "bad" or we feel like we are bad when we feel bad emotions. We seek out the experience of emotions we call "good." Instead, I'm encouraging you to get better at understanding the range of your emotions and what they are telling you about what you need.

R—Regular Breathing

When I started practicing yoga at sixteen years old I remember being shocked that I had never taken a conscious, deep, inhaled breath. Now I teach belly breathing to my clients and I see them have this same experience over and over. After ten breaths, people open their eyes in wonder and are shocked to feel they are breathing for the first time. Slow, deep breathing, especially into the belly, is foundational for stress regulation and for changing your brain toward more resilience long-term. Conscious, aware breathing rewires multiple brain areas, including your amygdala and prefrontal cortex, toward resilience and literally switches you into a safety state; see figure 26.[20] Directing your attention to your breath or to using your senses in the present moment exercises your brain like lifting a weight exercises your arm muscles. Every time you direct your attention to breathing or being present, it strengthens your brain. Plus, as you become a parent, your brain is more flexible and can benefit tremendously. It seems silly that we would have to learn something as simple as closing our eyes and breathing, but we do.

If you do no other practice, regular belly breathing will make a huge difference in your life. The reason deep belly breathing feels good is that this pattern of breathing stimulates relaxation areas in our brain. A study in an animal model found that breathing quickly into the chest activates cells in the survival brain, which go on to activate the emotional brain, and to launch the stress system to fight, flight, or freeze. When we

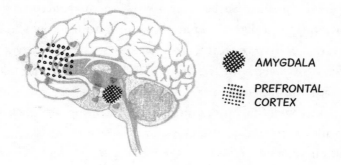

AMYGDALA

PREFRONTAL
CORTEX

Figure 26.

Practicing breathing can switch your brain into a safety state while growing your amygdala and prefrontal cortex toward resilience and wellness.

breathe slowly and deeply into our belly, however, cells in our survival brain signal to cells in our emotional brain to activate our safety state to connect, heal, rest, digest, and think.[21]

Belly breathing is a great example of how the physical body can change the mind and brain. Our belly is a sensitive, vulnerable place on our body, and when we are stressed we tend to protect it. When we sit comfortably, eyes closed, shoulders back, chest and belly wide, and breathe deeply, we send a signal from the body to the brain that we are safe and can rest.[22] It's amazing that just ten deep breaths into the belly can positively change the physiology of the body. Let's try it now.

1. Sit on a chair with your feet flat on the floor, one hand on your heart, and one hand on your belly.
2. Relax your shoulders, jaw, and belly. Lean back slightly and expose your belly.
3. Close your eyes and take ten deep breaths. On the inhale first fill up your chest so your hand on your heart moves, then fill up your belly so your hand on your belly moves. It is common to breathe into your chest, so make sure you breathe deeply and feel the hand on your belly move.

Deep belly breaths can be done anywhere, anytime, in any stressful situation. If you detect you are beginning to feel stress, take three belly breaths to attempt to reenter a safety state. If you detect you are highly stressed, start with ten deep belly breaths. You can take a few belly breaths throughout your day to maintain safety states. You can also practice extending to one minute of breathing and then to three minutes and up to twenty minutes per day. As you breathe, keep your attention on your breath. When you notice thoughts and feelings, that's okay, just direct your attention back to your breath. Take note of how you feel before and after.

Once you're comfortable with belly breathing you can try a body scan. For each belly breath, scan through each body part starting at your head and going down to your toes and back from your toes to your head. While you relax all the tension from each body part you can think, "My forehead is relaxing, my forehead is softening, my forehead is relaxed," and repeat for your whole body: eyes; ears; jaw; forehead; neck; shoulders; upper back; lower back; abdomen; left arm, wrist, and hand; right arm, wrist, and hand; pelvis; buttocks; left leg, ankle, and foot; right leg, ankle, and foot.

You can add vocalizing to your belly-breathing practice if it feels good to you. Vocalizing further stimulates your brain to increase relaxation and put the brain and body into a safety state. During belly breathing, try exhaling with a deep low noise that vibrates your throat. You can try an *Ommm, Mmmm, Haaa, Vuuu, Grrrr*, or any sound you like. I recommend making this sound for three exhales and then pausing and letting the sound resonate in and around you.

You may find that sitting still and breathing is not for you at all or some of the time. That's okay. Sometimes we need to move our bodies in order to register a sense of safety and regulation. Try a moving practice like walking slowly and mindfully around your block, nature walks, labyrinth walks, an ancient practice of contemplative walking into the center of a labyrinth (often made of rocks or stones and found in parks), turning around and walking out, or something more structured like gentle yoga, tai chi, or qi gong. During these practices your body moves but you are doing the same work of slow, deep breathing and relaxation. You may find that the help of body work like massage, acupuncture, craniosacral, reiki, or other treatments supports your breathing practices.

E—Evoke Compassion and Awe

When you feel good, your stress system can rest into safety. Practices that increase states of positive emotions like compassion and awe reshape circuits in the amygdala and prefrontal cortex to rewire the stress system toward resilience; see figure 27. Studies have shown that only twenty-one days of positive emotion practices enact measurable changes in the adult brain.[23] Our brains have strong negative filters, as we are always anticipating threats. We have to work to generate positive brain circuits, because our brain doesn't do it for us.

I'm not suggesting that you fake it and pretend everything is great if it feels awful—this is not about false optimism, toxic positivity, or bypassing negative-feeling emotions. Instead, I encourage you to learn how to feel all of your emotions and cultivate compassion for yourself,

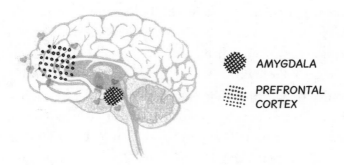

AMYGDALA

PREFRONTAL CORTEX

Figure 27.

A practice of evoking compassion and awe rewires your amygdala and prefrontal cortex toward resilience and wellness.

to form new brain circuitry you wouldn't otherwise have. Many of us have harsh or even cruel inner voices that we use to speak to ourselves. Your inner baby deserves to be spoken to with compassion. This practice of evoking gentle compassion for yourself, over time, will rewire your amygdala toward a higher threshold for alarm. You might say:

"Wow, you are a really good mom or dad. Your baby loves you."

"You must be so proud. That was a really hard moment and you did amazing."

"Your body is amazing! What a miracle it is to have a strong body to grow, feed, and take care of a baby."

"You worked so hard on that. What a success."

"You tried your best, and that is all you can ever do."

"You are wonderful just as you are."

"We all make mistakes. You are loved no matter what."

When you notice a harsh thought, follow it up with compassion. For example, if you think, "I look terrible today," follow it up with something like, "Anyone in my position would be having a hard time right now. I'm doing my best today and I'm proud of myself. I love my body for doing amazing things." Or, "I'm going through a big transition right now and it makes sense that things feel messy and unclear. I'm allowed to take my time. I'll get to where I need to be, in my own time." Really go overboard being nice to yourself. Tell yourself you're smart, you're an amazing parent, you're beautiful, you're strong, you're intuitive, you're creative, you're resilient, and you're really good at doing things that challenge your brain.

If you've done something you don't like, like yelled at your kid, thrown a toy across the room, or lashed out at your partner, it can help to describe your core self and return to that—"I'm a kind and loving person who did something unkind," or "I'm a good person having a hard time," or "I am worthy of love, in all of my emotions." This helps differentiate your behavior from yourself and can take you out of a shame spiral you may be stuck in.

Another way to cultivate positive emotions is to add them to a breathing exercise. Start by belly breathing, then think of something that makes you feel joy or safety—a special person, a special place, a special memory that brings you positive-feeling emotions. Breathe while you think of this for two minutes. Sense where you feel the joy of that person, place, or memory, and try to hold it—a warm feeling in your chest, for example, or a tingle in your belly. Can you put your energy there and help it radiate throughout your body?

I find that many of us would benefit from having compassion for our bodies during this stage in our lives. It may help to say to yourself, over and over, "I am beautiful. I love my body at every single stage. My body did something amazing. I grew a baby (or my body takes care of my baby, or my body gives me health). I can love my body right now, in any state, and still want to exercise or get stronger. My body is so freaking incredible."

This is a long-term practice. It will take time to start regularly saying nice things to yourself, but it's so worth it.

An Awe Practice

Awe is a feeling of amazement when we experience something overwhelming, vast, beautiful, or sacred. When something incredible happens, take a minute to feel the good feelings. When your baby does something new or amazing or brilliant, sit in the awe that you feel. When you and your baby connect in a deep way, sit in the connection. When you shift your stress responses, sit in the change. Pay attention to how you feel, what you think, and how your body feels. These moments are profound, and we benefit from being present for them.

You can also take a minute to remember a time when you felt awe or deep love, close your eyes, take some belly breaths, and think of the memory. For me, I think of waking up in the morning the summers I spent living in the woods, going outside my cabin and seeing a deer, a calm lake, and a loon. Evoking awe by remembering moments of awe or noticing awe changes our stress system toward more resilience. This makes us feel calm, connected, and regulated and can change our brain toward more regulation.

COMMITTING TO AN I CARE PRACTICE

Practicing I CARE every day will change your stress system to be more resilient and more nurturing. Think about how you can build this practice into your daily life. Some people like to set aside one part of their day to practice, first thing in the morning or before bedtime. Others like to practice throughout the day, for example, before every meal, or during scheduled breaks in their day. You can set a reminder on your phone if that helps.

Example plan—10–20 minutes

1. Pour yourself a glass of water and be curious about the feelings and sensations in your body.
2. Breathe for two-plus minutes. Option to add a body scan or positive emotion.
3. Say something nice to yourself or what you are grateful for.
4. Look at an emotions word list. Think about any feelings you have at the moment, or big feelings you might have experienced from the previous day or week.
5. Look at a needs list. Make a list of any unmet needs. Make plans to meet your needs.

Over time, I CARE practices can help build your nurture reservoir so you feel more at ease and less reactive to your baby's emotions and behaviors. So you can be the parent you want to be. Don't expect an instant transformation. It takes time for neuroplasticity to do its work on your nervous system. When you can't wait and need strategies to self-regulate right now, use my Growing SPACE practices.

GROWING SPACE: IN-THE-MOMENT STRATEGIES TO GUIDE YOU FROM STRESS STATES TO SAFETY STATES

Neurologist, psychiatrist, and writer Viktor Frankl recalled being inspired by a phrase he read while wandering the library: "Between stimulus and response there is a space. In that space is our power to choose our response. In our response lies our growth and our freedom."[24] Perhaps nowhere is this more relevant than in parenting infants. Many of us have difficulty creating a space between stimulus (like our baby whining) and our response (like us snapping). This is especially true if we have a narrow or shallow nurture reservoir, perhaps because our parents had no space between our emotions and their response to yell, silence, or ignore. Yet we don't have to repeat what happened to us. We can cultivate a space between our baby's behavior and our response so that we are more likely to respond from a safety state than from a stress state.

Growing SPACE has been one of the most challenging parts of nurture for me; it's something I am always working on. It is a part of nurture that reflects intense cycle-breaking, as patterns of no space have been modeled for generations. I do not want my son to live in fear of me snapping when he has big emotions. It's a scary way to live and develop. I want my son to have confidence that when he feels big emotions, I will be a safe, accepting presence. This is a safe way to live and grow.

As parents and caregivers, cultivating a space allows us to have freedom in our response—we can choose how we want to respond. We can choose nurture. When we practice Growing SPACE, over and over, the space gets bigger and easier and more accessible, and we can rewire our brain to engage brain circuits to enter a space versus an immediate response.

When your baby screams, throws something, hits you, runs away, or when someone has let you down—these can all be intense stimuli that send your stress way up high. When we have no space between the stimulus and response, we have no freedom or choice in how we respond. We might respond in ways we regret—yelling, grabbing, being scary, shutting down. When we create a space between stimulus and response, we gain freedom and choice in our response. Look at page 278 for a Growing SPACE resource that can help. Here's how we might achieve that:

Self-awareness: If you can notice when you are beginning to get stressed it is easier to grow a space to return to safety. When you wait until you are highly stressed, finding space is much harder, though still possible. Notice how it feels in your body when you start to feel stressed. Notice your thoughts and what emotions come up for you. Might you be entering a fight, flight, or freeze state? In fight-or-flight, you might feel angry, anxious, activated, energized, frazzled, tense, shortsighted. In freeze, you may feel sadness or fear, paralyzed, despondent, bored, depressed, immobile, tense. Notice what you think when you are in these states. Notice how your body feels. When you can be self-aware of your state, you can bring yourself back to a safety state.

Pause your immediate reaction: When you notice you are feeling stressed or feel yourself entering a fight, flight, or freeze response, try to interrupt the immediate response. This helps create a space and prevents you from a harsh immediate reaction. For example, your baby is banging their fork, throwing food, and screaming over and over again. You feel like you're going to scream, but you practice interrupting the immediate reaction by taking a big breath, singing, "This is a huge mess," or saying in a low voice, "I am having a hard time right now," or walking right out of the room. Once you interrupt an immediate reaction, you can take a few moments to build more space through a bottom-up approach from your body and a top-down approach from your mind.

Aware of the sensations: Feel the emotion, notice where the sensations in your body are. If you have thoughts, bring your attention back to your body for about ninety seconds. Most emotions, when we take time to experience them without judgment, last about ninety seconds.

Then they can pass if we sense our bodies, move with the emotion, and name the emotion, without attaching thoughts to the emotion.[25] Relax your jaw and shoulders, shift your body posture from closed to open, expose your belly, and breathe as you feel it.

Create movement: This is bottom-up regulation, or regulation from the body. Stay with the body. Move the energy from there. How can you release your stress from your body?

If you're in a fight-or-flight state—you feel tense, flooded, overwhelmed, you want to yell or run away—try:

- Physically moving: Shake your body, dance, jump, do jumping jacks, run, do squats, yawn. Movement uses the energy that is mobilized by the stress system to lower stress and make you feel calmer.
- Embodying your emotion: If your emotion had a physical movement or sound, what would it be? If you're feeling anxious, maybe shake your body or make a sound like *ooooooooo*. If you're angry, do you want to scream and punch with your fists? If you're sad, do you want to curl into a ball?[26]

If you're in a freeze state—you feel tense, flooded, overwhelmed; you want to hide, disappear, or go to sleep—try:

- Listening to music: Play your favorite song or play an instrument.
- Singing or humming: Sing or hum your favorite song.
- Gently moving: Sway slowly or dance.
- Crossing your midline: Do shoulder taps or thigh taps across your body, left arm to right side and right arm to left side.
- Shifting your body posture from closed to open: Expose your belly and breathe.

Emotion processing: This is top-down regulation—regulation from the thinking brain. It helps to have felt your emotions and moved your body first before engaging the thinking brain, because the thinking brain can make up elaborate stories that you get stuck in. Feel it and move from the body first and then name your feelings and needs. Use the lists on pages 269 and 274. You can then name your baby's feelings and needs, if appropriate. Finally, you can come up with a phrase or mantra that can help you through the experience.

Here is how the whole process might look. You encounter a stimulus—perhaps your baby will not eat; they keep saying, "Different food, different food"—and you don't have any other food in your house.

Self-awareness: You feel your body get tense, you feel a pain in your neck—you are self-aware that your stress is building, you're entering a state of fight stress.

Pause your immediate reaction: You want to scream, "I don't have any other food!," but you have paused. You sing, "This is all the food I have, baby; I need a minute." You get up and leave the table.

Aware of the sensations: You breathe, you feel the tension in your body rise and fall, you feel a burning in your neck and throat. You relax your shoulders, jaw, and pelvic floor and expose your belly as you keep breathing. You could also communicate to your baby, "I'm feeling my big feelings."

Create movement: You continue to feel the energy from the emotion, but now you also make a low deep *Ommmmmm* sound while you move your arms up and down. You might tell your baby, "I'm moving my big feelings."

Emotion processing: Now that you've moved through the stress, you have access to your thinking brain. You look at your emotions list that you've stuck to the fridge, and you see what you're feeling. You use nurtured empathy and reflect, "My baby is having a hard time, saying, 'Different food,' and I am having a hard time feeling fight energy, stressed, exasperated, annoyed, furious. I have moved through the emotions and I'm back in a safety state. I can do this; my baby's emotion will not last forever, and I can help them through this."

Response with a SPACE

Now you can respond to your baby with nurtured empathy. "I hear you saying, 'Different food' (behavior). I'm wondering if you're feeling hungry and stressed (feeling). I'm wondering if you're needing some help to feel safe (need). Let me put you on my lap and we can have some bites together."

This in-the-moment practice will move slowly at first. It may feel awkward and ridiculous. You may resist doing it. You may not want to. You may feel embarrassed or silly doing it. The thought of it may make you feel tired or angry. You might feel you don't have the time because your baby is having a meltdown. That's all normal and part of the process of growing your awareness of your state. Try to stay with your bodily sensations as much as you can. Sense yourself from the inside. It will get smoother and faster with time. Your state and your emotions and needs will get clearer with time.

Most families I work with discover that their babies love this. They are curious about the *Ommmmmm* sound or giggle and join in with dancing or pushing the wall. They are learning from you how to be with their sensations and their feelings. You can both be new at it! It's okay to be in the process with them. You can say, "Oops, I needed water and a few minutes to myself, but I didn't take them and then I got really grumpy when you wanted to play. Let me take a few minutes now and then let's do that puzzle together." Or, "You needed to be held and I felt annoyed because I didn't realize I needed to eat something first. I'm sorry—let me grab a snack and then I can't wait to pick you up."

It's hard to nurture from an empty nurture reservoir. It's hard to feel connected and be in relationship when your nurture reservoir is depleted and you're in a threat state. Don't put that pressure on yourself to say or do the right things when you don't feel good, supported, calm, or present inside. You can be human with your child. A work in progress. Whatever capacity you have to feel regulated and at ease you can use now, even as you grow that capacity through practice. Your parent brain is in a beautiful process of transformation that offers you a powerful opportunity to nurture yourself the way you nurture your baby, the way you wish you were nurtured as a child, or the way you were nurtured as a child. The true foundation of the nurture revolution is a generation of parents who are doing the profound, messy, and joyful work of attuning to themselves in order to nurture their babies. Welcome.

CONCLUSION

A Nurtured Future to Revolutionize Mental Health

I wrote much of the material for this book during the height of the COVID-19 pandemic while my baby was still in the precious season of infancy. There were plenty of stops and starts in the writing process because my son would be home from preschool needing a COVID test every time he had a runny nose or sneezed. My husband and I juggled full-time parenting and work. As I struggled to be a nurturing, regulated presence for my son, to find time to nurture my parent brain, and to make progress on my work—largely in isolation—I couldn't help but reflect on how lonely and unsupported the work of nurturing young children is. At the time of writing, as the world opens back up without a foreseeable end to this crisis in public health and health care, parents of infants remain in a kind of liminal no-man's-land. We're desperately trying to care for our young and ourselves with very little support while we also still have to show up for work on time, and every decision to get ourselves and our babies social connection or professional services is burdened with our own individual risk assessment. In truth, this is not so different than parenting infants pre-pandemic; this public health crisis heightened the stakes in an already overwhelming situation. From a social and institutional perspective, if you've got small children, you're pretty much on your own.

It's no wonder that forced independence, unrealistic expectations for emotional maturity, sleep training, rejecting negative-feeling emotions, low touch, and fear of spoiling are powerfully compelling low-nurture practices pervading norms of infancy and parenthood. As if to say, "Hurry and grow up; we don't have the resources, the time, or the knowledge to support your extended stay in this phase." At the same time, many parents in the pandemic shared with me that while the loss of in-person professional and social support was devastating, nurturing was easier because societal pressure was out of the picture. No one questioned or shamed parents for holding their babies, sleeping close to their babies, feeding their babies, responding unconditionally to their babies, or accepting their babies' full range of emotions. They felt liberated from our powerful cultural pressure to provide low nurture. A society built on low nurture shames, rejects, and stresses out babies and parents who need nurture to build their brains into health. A society built on ignoring babies' emotions, shaming stress, forcing independent sleep, and focusing on cognition and flash cards has failed the health of our brains and bodies. Look at where the last hundred years of low nurture have taken us: Mental health is at an all-time low and we continue to suffer worse than ever at younger and younger ages.

What if we pivot right now together, support each other, spread knowledge, and empower new parents to nurture? A revolution of nurture. Simultaneously we can transform our parent brains as we build a society of humans who had the gift of nurture in their infancy.

I often wished I were writing this book in a different cultural landscape. If only I were encouraging you to nurture your babies in a society that offered you real and robust parental leave; easy access to trauma-informed mental health practitioners; infant and family sleep specialists for every family; educational, emotional, and physical support for conception, loss, pregnancy, birth, postpartum, and infancy; pelvic floor physiotherapy for all mothers and birthing people; universal birth doulas and lactation consultants; body work, massage, and craniosacral therapy for every family; postpartum home support for the first four months at minimum; and quality childcare that is nurture-based and child-led, all affordable or even free to all. How much easier it would be to embrace what research shows us is good for our babies' brains! Babies and parents have lower stress, higher oxytocin, and improved mental health and brain development with these supports.[1]

Fighting for those programs and policies is absolutely part of the nurture revolution. We can't do it all and we can't do it alone. We need a society that's structured to support nurturing our young's developing brains. A society that honors and supports this season of beautiful neuroplasticity in infants and parents will benefit us all, including the child-free. There is even a strong research-backed economic argument for investing in infancy—for every dollar invested in infancy, society gets a $4–$9 return.[2] Wouldn't it be nice if our politicians invested our tax money into truly helping us in the long run versus enacting change within the time limits they get credit for? We need leaders and citizens who can regulate their stress, be comfortable with emotions, are good at relationships, and use their thinking brains and emotional brains in balance. We need a nurtured future. We need a society built on healthy baby brains.

That kind of change takes time, but your baby doesn't have to wait. While we advocate for those public programs and policies for tomorrow, we need to nurture ourselves and our babies the best we can today, even despite the lack of public resources. It is hard work to nurture in a low-nurture culture. And that makes your nurture extraordinary and revolutionary. You don't have to be perfect. Every time you soothe your baby back to sleep, every time you practice nurtured connection, every time you self-regulate so you can co-regulate your baby's stress, you participate in collective healing for us and preventive medicine for our babies. Every time you nurture your inner baby, you say, "This ends with me," and the suffering from our childhoods, our wounds, the loss of joy and opportunities we endured are silenced that much more.

A pregnant friend once told me she knew she could never undo all of the unwellness her mother passed on to her. It was overwhelming and impossible. I told her: We don't have to carry the pressure to heal it all. If you're carrying a hundred painful things from your childhood and you heal just five, that makes a world of difference for your child. If you only get a little better at regulating, a little better at repair, or a little better at connecting, you are a cycle breaker, an intergenerational healer, and a new cycle starter. Your changes make an enormous difference and will snowball into bigger changes. Any amount we nurture matters to our babies. There is no such thing as a perfect brain. The more we build our capacity to be in relationship with our babies, to see and value them for who they are, and to support their need for closeness and stress support, the more we grow their resilience.

I hope this book will guide you to use your nurturing intuition in all the funny, painful, loving, frustrating, and fun situations you encounter with your baby. I hope it will give you a strong foundation from which to make all your other decisions with your baby. As long as nurture is the through line, you can get through any situation and make choices that are the most brain healthy for your baby.

I hope that this foundation in the season of infancy continues for your baby's childhood, adolescence, and adulthood. Your child at all ages will need: nurtured presence (accepting all of your child's emotions); nurtured empathy (getting behind your child's eyes); keeping a nurtured connection (face-to-face interaction); nurtured exploration (cheering on your child as they explore the world and being a safe place to return to); nurtured stress (being the one your child can always go to when overwhelmed, to feel safe again); and nurtured sleep (providing lifelong safe sleep). These practices not only build your baby's brain but are the foundation of an emotionally connected child-brain-to-parent-brain connection for life. This relationship is the bedrock of mental health for your baby's entire life and can restore mental health for you. I bet this type of relationship will fulfill the biggest wishes and dreams you had when having a baby. Nurture lets us be the parent we want to be, lets us be the parent we wish we had, and gives our baby the parent of their dreams. Our need for connection and co-regulation, especially with our parents, remains for life.

I also hope it translates to your other relationships so you can connect and support stress for others. And I hope it comes back to you so others connect with you and support you. I hope it feels really good sometimes to nurture. I hope you can feel powerful and radical in your nurturing. I hope you find moments when nurturing feels delicious, ecstatic, and liberating—an oxytocin cascade that is a direct refusal of low-nurture culture.

I hope this book speaks for the babies, the most vulnerable people, who have strong communication but whose voices have been ignored for a century. Our babies need their human rights restored; they need us to know about their developing brains. When we learn to listen to them, we will hear their voices loud and clear. If you are ever in doubt, take a breath and listen to your baby. They will be saying something important.

The science is clear that nurture is a gift like no other; it is the most dramatic life-shifting advantage a human can have. Nurture is invisible, hidden inside the brain, and yet so visible in the everyday moments in the life of a human being. If we receive nurture in infancy, we are gifted with the most valuable offering on Earth.

Nurture for our babies and for us as parents is worth working for, fighting for, going to sleep early for, returning to connection for, learning emotions for, repairing for, getting behind our baby's eyes for, taking care of ourselves for, and reshaping ourselves for.

One of my favorite parts of the Talmud reads, "Anyone who saves a life is as if they save an entire world." I like to think of nurture this way, too. Anyone who nurtures a life is as if they nurture an entire world.

NOTES

Introduction

1. Kessler, R. C., et al. Lifetime prevalence and age-of-onset distributions of DSM-IV disorders in the National Comorbidity Survey Replication. *Arch Gen Psychiat* 62, 593–602 (2005).
2. MHC of Canada. Making the Case for Investing in Mental Health in Canada. https://mentalhealthcommission.ca/resource/making-the-case-for-investing-in-mental-health-in-canada/ (2013); NIMH. Mental Health Information. www.nimh.nih.gov/health/statistics/mental-illness.shtml (2013).
3. Schaefer, J. D., et al. Enduring mental health: Prevalence and prediction. *J Abnorm Psychol* 126, 212–224 (2017); Kessler, R. C., Angermeyer, M., Anthony, J. C., et al. Lifetime prevalence and age-of-onset distributions of mental disorders in the World Health Organization's World Mental Health Survey Initiative. *World Psychiatry* 6(3), 168–176 (2007).
4. NIH. *NIH Curriculum Supplement Series* (2007).
5. WHO. Mental Health. www.who.int/health-topics/mental-health#tab=tab_2.
6. Bale, T. L., et al. Early life programming and neurodevelopmental disorders. *Biol Psychiat* 68, 314–319 (2010); Fareri, D. S. & Tottenham, N. Effects of early life stress on amygdala and striatal development. *Developmental Cognitive Neuroscience,* 19, 233–247 (2015); Shackman, A. J., Fox, A. S. & Seminowicz, D. A. The cognitive-emotional brain: Opportunities and challenges for understanding neuropsychiatric disorders. *Behav Brain Sci* 38, e86 (2015).
7. Swaab, D. F. Development of the human hypothalamus. *Neurochem Res* 20, 509–519 (1995); Utsunomiya, H., Takano, K., Okazaki, M. & Mitsudome, A. Development of the temporal lobe in infants and children: Analysis by MR-based volumetry. *Am J Neuroradiol* 20, 717–723 (1999); Gabard-Durnam, L. J., et al. Human amygdala functional network development: A cross-sectional study from 3 months to 5 years of age. *Dev Cogn Neurosci* 34, 63–74 (2018); Teffer, K. & Semendeferi, K. Human prefrontal cortex: Evolution, development, and pathology. *Prog Brain Res* 195, 191–218 (2012); Hornung, J.-P. The human raphe nuclei and the serotonergic system. *J Chem Neuroanat* 26, 331–343 (2003); Salgado, S. & Kaplitt, M. G. The nucleus accumbens: A comprehensive review. *Stereotact Funct Neurosurg* 93, 75–93 (2015).
8. Harvard Center on the Developing Child. Brain Architecture. https://developingchild.harvard.edu/science/key-concepts/brain-architecture/.

9. Harvard Center on the Developing Child. InBrief: Early Childhood Mental Health. https://developingchild.harvard.edu/resources/inbrief-early-childhood-mental-health/.

10. Holt, L. E. *The Care and Feeding of Children* (Appleton and Company, 1895); Spock, B. *The Common Sense Book of Baby and Child Care* (Duell, Sloan and Pearce, 1946); Ferber, R. *Solve Your Child's Sleep Problems: A Practical and Comprehensive Guide for Parents* (Fireside, 1986); Weissbluth, M. *Healthy Sleep Habits, Happy Child* (Random House, 1987); Watson, J. B. *Psychological Care of Infant and Child* (Arno Press, 1976); Ezzo, G. & Bucknam, R. *On Becoming Baby Wise* (Multnomah, 1995).

11. Sears, W. & Sears, M. *The Baby Book: Everything You Need to Know About Your Baby from Birth to Age Two* (Little, Brown, 1993); Sears, W. & Sears, M. *The Attachment Parenting Book: A Commonsense Guide to Understanding and Nurturing Your Baby* (Word Alive, 2001).

12. Brazelton, T. B. & Cramer, B. G. *The Earliest Relationship: Parents, Infants, and the Drama of Early Attachment* (Da Capo Lifelong Books, 1991).

Chapter 1. A Season for Nurture

1. Fong, M., Mitchell, D. E., Duffy, K. R. & Bear, M. F. Rapid recovery from the effects of early monocular deprivation is enabled by temporary inactivation of the retinas. *Proc Natl Acad Sci USA* 113, 14139–14144 (2016).

2. Reh, R. K., et al. Critical period regulation across multiple timescales. *Proc Natl Acad Sci USA* 117, 23242–23251 (2020); Tottenham, N. Early adversity and the neotenous human brain. *Biol Psychiat* 87, 350–358 (2019); Miguel, P. M., Pereira, L. O., Silveira, P. P. & Meaney, M. J. Early environmental influences on the development of children's brain structure and function. *Dev Medicine Child Neurology* 61, 1127–1133 (2019).

3. Azevedo, F. A. C., et al. Equal numbers of neuronal and nonneuronal cells make the human brain an isometrically scaled-up primate brain. *J Comp Neurology* 513, 532–541 (2009).

4. Rakic, P. Neuroscience. No more cortical neurons for you. *Science* 313, 928–929 (2006); Gilmore, J. H., et al. Regional gray matter growth, sexual dimorphism, and cerebral asymmetry in the neonatal brain. 27; Nowakowski, R. S. Stable neuron numbers from cradle to grave. *Proc Natl Acad Sci USA* 103, 12219–12220 (2006).

5. Nowakowski. Stable neuron numbers from cradle to grave.

6. Kolb, B. Neuroanatomy and development overview. In *The Role of Early Experience in Infant Development*. Johnson & Johnson Pediatric Round Table Series (eds. Fox, N., Leavitt, L. A. & Warhol, J. G.); Tau, G. Z. & Peterson, B. S. Normal development of brain circuits. *Neuropsychopharmacol* 35, 147–168 (2010); Lagercrantz, H. & Ringstedt, T. Organization of the neuronal circuits in the central nervous system during development. *Acta Pædiatrica* 90, 707–715 (2001); Anusuya, M. A. & Katt, S. K. Superficial analogies and differences between the human brain and the computer. *International Journal of Computer Science and Network Security* 10, 196–201 (2010); Lenroot, R. K. & Giedd, J. N. The changing impact of genes and environment on brain development

during childhood and adolescence: initial findings from a neuroimaging study of pediatric twins. *Dev Psychopathol* 20, 1161–1175 (2008); Huttenlocher, P. Synaptogenesis in human cerebral cortex and the concept of crucial periods. In *The Role of Early Experience in Infant Development*; Tang, Y., Nyengaard, J. R., Groot, D. M. G. D. & Gundersen, H. J. G. Total regional and global number of synapses in the human brain neocortex. *Synapse* 41, 258–273 (2001).

7. Rakic, P. Neuroscience. No more cortical neurons for you. *Science* 313, 928–929 (2006); Gilmore, J. H., et al. Regional gray matter growth, sexual dimorphism, and cerebral asymmetry in the neonatal brain. *J Neurosci* 27, 1255–1260 (2007); Knickmeyer, R. C., et al. A structural MRI study of human brain development from birth to 2 years. *J Neurosci* 28, 12176–12182 (2008); Nowakowski, R. S. Stable neuron numbers from cradle to grave. *Proc Natl Acad Sci USA* 103, 12219–12220 (2006); NIH, "NIH MRI Study of Normal Brain Development." https://neuroscienceblueprint.nih.gov/resources-tools/blueprint-resources-tools -library/nih-mri-study-normal-brain-development.

8. Miguel, P. M., Pereira, L. O., Silveira, P. P. & Meaney, M. J. Early environmental influences on the development of children's brain structure and function. *Dev Medicine Child Neurology* 61, 1127–1133 (2019).

9. Valkanova, V., Rodriguez, R. E. & Ebmeier, K. P. Mind over matter—what do we know about neuroplasticity in adults? *Int Psychogeriatr* 26, 891–909 (2014); Tang, Y.-Y., Hölzel, B. K. & Posner, M. I. The neuroscience of mindfulness meditation. *Nat Rev Neurosci* 16, 213–225 (2015).

10. Reh, R. K., et al. Critical period regulation across multiple timescales. *Proc Natl Acad Sci USA* 117, 23242–23251 (2020); Mataga, N., Mizuguchi, Y. & Hensch, T. K. Experience-dependent pruning of dendritic spines in visual cortex by tissue plasminogen activator. *Neuron* 44, 1031–1041 (2004); Laham, B. J. & Gould, E. How stress influences the dynamic plasticity of the brain's extracellular matrix. *Front Cell Neurosci* 15, 814287 (2022); Huttenlocher, P. R. *Neural Plasticity: The Effects of Environment on the Development of the Cerebral Cortex* (Harvard University Press, 2002); Andersen, S. L. Trajectories of brain development: Point of vulnerability or window of opportunity? *Neurosci Biobehav Rev* 27, 3–18 (2003).

11. Kuhl, P. K., Tsao, F.-M. & Liu, H.-M. Foreign-language experience in infancy: Effects of short-term exposure and social interaction on phonetic learning. *Proc Natl Acad Sci USA* 100, 9096–9101 (2003).

12. Shatz, C. J. The developing brain. *Sci Am* 267, 60–67 (1992).

13. Andersen, S. L. Trajectories of brain development: Point of vulnerability or window of opportunity? *Neurosci Biobehav Rev* 27, 3–18 (2003); Hensch, T. K. Critical period regulation. *Annu Rev Neurosci* 27, 549–579 (2004); Tooley, U. A., Bassett, D. S. & Mackey, A. P. Environmental influences on the pace of brain development. *Nat Rev Neurosci* 22, 372–384 (2021); Gilmore, J. H., Knickmeyer, R. C. & Gao, W. Imaging structural and functional brain development in early childhood. *Nat Rev Neurosci* 19, 123–137 (2018).

14. Swaab, D. F. Development of the human hypothalamus. *Neurochem Res* 20, 509–519 (1995); Utsunomiya, H., Takano, K., Okazaki, M. & Mitsudome, A. Development

of the temporal lobe in infants and children: Analysis by MR-based volumetry. *Am J Neuroradiol* 20, 717–723 (1999); Gabard-Durnam, L. J., et al. Human amygdala functional network development: A cross-sectional study from 3 months to 5 years of age. *Dev Cogn Neurosci* 34, 63–74 (2018); Teffer, K. & Semendeferi, K. Human prefrontal cortex: Evolution, development, and pathology. *Prog Brain Res* 195, 191–218 (2012); LeMoult, J., et al. Meta-analysis: Exposure to early life stress and risk for depression in childhood and adolescence. *J Am Acad Child Adolesc Psychiatry* 59, 842–855 (2020); Chen, L.-Z., Holmes, A. J., Zuo, X.-N. & Dong, Q. Neuroimaging brain growth charts: A road to mental health. *Psychoradiology* 1, 272–286 (2021); Van den Bergh, B. R. H., et al. Prenatal developmental origins of behavior and mental health: The influence of maternal stress in pregnancy. *Neurosci Biobehav Rev* 117, 26–64 (2016); Hornung, J.-P. The human raphe nuclei and the serotonergic system. *J Chem Neuroanat* 26, 331–343 (2003); Salgado, S. & Kaplitt, M. G. The nucleus accumbens: A comprehensive review. *Stereotact Funct Neurosurg* 93, 75–93 (2015).

15. Cuijpers, P., et al. Adding psychotherapy to antidepressant medication in depression and anxiety disorders: A meta-analysis. *World Psychiatry* 13, 56–67 (2014).

16. Vittner, D., et al. Increase in oxytocin from skin-to-skin contact enhances development of parent-infant relationship. *Biol Res Nurs* 20, 54–62 (2017); Moberg, K. U. & Prime, D. K. Oxytocin effects in mothers and infants during breastfeeding. *Infant* 6, 201–206 (2013); Moberg, K. U. *Oxytocin: The Biological Guide to Motherhood* (Praeclarus Press, 2014); Maruyama, K., Shimoju, R., Ohkubo, M., Maruyama, H. & Kurosawa, M. Tactile skin stimulation increases dopamine release in the nucleus accumbens in rats. *J Physiological Sci* 62, 259–266 (2011).

17. Smith, A. K., Mick, E. & Faraone, S. V. Advances in genetic studies of attention deficit/hyperactivity disorder. *Curr Psychiat Rep* 11, 143–148 (2009); Lester, B. M., Marsit, C. J., Conradt, E., Bromer, C. & Padbury, J. F. Behavioral epigenetics and the developmental origins of child mental health disorders. *J Dev Orig Hlth Dis* 3, 395–408 (2012); McLaughlin, K. A., et al. Causal effects of the early caregiving environment on development of stress response systems in children. *Proc Natl Acad Sci USA* 112, 5637–5642 (2015); Koss, K. J., Mliner, S. B., Donzella, B. & Gunnar, M. R. Early adversity, hypocortisolism, and behavior problems at school entry: A study of internationally adopted children. *Psychoneuroendocrinology* 66, 31–38 (2016); Gunnar, M. R., Frenn, K., Wewerka, S. S. & Ryzin, M. J. V. Moderate versus severe early life stress: Associations with stress reactivity and regulation in 10–12-year-old children. *Psychoneuroendocrinology* 34, 62–75 (2009); Felitti, V. J., et al. Relationship of childhood abuse and household dysfunction to many of the leading causes of death in adults. The Adverse Childhood Experiences (ACE) Study. *Am J Prev Med* 14, 245–258 (1998); Gunnar, M. R. & Donzella, B. Social regulation of the cortisol levels in early human development. *Psychoneuroendocrinology* 27, 199–220 (2002); Hostinar, C. E. & Gunnar, M. R. The developmental effects of early life stress: An overview of current theoretical frameworks. *Curr Dir Psychol Sci* 22, 400–406 (2013); Hughes, K., et al. The effect of multiple adverse childhood experiences on health: A systematic review and meta-analysis. *Lancet Public Health* 2, e356–e366 (2017); Heim, C., Newport, D. J., Mletzko, T., Miller, A. H. & Nemeroff, C. B.

The link between childhood trauma and depression: Insights from HPA axis studies in humans. *Psychoneuroendocrinology* 33, 693–710 (2008); Felitti, V. J. The relation between adverse childhood experiences and adult health: Turning gold into lead. *Perm J* 6, 44–47 (2002); Heim, C. & Nemeroff, C. B. The role of childhood trauma in the neurobiology of mood and anxiety disorders: Preclinical and clinical studies. *Biol Psychiat* 49, 1023–1039 (2001); Merrick, M. T., et al. Unpacking the impact of adverse childhood experiences on adult mental health. *Child Abuse Neglect* 69, 10–19 (2016); Sapolsky, R. *Why Zebras Don't Get Ulcers* (Henry Holt and Co., 2004); Sumner, J. A., et al. Epigenetics of early-life adversity in youth: Cross-sectional and longitudinal associations. *Clin Epigenetics* 14, 48 (2021); Ellis, B. J., Sheridan, M. A., Belsky, J. & McLaughlin, K. A. Why and how does early adversity influence development? Toward an integrated model of dimensions of environmental experience. *Dev Psychopathol* 34, 447–471 (2022); Schafer, J. L., et al. Threat and deprivation are associated with distinct aspects of cognition, emotional processing, and psychopathology in children and adolescents. *Developmental Sci* e13267 (2022) doi:10.1111/desc.13267; Murphy, Y. E., Zhang, X. & Gatzke-Kopp, L. The developmental cascade of early parenting, emergence of executive functioning, and emotional symptoms across childhood. *Infant Ment Health* J 42, 331–345 (2021); Reid, B. M., et al. Pathways to inflammation in adolescence through early adversity, childhood depressive symptoms, and body mass index: A prospective longitudinal study of Chilean infants. *Brain Behav Immun* 86, 4–13 (2018).

18. Squire, L. R. & Dede, A. J. O. Conscious and unconscious memory systems. *Cold Spring Harb Perspect Biol* 7, a021667 (2015).

19. Alberini, C. M. & Travaglia, A. Infantile amnesia: A critical period of learning to learn and remember. *J Neurosci* 37, 5783–5795 (2017); Akers, K. G., et al. Hippocampal neurogenesis regulates forgetting during adulthood and infancy. *Science* 344, 598–602 (2014).

20. Vöhringer, I. A., et al. The development of implicit memory from infancy to childhood: On average performance levels and interindividual differences. *Child Dev* 89, 370–382 (2017).

21. Cozolino, L. *The Neuroscience of Human Relationships: Attachment and the Developing Social Brain* (Norton, 2006).

Chapter 2. Babies Need to Borrow Your Brain

1. Vittner, D., et al. Increase in oxytocin from skin-to-skin contact enhances development of parent-infant relationship. *Biol Res Nurs* 20, 54–62 (2017); Moberg, K. U. & Prime, D. Oxytocin effects in mothers and infants during breastfeeding. *Infant* 6, 201–206 (2013); Moberg, K. U. *Oxytocin: The Biological Guide to Motherhood* (Praeclarus Press, 2014); Maruyama, K., Shimoju, R., Ohkubo, M., Maruyama, H. & Kurosawa, M. Tactile skin stimulation increases dopamine release in the nucleus accumbens in rats. *J Physiological Sci* 62, 259–266 (2011).

2. Gunnar, M. R., Frenn, K., Wewerka, S. S. & Ryzin, M. J. V. Moderate versus severe early life stress: Associations with stress reactivity and regulation in 10–12-year-old

children. *Psychoneuroendocrinology* 34, 62–75 (2009); Sackett, G. P., Bowman, R. E., Meyer, J. S., Tripp, R. L. & Grady, S. S. Adrenocortical and behavioral reactions by differentially raised rhesus monkeys. *Physiol Psychol* 1, 209–212 (1973); Benmhammed, H., et al. Animal models of early-life adversity. *Methods Mol Biol* 2011, 143–161 (2019); Gordis, E. B., Granger, D. A., Susman, E. J. & Trickett, P. K. Asymmetry between salivary cortisol and α-amylase reactivity to stress: Relation to aggressive behavior in adolescents. *Psychoneuroendocrinology* 31, 976–987 (2006); Oosterman, M., Schipper, J. C. D., Fisher, P., Dozier, M. & Schuengel, C. Autonomic reactivity in relation to attachment and early adversity among foster children. *Dev Psychopathol* 22, 109–118 (2010); Meyer, J. S., Novak, M. A., Bowman, R. E. & Harlow, H. F. Behavioral and hormonal effects of attachment object separation in surrogate-peer-reared and mother-reared infant rhesus monkeys. *Dev Psychobiol* 8, 425–435 (1975); Harkness, K. L., Stewart, J. G. & Wynne-Edwards, K. E. Cortisol reactivity to social stress in adolescents: Role of depression severity and child maltreatment. *Psychoneuroendocrinology* 36, 173–181 (2011); Mac-Millan, H. L., et al. Cortisol response to stress in female youths exposed to childhood maltreatment: Results of the Youth Mood Project. *Biol Psychiat* 66, 62–68 (2009); Sánchez, M. M., Ladd, C. O. & Plotsky, P. M. Early adverse experience as a developmental risk factor for later psychopathology: Evidence from rodent and primate models. *Dev Psychopathol* 13, 419–449 (2001); Lyons, D. M., Yang, C., Mobley, B. W., Nickerson, J. T. & Schatzberg, A. F. Early environmental regulation of glucocorticoid feedback sensitivity in young adult monkeys. *J Neuroendocrinol* 12, 723–728 (2000); Van der Vegt, E. J. M., Van der Ende, J., Kirschbaum, C., Verhulst, F. C. & Tiemeier, H. Early neglect and abuse predict diurnal cortisol patterns in adults: A study of international adoptees. *Psychoneuroendocrinology* 34, 660–669 (2009); Plotsky, P. M. & Meaney, M. J. Early, postnatal experience alters hypothalamic corticotropin-releasing factor (CRF) mRNA, median eminence CRF content and stress-induced release in adult rats. *Mol Brain Res* 18, 195–200 (1993); Nishi, M. Effects of early-life stress on the brain and behaviors: Implications of early maternal separation in rodents. *Int J Mol Sci* 21, 7212 (2020); Champoux, M., Coe, C. L., Schanberg, S. M., Kuhn, C. M. & Suomi, S. J. Hormonal effects of early rearing conditions in the infant rhesus monkey. *Am J Primatol* 19, 111–117 (1989); Bayart, F., Hayashi, K. T., Faull, K. F., Barchas, J. D. & Levine, S. Influence of maternal proximity on behavioral and physiological responses to separation in infant rhesus monkeys (*Macaca mulatta*). *Behav Neurosci* 104, 98–107 (1990); Liu, D., et al. Maternal Care, hippocampal glucocorticoid receptors, and hypothalamic-pituitary-adrenal responses to stress. *Science* 277, 1659–1662 (1997); Bodegom, M. van, Homberg, J. R. & Henckens, M. J. A. G. Modulation of the hypothalamic-pituitary-adrenal axis by early life stress exposure. *Front Cell Neurosci* 11, 87 (2017); Bruce, J., Fisher, P. A., Pears, K. C. & Levine, S. Morning cortisol levels in preschool-aged foster children: Differential effects of maltreatment type. *Dev Psychobiol* 51, 14–23 (2009); Fries, A. B. W., Shirtcliff, E. A. & Pollak, S. D. Neuroendocrine dysregulation following early social deprivation in children. *Dev Psychobiol* 50, 588–599 (2008); Ladd, C. O. Persistent changes in corticotropin-releasing factor neuronal systems induced by maternal deprivation. *Endocrinology* 137, 1212–1218 (1996); Heim, C., et al. Pituitary-adrenal and autonomic responses to stress in women after sexual and physical abuse in childhood. *JAMA* 284, 592–597 (2000); Capitanio, J. P., Mendoza, S. P., Mason, W. A. & Maninger, N. Rearing environment and hypothalamic-pituitary-adrenal regulation in young rhesus monkeys (*Macaca mulatta*). *Dev Psychobiol* 46, 318–330 (2005); Gunnar, M. R., Morison, S. J., Chisholm, K. & Schuder, M. Salivary cortisol levels in children adopted from Romanian orphanages. *Dev Psychopathol* 13, 611–628 (2001); Kaufman, J., et al. The corticotropin-releasing hormone challenge in depressed abused, depressed nonabused, and normal control children. *Biol Psychiat* 42, 669–679 (1997); Levine, S. The influence of social factors on the response to stress. *Psychother Psychosom* 60, 33–38 (1993).

3. McLaughlin, K. A., et al. Causal effects of the early caregiving environment on development of stress response systems in children. *Proc Natl Acad Sci USA* 112, 5637–5642 (2015); Koss, K. J., Mliner, S. B., Donzella, B. & Gunnar, M. R. Early adversity, hypocortisolism, and behavior problems at school entry: A study of internationally adopted children. *Psychoneuroendocrinology* 66, 31–38 (2016); Gunnar, M. R., Frenn, K., Wewerka, S. S. & Ryzin, M. J. V. Moderate versus severe early life stress: Associations with stress reactivity and regulation in 10–12-year-old children. *Psychoneuroendocrinology* 34, 62–75 (2009); Felitti, V. J., et al. Relationship of childhood abuse and household dysfunction to many of the leading causes of death in adults. The Adverse Childhood Experiences (ACE) Study. *Am J Prev Med* 14, 245–258 (1998); Merrick, M. T., et al. Unpacking the impact of adverse childhood experiences on adult mental health. *Child Abuse Neglect* 69, 10–19 (2016); Fries, E., Hesse, J., Hellhammer, J. & Hellhammer, D. H. A new view on hypocortisolism. *Psychoneuroendocrinology* 30, 1010–1016 (2005); Yehuda, R., Yang, R.-K., Buchsbaum, M. S. & Golier, J. A. Alterations in cortisol negative feedback inhibition as examined using the ACTH response to cortisol administration in PTSD. *Psychoneuroendocrinology* 31, 447–451 (2006); Gunnar, M. R. & Quevedo, K. M. Early care experiences and HPA axis regulation in children: A mechanism for later trauma vulnerability. *Prog Brain Res* 167, 137–149 (2007); McGowan, P. O., et al. Epigenetic regulation of the glucocorticoid receptor in human brain associates with childhood abuse. *Nat Neurosci* 12, 342–348 (2009); Jones, N. A., Field, T. & Davalos, M. Right frontal EEG asymmetry and lack of empathy in preschool children of depressed mothers. *Child Psychiatry Hum Dev* 30, 189–204 (2000).

4. Gunnar, M. R. & Donzella, B. Social regulation of the cortisol levels in early human development. *Psychoneuroendocrinology* 27, 199–220 (2002); Gunnar, M. R. & Cheatham, C. L. Brain and behavior interface: Stress and the developing brain. *Infant Ment Health J* 24, 195–211 (2003); Packard, K., Opendak, M., Soper, C. D., Sardar, H. & Sullivan, R. M. Infant attachment and social modification of stress neurobiology. *Frontiers Syst Neurosci* 15, 718198 (2021); Ilyka, D., Johnson, M. H. & Lloyd-Fox, S. Infant social interactions and brain development: A systematic review. *Neurosci Biobehav Rev* 130, 448–469 (2021); Gee, D. G., et al. Maternal buffering of human amygdala-prefrontal circuitry during childhood but not during adolescence. *Psychol Sci* 25, 2067–2078 (2014); Lee, A., et al. Maternal care in infancy and the

course of limbic development. *Dev Cogn Neurosci* 40, 100714 (2019); Hostinar, C. E., Johnson, A. E. & Gunnar, M. R. Parent support is less effective in buffering cortisol stress reactivity for adolescents compared to children. *Developmental Sci* 18, 281–297 (2015); Hostinar, C. E., Sullivan, R. M. & Gunnar, M. R. Psychobiological mechanisms underlying the social buffering of the hypothalamic-pituitary-adrenocortical axis: A review of animal models and human studies across development. *Psychol Bull* 140, 256–282 (2014); Sullivan, R. M. & Holman, P. J. Transitions in sensitive period attachment learning in infancy: The role of corticosterone. *Neurosci Biobehav Rev* 34, 835–844 (2010).

5. Gilmore, J. H., Knickmeyer, R. C. & Gao, W. Imaging structural and functional brain development in early childhood. *Nat Rev Neurosci* 19, 123–137 (2018); Tierney, A. L. & Nelson, C. A. Brain development and the role of experience in the early years. *Zero Three* 30, 9–13 (2009); Vasung, L., et al. Exploring early human brain development with structural and physiological neuroimaging. *Neuroimage* 187, 226–254 (2019); Farber, M. J., Kim, M. J., Knodt, A. R. & Hariri, A. R. Maternal overprotection in childhood is associated with amygdala reactivity and structural connectivity in adulthood. *Dev Cogn Neurosci* 40, 100711 (2019); Sharma, S., et al. Maturation of the adolescent brain. *Neuropsych Dis Treat* 9, 449 (2013); Uytun, M. C. Development period of prefrontal cortext. In *Prefrontal Cortex* (2018) doi:10.5772/intechopen.78697.

6. Kelley, N. J., Gallucci, A., Riva, P., Lauro, L. J. R. & Schmeichel, B. J. Stimulating self-regulation: A review of non-invasive brain stimulation studies of goal-directed behavior. *Front Behav Neurosci* 12, 337 (2019).

7. Perry, B. D. Childhood experience and the expression of genetic potential: What childhood neglect tells us about nature and nurture. *Brain and Mind* 3, 79–100 (2002); Nelson, C. A., et al. Cognitive recovery in socially deprived young children: the Bucharest Early Intervention Project. *Science* 318, 1937–1940 (2007); Bruce, J., Gunnar, M. R., Pears, K. C. & Fisher, P. A. Early adverse care, stress neurobiology, and prevention science: Lessons learned. *Prev Sci* 14, 247–256 (2013); Mackes, N. K., et al. Early childhood deprivation is associated with alterations in adult brain structure despite subsequent environmental enrichment. *Proc Natl Acad Sci USA* 117, 641–649 (2020); Nelson, C. A., Fox, N. A. & Zeanah, C. H. *Romania's Abandoned Children: Deprivation, Brain Development, and the Struggle for Recovery* (Harvard University Press, 2014).

8. Gunnar, M. R., DePasquale, C. E., Reid, B. M., Donzella, B. & Miller, B. S. Pubertal stress recalibration reverses the effects of early life stress in postinstitutionalized children. *Proc Natl Acad Sci USA* 116, 23984–23988 (2019); Perry, N. B., Donzella, B. & Gunnar, M. R. Pubertal stress recalibration and later social and emotional adjustment among adolescents: The role of early life stress. *Psychoneuroendocrinology* 135, 105578 (2021).

9. Egeland, B. & Farber, E. A. Infant-mother attachment: Factors related to its development and changes over time. *Child Dev* 55, 753–771 (1984); Tronick, E. Z. & Gianino, A. F. The transmission of maternal disturbance to the infant. *New Dir Child Adoles* 1986, 5–11 (1986).

10. Wu, Q. & Feng, X. Infant emotion regulation and cortisol response during the first 2 years of life: Association with maternal parenting profiles. *Dev Psychobiol* 62, 1076–1091 (2020).

11. Egeland & Farber. Infant-mother attachment; Tronick & Gianino. The transmission of maternal disturbance to the infant.

12. Wu & Feng. Infant emotion regulation and cortisol response during the first 2 years of life.

13. Egeland & Farber. Infant-mother attachment; Tronick & Gianino. The transmission of maternal disturbance to the infant.

14. Sharma, S., et al. Maturation of the adolescent brain. *Neuropsych Dis Treat* 9, 449 (2013).

15. Roozendaal, B., McEwen, B. S. & Chattarji, S. Stress, memory and the amygdala. *Nat Rev Neurosci* 10, 423–433 (2009).

16. Tottenham, N. Early adversity and the neotenous human brain. *Biol Psychiat* 87, 350–358 (2019); Gee, D. G., et al. Early developmental emergence of human amygdala–prefrontal connectivity after maternal deprivation. *Proc Natl Acad Sci USA* 110, 15638–15643 (2013). Cohen, M. M., et al. Early-life stress has persistent effects on amygdala function and development in mice and humans. *Proc Natl Acad Sci USA* 110, 18274–18278 (2013).

17. Ciernia, A. V., et al. Experience-dependent neuroplasticity of the developing hypothalamus: Integrative epigenomic approaches. *Epigenetics* 13, 318–330 (2018); Korosi, A. & Baram, T. Z. Plasticity of the stress response early in life: Mechanisms and significance. *Dev Psychobiol* 52, 661–670 (2010).

18. Leslie, A. T., et al. Impact of early adverse experience on complexity of adult-generated neurons. *Transl Psychiat* 1, e35 (2011); Lester, B. M., et al. Epigenetic programming by maternal behavior in the human infant. *Pediatrics* 142, e20171890 (2018); Zhang, T. Y., Labont., B., Wen, X. L., Turecki, G. & Meaney, M. J. Epigenetic mechanisms for the early environmental regulation of hippocampal glucocorticoid receptor gene expression in rodents and humans. *Neuropsychopharmacol* 38, 111–123 (2012); Mirescu, C., Peters, J. D. & Gould, E. Early life experience alters response of adult neurogenesis to stress. *Nat Neurosci* 7, 841–846 (2004); Luby, J. L., et al. Maternal support in early childhood predicts larger hippocampal volumes at school age. *Proc Natl Acad Sci USA* 109, 2854–2859 (2012).

19. Knickmeyer, R. C., et al. A structural MRI study of human brain development from birth to 2 years. *J Neurosci* 28, 12176–12182 (2008); Sapolsky, R. M., Meaney, M. J. & McEwen, B. S. The development of the glucocorticoid receptor system in the rat limbic brain. III. Negative-feedback regulation. *Dev Brain Res* 18, 169–173 (1985); Giedd, J. N., et al. Quantitative magnetic resonance imaging of human brain development: Ages 4–18. *Cereb Cortex* 6, 551–560 (1996); Meaney, M. J., et al. Early environmental regulation of forebrain glucocorticoid receptor gene expression: Implications for adrenocortical responses to stress. *Dev Neurosci* 18, 49–60 (1996); Gogtay, N., et al. Dynamic mapping of normal human hippocampal development. *Hippocampus* 16, 664–672 (2006).

20. Lester, B. M., et al. Epigenetic programming by maternal behavior in the human infant. *Pediatrics* 142, e20171890 (2018); Perkeybile, A. M., et al. Early nurture

epigenetically tunes the oxytocin receptor. *Psychoneuroendocrinology* 99, 128–136 (2019); Krol, K. M., Moulder, R. G., Lillard, T. S., Grossmann, T. & Connelly, J. J. Epigenetic dynamics in infancy and the impact of maternal engagement. *Sci Adv* 5, eaay0680 (2019); Winberg, J. Mother and newborn baby: Mutual regulation of physiology and behavior—A selective review. *Dev Psychobiol* 47, 217–229 (2005); Scatliffe, N., Casavant, S., Vittner, D. & Cong, X. Oxytocin and early parent-infant interactions: A systematic review. *Int J Nurs Sci* 6, 445–453 (2019); Seltzer, L. J., Ziegler, T. E. & Pollak, S. D. Social vocalizations can release oxytocin in humans. *Proc Biological Sci* 277, 2661–2666 (2010); Maud, C., Ryan, J., McIntosh, J. E. & Olsson, C. A. The role of oxytocin receptor gene (OXTR) DNA methylation (DNAm) in human social and emotional functioning: A systematic narrative review. *BMC Psychiatry* 18, 154 (2018); Moore, S. R., et al. Epigenetic correlates of neonatal contact in humans. *Dev Psychopathol* 29, 1517–1538 (2017).

21. Benmhammed, H., et al. Animal models of early-life adversity. *Methods Mol Biology* 2011, 143–161 (2019); Nishi, M. Effects of early-life stress on the brain and behaviors: Implications of early maternal separation in rodents. *Int J Mol Sci* 21, 7212 (2020); Bodegom, M. van, Homberg, J. R. & Henckens, M. J. A. G. Modulation of the hypothalamic-pituitary-adrenal axis by early life stress exposure. *Front Cell Neurosci* 11, 87 (2017); Rattaz, V., Puglisi, N., Tissot, H. & Favez, N. Associations between parent–infant interactions, cortisol and vagal regulation in infants, and socioemotional outcomes: A systematic review. *Infant Behav Dev* 67, 101687 (2022); Kirsch, D. E. & Lippard, E. T. C. Early life stress and substance use disorders: The critical role of adolescent substance use. *Pharmacol Biochem Behav* 215, 173360 (2021); Tost, H., Champagne, F. A. & Meyer-Lindenberg, A. Environmental influence in the brain, human welfare and mental health. *Nat Neurosci* 18, 1421–1431 (2015); Lillas, C. & Turnbull, J. *Infant Child Mental Health Early Intervention: A Neurorelational Framework for Interdisciplinary Practice* (Norton, 2009); Cattane, N., et al. Preclinical animal models of mental illnesses to translate findings from the bench to the bedside: Molecular brain mechanisms and peripheral biomarkers associated to early life stress or immune challenges. *Eur Neuropsychopharm* 58, 55–79 (2022).

22. Leslie, A. T., et al. Impact of early adverse experience on complexity of adult-generated neurons. *Transl Psychiat* 1, e35 (2011); Lester, B. M., et al. Epigenetic programming by maternal behavior in the human infant. *Pediatrics* 142, e20171890 (2018); Zhang, T. Y., Labont, B., Wen, X. L., Turecki, G. & Meaney, M. J. Epigenetic mechanisms for the early environmental regulation of hippocampal glucocorticoid receptor gene expression in rodents and humans. *Neuropsychopharmacol* 38, 111–123 (2012); Mirescu, C., Peters, J. D. & Gould, E. Early life experience alters response of adult neurogenesis to stress. *Nat Neurosci* 7, 841–846 (2004); Luby, J. L., et al. Maternal support in early childhood predicts larger hippocampal volumes at school age. *Proc Natl Acad Sci USA* 109, 2854–2859 (2012).

23. Felitti, V. J., et al. REPRINT OF: Relationship of childhood abuse and household dysfunction to many of the leading causes of death in adults: The Adverse Childhood Experiences (ACE) Study. *Am J Prev Med* 56, 774–786 (2019).

Chapter 3. Nurtured Nature

1. Cash-Padgett, T. & Jaaro-Peled, H. DISC1 mouse models as a tool to decipher gene environment interactions in psychiatric disorders. *Front Behav Neurosci* 7, 113 (2013); Smeeth, D., Beck, S., Karam, E. G. & Pluess, M. The role of epigenetics in psychological resilience. *Lancet Psychiatry* 8, 620–629 (2021).

2. Lenroot, R. K. & Giedd, J. N. The changing impact of genes and environment on brain development during childhood and adolescence: Initial findings from a neuroimaging study of pediatric twins. *Dev Psychopathol* 20, 1161–1175 (2008).

3. Letourneau, N. *Scientific Parenting: What Science Reveals About Parental Influence* (Dundurn Press, 2013).

4. Cash-Padgett, T. & Jaaro-Peled, H. DISC1 mouse models as a tool to decipher gene environment interactions in psychiatric disorders. *Front Behav Neurosci* 7, 113 (2013).

5. Letourneau, N. *Scientific Parenting*; Belsky, J., et al. Vulnerability genes or plasticity genes? *Mol Psychiatr* 14, 746–754 (2009); Lavigne, J. V., et al. Gene × environment effects of serotonin transporter, dopamine receptor D4, and monoamine oxidase A genes with contextual and parenting risk factors on symptoms of oppositional defiant disorder, anxiety, and depression in a community sample of 4-year-old children. *Dev Psychopathol* 25, 555–575 (2013); Zhang, X., Widaman, K. & Belsky, J. Beyond orchids and dandelions: Susceptibility to environmental influences is not bimodal. *Dev Psychopathol* 1–13 (2021) doi:10.1017/s0954579421000821; IJzendoorn, M. H. van, Belsky, J. & Bakermans-Kranenburg, M. J. Serotonin transporter genotype 5HTTLPR as a marker of differential susceptibility? A meta-analysis of child and adolescent gene-by-environment studies. *Transl Psychiat* 2, e147 (2012); Belsky, J. & Hartman, S. Gene-environment interaction in evolutionary perspective: differential susceptibility to environmental influences. *World Psychiatry* 13, 87–89 (2014); Belsky, J., Zhang, X. & Sayler, K. Differential susceptibility 2.0: Are the same children affected by different experiences and exposures? *Dev Psychopathol* 1–9 (2021) doi:10.1017/s0954579420002205.

6. Nachmias, M., Gunnar, M., Mangelsdorf, S., Parritz, R. H. & Buss, K. Behavioral inhibition and stress reactivity: The moderating role of attachment security. *Child Dev* 67, 508–522 (1996).

7. Letourneau, N. *Scientific Parenting*; Bakermans-Kranenburg, M. J. & IJzendoorn, M. H. van. Gene-environment interaction of the dopamine D4 receptor (DRD4) and observed maternal insensitivity predicting externalizing behavior in preschoolers. *Dev Psychobiol* 48, 406–409 (2006).

8. Meaney, M. J. Maternal care, gene expression, and the transmission of individual differences in stress reactivity across generations. *Annu Rev Neurosci* 24, 1161–1192 (2001); Weaver, I. C. G., et al. Epigenetic programming by maternal behavior. *Nat Neurosci* 7, 847–854 (2004).

9. Lester, B. M., et al. Epigenetic programming by maternal behavior in the human infant. *Pediatrics* 142, e20171890 (2018); Krol, K. M., Moulder, R. G., Lillard, T. S., Grossmann, T. & Connelly, J. J. Epigenetic dynamics in infancy and the impact of maternal engagement. *Sci Adv* 5, eaay0680 (2019); Moore, S. R., et al.

Epigenetic correlates of neonatal contact in humans. *Dev Psychopathol* 29, 1517–1538 (2017); Labont, B., et al. Genome-wide epigenetic regulation by early-life trauma. *Arch Gen Psychiat* 69, 722–731 (2012); Tomassi, S. & Tosato, S. Epigenetics and gene expression profile in first-episode psychosis: The role of childhood trauma. *Neurosci Biobehav Rev* 83, 226–237 (2017).

10. BABY ACES: When we consider the traumas that qualify as ACEs, babies need their own list. PACES Connection. www.pacesconnection.com/blog/baby-aces -when-we-considerthe-traumas-that-qualify-as-aces-babies-need-their-own-list; Porges, S. W. Social engagement and attachment: A phylogenetic perspective. *Ann NY Acad Sci* 1008, 31–47 (2003). https://www.pacesconnection.com/blog/baby-aces -when-we-consider-the-traumas-that-qualify-as-aces-babies-need-their-own-list.

11. Mashoodh, R., Habrylo, I. B., Gudsnuk, K. M., Pelle, G. & Champagne, F. A. Maternal modulation of paternal effects on offspring development. *Proc Biological Sci* 285, 20180118 (2018); Curley, J. P., Mashoodh, R. & Champagne, F. A. Epigenetics and the origins of paternal effects. *Horm Behav* 59, 306–314 (2011); Chan, J. C., Nugent, B. M. & Bale, T. L. Parental advisory: Maternal and paternal stress can impact offspring neurodevelopment. *Biol Psychiat* 83, 886–894 (2018).

12. Chan, Nugent & Bale. Parental advisory; Bale, T. L. Epigenetic and transgenerational reprogramming of brain development. *Nat Rev Neurosci* 16, 332–344 (2015); Bale, T. L., et al. Early life programming and neurodevelopmental disorders. *Biol Psychiat* 68, 314–319 (2010).

13. Meaney, M. J. Maternal care, gene expression, and the transmission of individual differences in stress reactivity across generations. *Annu Rev Neurosci* 24, 1161–1192 (2001); Franklin, T. B., et al. Epigenetic transmission of the impact of early stress across generations. *Biol Psychiat* 68, 408–415 (2010); Maestripieri, D. Early experience affects the intergenerational transmission of infant abuse in rhesus monkeys. *Proc Natl Acad Sci USA* 102, 9726–9729 (2005); Widom, C. S., Czaja, S. J. & DuMont, K. A. Intergenerational transmission of child abuse and neglect: Real or detection bias? *Science* 347, 1480–1485 (2015); Champagne, F. A. Epigenetic mechanisms and the transgenerational effects of maternal care. *Front Neuroendocrinol* 29, 386–397 (2007); Dettmer, A., Heckman, J., Pantano, J., Ronda, V. & Suomi, S. Intergenerational effects of early-life advantage: Lessons from a primate study. NBER working paper 27737 (2020) doi:10.3386/w27737.

14. Doherty, T. S., Forster, A. & Roth, T. L. Global and gene-specific DNA methylation alterations in the adolescent amygdala and hippocampus in an animal model of caregiver maltreatment. *Behav Brain Res* 298, 55–61 (2016).

15. Ciernia, A. V., et al. Experience-dependent neuroplasticity of the developing hypothalamus: Integrative epigenomic approaches. *Epigenetics* 13, 318–330 (2018); Singh-Taylor, A., et al. NRSF-dependent epigenetic mechanisms contribute to programming of stress-sensitive neurons by neonatal experience, promoting resilience. *Mol Psychiatr* 23, 648–657 (2017); Korosi, A., et al. Early-life experience reduces excitation to stress-responsive hypothalamic neurons and reprograms the expression of corticotropin-releasing hormone. *J Neurosci* 30, 703–713 (2010).

16. Lester, B. M., et al. Epigenetic programming by maternal behavior in the human infant. *Pediatrics* 142, e20171890 (2018); Zhang, T. Y., Labont., B., Wen, X. L., Turecki, G. & Meaney, M. J. Epigenetic mechanisms for the early environmental regulation of hippocampal glucocorticoid receptor gene expression in rodents and humans. *Neuropsychopharmacol* 38, 111–123 (2012); Weaver, I. C. G., et al. Epigenetic programming by maternal behavior. *Nat Neurosci* 7, 847–854 (2004).

17. Blaze, J., Scheuing, L. & Roth, T. L. Differential methylation of genes in the medial prefrontal cortex of developing and adult rats following exposure to maltreatment or nurturing care during infancy. *Dev Neurosci* 35, 306–316 (2013).

18. Perkeybile, A. M., et al. Early nurture epigenetically tunes the oxytocin receptor. *Psychoneuroendocrinology* 99, 128–136 (2019); Maud, C., Ryan, J., McIntosh, J. E. & Olsson, C. A. The role of oxytocin receptor gene (OXTR) DNA methylation (DNAm) in human social and emotional functioning: A systematic narrative review. *BMC Psychiatry* 18, 154 (2018).

19. Krol, K. M., Moulder, R. G., Lillard, T. S., Grossmann, T. & Connelly, J. J. Epigenetic dynamics in infancy and the impact of maternal engagement. *Sci Adv* 5, eaay0680 (2019); Pena, C. J., Neugut, Y. D. & Champagne, F. A. Developmental timing of the effects of maternal care on gene expression and epigenetic regulation of hormone receptor levels in female rats. *Endocrinology* 154, 4340–4351 (2013).

Chapter 4. Superpowers of the Parent Brain

1. Seifritz, E., et al. Differential sex-independent amygdala response to infant crying and laughing in parents versus nonparents. *Biol Psychiat* 54, 1367–1375 (2003); Glasper, E. R., Kenkel, W. M., Bick, J. & Rilling, J. K. More than just mothers: The neurobiological and neuroendocrine underpinnings of allomaternal caregiving. *Front Neuroendocrinol* 53, 100741 (2019); Feldman, R. The adaptive human parental brain: Implications for children's social development. *Trends Neurosci* 38, 387–399 (2015); Young, K. S., et al. The neural basis of responsive caregiving behavior: Investigating temporal dynamics within the parental brain. *Behav Brain Res* 325, 105–116 (2016).

2. Feldman, R., Braun, K. & Champagne, F. A. The neural mechanisms and consequences of paternal caregiving. *Nat Rev Neurosci* 20, 205–224 (2019).

3. Hoekzema, E., et al. Pregnancy leads to long-lasting changes in human brain structure. *Nat Neurosci* 20, 287–296 (2016).

4. Glasper, E. R., Kenkel, W. M., Bick, J. & Rilling, J. K. More than just mothers: The neurobiological and neuroendocrine underpinnings of allomaternal caregiving. *Front Neuroendocrinol* 53, 100741 (2019); Hernández-González, M., Hidalgo-Aguirre, R. M., Guevara, M. A., Pérez-Hernández, M. & Amezcua-Gutiérrez, C. Observing videos of a baby crying or smiling induces similar, but not identical, electroencephalographic responses in biological and adoptive mothers. *Infant Behav Dev* 42, 1–10 (2015); Grasso, D. J., Moser, J. S., Dozier, M. & Simons, R. ERP correlates of attention allocation in mothers processing faces of their children. *Biol Psychol* 81, 95–102

(2008); Abraham, E. & Feldman, R. The neurobiology of human allomaternal care: Implications for fathering, coparenting, and children's social development. *Physiol Behav* 193, 25–34 (2018).

5. Williams, L. R. & Turner, P. R. Infant carrying as a tool to promote secure attachments in young mothers: Comparing intervention and control infants during the still-face paradigm. *Infant Behav Dev* 58, 101413 (2020); Williams, L. R. The impact of infant carrying on adolescent mother–infant interactions during the still-face task. *Infant Child Dev* 29, (2020); Williams, L. R. & Turner, P. R. Experiences with "babywearing": Trendy parenting gear or a developmentally attuned parenting tool? *Child Youth Serv Rev* 112, 104918 (2020); Williams, L. R., Gebler-Wolfe, M., Grisham, L. M. & Bader, M. Y. "Babywearing" in the NICU: An intervention for infants with neonatal abstinence syndrome. *Adv Neonatal Care* 20, 440–449 (2020).

6. Kim, P., et al. Neural plasticity in fathers of human infants. *Soc Neurosci* 9, 522–535 (2014).

7. Feldman, R. The adaptive human parental brain: Implications for children's social development. *Trends Neurosci* 38, 387–399 (2015); Feldman, R., Braun, K. & Champagne, F. A. The neural mechanisms and consequences of paternal caregiving. *Nat Rev Neurosci* 20, 205–224 (2019); Pawluski, J. L., Hoekzema, E., Leuner, B. & Lonstein, J. S. Less can be more: Fine tuning the maternal brain. *Neurosci Biobehav Rev* 133, 104475 (2022); Abraham, E., et al. Father's brain is sensitive to childcare experiences. *Proc National Acad Sci USA* 111, 9792–9797 (2014); Carmona, S., et al. Pregnancy and adolescence entail similar neuroanatomical adaptations: A comparative analysis of cerebral morphometric changes. *Hum Brain Mapp* 40, 2143–2152 (2019).

8. Mundorf, A., Bölükbas, I. & Freund, N. Maternal separation: Does it hold the potential to model consequences of postpartum depression? *Dev Psychobiol* 64, e22219 (2022).

9. Numan, M. & Insel, T. R. The neurobiology of parental behavior. *Hormones Brain Behav* (2003) doi:10.1007/b97533.

10. Hoekzema, E., et al. Pregnancy leads to long-lasting changes in human brain structure. *Nat Neurosci* 20, 287–296 (2016); Pawluski, J. L., Hoekzema, E., Leuner, B. & Lonstein, J. S. Less can be more: Fine tuning the maternal brain. *Neurosci Biobehav Rev* 133, 104475 (2022); Hoekzema, E., et al. Becoming a mother entails anatomical changes in the ventral striatum of the human brain that facilitate its responsiveness to offspring cues. *Psychoneuroendocrinology* 112, 104507 (2019).

11. Boddy, A. M., Fortunato, A., Sayres, M. W. & Aktipis, A. Fetal microchimerism and maternal health: A review and evolutionary analysis of cooperation and conflict beyond the womb. *Bioessays* 37, 1106–1118 (2015).

12. Numan, M. & Insel, T. R. The neurobiology of parental behavior. *Hormones Brain Behav* (2003) doi:10.1007/b97533; Gettler, L. T., et al. Fathers' oxytocin responses to first holding their newborns: Interactions with testosterone reactivity to predict later parenting behavior and father-infant bonds. *Dev Psychobiol* 63, 1384–1398 (2021); Wynne-Edwards, K. E. Hormonal changes in mammalian fathers. *Horm Behav* 40, 139–145 (2001).

13. Plantin, L., Olukoya, A. A. & Ny, P. Positive health outcomes of fathers' involvement in pregnancy and childbirth paternal support: A scope study literature review. *Fathering* 9, 87–102 (2011).

14. Kim, P., et al. Neural plasticity in fathers of human infants. *Soc Neurosci* 9, 522–535 (2014).

15. Abraham, E., et al. Father's brain is sensitive to childcare experiences. *Proc National Acad Sci USA* 111, 9792–9797 (2014).

16. Farren, J., et al. Posttraumatic stress, anxiety and depression following miscarriage and ectopic pregnancy: A multicenter, prospective, cohort study. *Am J Obstet Gynecol* 222, 367.e1–367.e22 (2019).

17. Feldman, R., Braun, K. & Champagne, F. A. The neural mechanisms and consequences of paternal caregiving. *Nat Rev Neurosci* 20, 205–224 (2019); Barba-Müller, E., Craddock, S., Carmona, S. & Hoekzema, E. Brain plasticity in pregnancy and the postpartum period: Links to maternal caregiving and mental health. *Archives Women's Ment Health* 22, 289–299 (2018).

18. Marlin, B. J., Mitre, M., D'amour, J. A., Chao, M. V. & Froemke, R. C. Oxytocin enables maternal behaviour by balancing cortical inhibition. *Nature* 520, 499–504 (2014); Pisapia, N. D., et al. Sex differences in directional brain responses to infant hunger cries. *Neuroreport* 24, 142–146 (2013).

19. Kim, P., et al. Neural plasticity in fathers of human infants. *Soc Neurosci* 9, 522–535 (2014); Paternina-Die, M., et al. The paternal transition entails neuroanatomic adaptations that are associated with the father's brain response to his infant cues. *Cereb Cortex Commun* 1, tgaa082 (2020).

20. Seifritz, E., et al. Differential sex-independent amygdala response to infant crying and laughing in parents versus nonparents. *Biol Psychiat* 54, 1367–1375 (2003).

21. Pisapia, N. D., et al. Sex differences in directional brain responses to infant hunger cries. *Neuroreport* 24, 142–146 (2013).

22. Schiavo, J. K., et al. Innate and plastic mechanisms for maternal behavior in auditory cortex. *Nature* 587, 426–431 (2019).

23. Hoekzema, E., et al. Pregnancy leads to long-lasting changes in human brain structure. *Nat Neurosci* 20, 287–296 (2016); Kim, P., et al. Neural plasticity in fathers of human infants. *Soc Neurosci* 9, 522–535 (2014).

24. Abraham, E., Raz, G., Zagoory-Sharon, O. & Feldman, R. Empathy networks in the parental brain and their long-term effects on children's stress reactivity and behavior adaptation. *Neuropsychologia* 116, 75–85 (2018); McMahon, C. A. & Bernier, A. Twenty years of research on parental mind-mindedness: Empirical findings, theoretical and methodological challenges, and new directions. *Dev Rev* 46, 54–80 (2017); Farrow, C. & Blissett, J. Maternal mind-mindedness during infancy, general parenting sensitivity and observed child feeding behavior: A longitudinal study. *Attach Hum Dev* 16, 230–241 (2014); McMahon, C. A. & Meins, E. Mind-mindedness, parenting stress, and emotional availability in mothers of preschoolers. *Early Child Res Q* 27, 245–252 (2012); Laranjo, J., Bernier, A. & Meins, E. Associations between maternal mind-mindedness and infant attachment security: Investigating the mediating role of maternal sensitivity. *Infant Behav Dev* 31, 688–695 (2008).

25. Seifritz, E., et al. Differential sex-independent amygdala response to infant crying and laughing in parents versus nonparents. *Biol Psychiat* 54, 1367–1375 (2003); Noriuchi, M., Kikuchi, Y. & Senoo, A. The functional neuroanatomy of maternal love: Mother's response to infant's attachment behaviors. *Biol Psychiat* 63, 415–423 (2007).

26. Hoekzema, E., et al. Becoming a mother entails anatomical changes in the ventral striatum of the human brain that facilitate its responsiveness to offspring cues. *Psychoneuroendocrinology* 112, 104507 (2019); Rincon-Cortes, M. & Grace, A. A. Adaptations in reward-related behaviors and mesolimbic dopamine function during motherhood and the postpartum period. *Front Neuroendocrinol* 57, 100839 (2020); Bartels, A. & Zeki, S. The neural correlates of maternal and romantic love. *Neuroimage* 21, 1155–1166 (2004); Atzil, S., et al. Dopamine in the medial amygdala network mediates human bonding. *Proc Natl Acad Sci USA* 114, 2361–2366 (2017).

27. Abraham, E., et al. Father's brain is sensitive to childcare experiences. *Proc Natl Acad Sci USA* 111, 9792–9797 (2014).

28. Small, M. *Our Babies, Ourselves: How Biology and Culture Shape the Way We Parent* (Anchor, 1999).

29. Leuner, B., Glasper, E. R. & Gould, E. Parenting and plasticity. *Trends Neurosci* 33, 465–473 (2010).

Chapter 5. How to Nurture

1. Close, N. Wondering How Your Children Are Doing During COVID-19? Watch Them Play. Yale School of Medicine. https://medicine.yale.edu/news-article /wondering-how-your-children-are-doing-duringcovid-19-watch-them-play/ (2020).

2. Moberg, K. U. *Oxytocin: The Biological Guide to Motherhood* (Praeclarus Press, 2014); Seltzer, L. J., Ziegler, T. E. & Pollak, S. D. Social vocalizations can release oxytocin in humans. *Proc Biological Sci* 277, 2661–2666 (2010).

3. Herreman, C., Gojman-de-Millan, S. & Sroufe, L. A., eds. *Attachment Across Clinical and Cultural Perspectives: A Relational Psychoanalytic Approach* (Routledge, 2016) doi:10.4324/9781315658100.

4. Endevelt-Shapira, Y., Djalovski, A., Dumas, G. & Feldman, R. Maternal chemosignals enhance infant-adult brain-to-brain synchrony. *Sci Adv* 7, eabg6867 (2021).

5. Slade, A. Parental reflective functioning: An introduction. *Attach Hum Dev* 7, 269–281 (2005).

6. Grienenberger, J. F., Kelly, K. & Slade, A. Maternal reflective functioning, mother-infant affective communication, and infant attachment: Exploring the link between mental states and observed caregiving behavior in the intergenerational transmission of attachment. *Attach Hum Dev* 7, 299–311 (2005); Slade, A., Grienenberger, J., Bernbach, E., Levy, D. & Locker, A. Maternal reflective functioning, attachment, and the transmission gap: A preliminary study. *Attach Hum Dev* 7, 283–298 (2005).

7. Slade. Parental reflective functioning.

8. Slade. Parental reflective functioning.

9. Wu, Q. & Feng, X. Infant emotion regulation and cortisol response during the first 2 years of life: Association with maternal parenting profiles. *Dev Psychobiol* 62, 1076–1091 (2020).

10. Salomonsson, B. Psychodynamic therapies with infants and parents: A critical review of treatment methods. *Psychodyn Psychiatry* 42, 203–234 (2014).

Chapter 6. When Your Baby Is Calm and Alert: Nurturing Through Connection

1. Perkeybile, A. M., et al. Early nurture epigenetically tunes the oxytocin receptor. *Psychoneuroendocrinology* 99, 128–136 (2019); Albers, E. M., Riksen-Walraven, J. M., Sweep, F. C. G. J. & Weerth, C. de. Maternal behavior predicts infant cortisol recovery from a mild everyday stressor. *J Child Psychol Psychiatry* 49, 97–103 (2008); Grant, K.-A., et al. Maternal prenatal anxiety, postnatal caregiving and infants' cortisol responses to the still-face procedure. *Dev Psychobiol* 51, 625–637 (2009); Kok, R., et al. Normal variation in early parental sensitivity predicts child structural brain development. *J Am Acad Child Adolesc Psychiatry* 54, 824–831.e1 (2015); Sethna, V., et al. Mother–infant interactions and regional brain volumes in infancy: An MRI study. *Brain Struct Funct* 222, 2379–2388 (2016); Rifkin-Graboi, A., et al. Maternal sensitivity, infant limbic structure volume and functional connectivity: a preliminary study. *Transl Psychiat* 5, e668 (2015); Levy, J., Goldstein, A. & Feldman, R. The neural development of empathy is sensitive to caregiving and early trauma. *Nat Commun* 10, 1905 (2019); Feldman, R., Gordon, I., Schneiderman, I., Weisman, O. & Zagoory-Sharon, O. Natural variations in maternal and paternal care are associated with systematic changes in oxytocin following parent–infant contact. *Psychoneuroendocrinology* 35, 1133–1141 (2010); Beebe, B., Cohen, B. P. & Lachmann, B. F. *The Mother-Infant Interaction Picture Book: Origins of Attachment* (Norton, 2016); Gerhardt, S. *Why Love Matters: How Affection Shapes a Baby's Brain* (Routledge, 2014); Feldman, R. The development of regulatory functions from birth to 5 years: Insights from premature infants. *Child Dev* 80, 544–561 (2009).

2. Porges, S. W. Polyvagal theory: A biobehavioral journey to sociality. *Compr Psychoneuroendocrinology* 7, 100069 (2021); Porges, S. W. Polyvagal theory: A science of safety. *Frontiers Integr Neurosci* 16, 871227 (2022).

3. Feldman, R. Parent-infant synchrony: A biobehavioral model of mutual influences in the formation of affiliative bonds. *Monogr Soc Res Child* 77, 42–51 (2012); Feldman, R. Sensitive periods in human social development: New insights from research on oxytocin, synchrony, and high-risk parenting. *Dev Psychopathol* 27, 369–395 (2015); Schore, A. N. Effects of a secure attachment relationship on right brain development, affect regulation, and infant mental health. *Infant Ment Health J* 22, 7–66 (2001); Tronick, E. Z. Emotions and emotional communication in infants. *Am Psychol* 44, 112–119 (1989).

4. Beebe, Cohen & Lachmann. *The Mother-Infant Interaction Picture Book*; Tronick. Emotions and emotional communication in infants; Tronick, E. Z. & Cohn, J. F.

Infant-mother face-to-face interaction: Age and gender differences in coordination and the occurrence of miscoordination. *Child Dev* 60, 85 (1989).

5. White-Traut, R. C., Schwertz, D., McFarlin, B. & Kogan, J. Salivary cortisol and behavioral state responses of healthy newborn infants to tactile-only and multisensory interventions. *J Obstetric Gynecol Neonatal Nurs* 38, 22–34 (2009).

6. Endevelt-Shapira, Y., Djalovski, A., Dumas, G. & Feldman, R. Maternal chemosignals enhance infant-adult brain-to-brain synchrony. *Sci Adv* 7, eabg6867 (2021).

7. Debiec, J. & Sullivan, R. M. The neurobiology of safety and threat learning in infancy. *Neurobiol Learn Mem* 143, 49–58 (2016).

8. Lundström, J. N., et al. Maternal status regulates cortical responses to the body odor of newborns. *Front Psychol* 4, 597 (2013).

9. Ali, N. A. & Khoja, A. Growing evidence for the impact of air pollution on depression. *Ochsner J* 19, 4 (2019); Kougias, D. G., Sellinger, E. P., Willing, J. & Juraska, J. M. Perinatal exposure to an environmentally relevant mixture of phthalates results in a lower number of neurons and synapses in the medial prefrontal cortex and decreased cognitive flexibility in adult male and female rats. *J Neurosci* 38, 6864–6872 (2018); Ejaredar, M., Nyanza, E. C., Eycke, K. T. & Dewey, D. Phthalate exposure and childrens neurodevelopment: A systematic review. *Environ Res* 142, 51–60 (2015); Holahan, M. R. & Smith, C. A. Phthalates and neurotoxic effects on hippocampal network plasticity. *Neurotoxicology* 48, 21–34 (2015); Taylor, K. M., Weisskopf, M. & Shine, J. Human exposure to nitro musks and the evaluation of their potential toxicity: An overview. *Environ Health* 13, 14 (2014); Diamanti-Kandarakis, E., et al. Endocrine-disrupting chemicals: An Endocrine Society scientific statement. *Endocr Rev* 30, 293–342 (2009).

10. Feldman, R. Parent-infant synchrony: A biobehavioral model of mutual influences in the formation of affiliative bonds. *Monogr Soc Res Child* 77, 42–51 (2012); Feldman, R. Sensitive periods in human social development: New insights from research on oxytocin, synchrony, and high-risk parenting. *Dev Psychopathol* 27, 369–395 (2015).

11. Bonyata, K. Hunger Cues—When do I feed baby? https://kellymom.com/bf/normal/hungercues/ (2018).

12. Graven, S. N. & Browne, J. V. Auditory development in the fetus and infant. *Newborn Infant Nurs Rev* 8, 187–193 (2008); Webb, A. R., Heller, H. T., Benson, C. B. & Lahav, A. Mother's voice and heartbeat sounds elicit auditory plasticity in the human brain before full gestation. *Proc Natl Acad Sci USA* 112, 3152–3157 (2015); Moon, C., Lagercrantz, H. & Kuhl, P. K. Language experienced *in utero* affects vowel perception after birth: A two-country study. *Acta Paediatrica* 102, 156–160 (2013); Mampe, B., Friederici, A. D., Christophe, A. & Wermke, K. Newborns' cry melody is shaped by their native language. *Curr Biol* 19, 1994–1997 (2009).

13. DeCasper, A. J. & Spence, M. J. Prenatal maternal speech influences newborns' perception of speech sounds. *Infant Behav Dev* 9, 133–150 (1986).

14. Marx, V. & Nagy, E. Fetal behavioral responses to the touch of the mother's abdomen: A frame-by-frame analysis. *Infant Behav Dev* 47, 83–91 (2017).

15. Mennella, J. A., Jagnow, C. P. & Beauchamp, G. K. Prenatal and postnatal flavor learning by human infants. *Pediatrics* 107, E88 (2001); Spahn, J. M., et al. Influence

of maternal diet on flavor transfer to amniotic fluid and breast milk and children's responses: A systematic review. *Am J Clin Nutrition* 109, 1003S–1026S (2018).

16. DeCasper, A. J. & Fifer, W. P. Of human bonding: Newborns prefer their mothers' voices. *Science* 208, 1174–1176 (1980).

17. Seltzer, L. J., Ziegler, T. E. & Pollak, S. D. Social vocalizations can release oxytocin in humans. *Proc Biological Sci* 277, 2661–2666 (2010); Liebenthal, E., Silbersweig, D. A. & Stern, E. The language, tone and prosody of emotions: Neural substrates and dynamics of spoken-word emotion perception. *Front Neurosci* 10, 506 (2016); Grossmann, T., Oberecker, R., Koch, S. P. & Friederici, A. D. The developmental origins of voice processing in the human brain. *Neuron* 65, 852–858 (2010).

18. Corbeil, M., Trehub, S. E. & Peretz, I. Singing delays the onset of infant distress. *Infancy* 21, 373–391 (2015); Loewy, J., Stewart, K., Dassler, A.-M., Telsey, A. & Homel, P. The effects of music therapy on vital signs, feeding, and sleep in premature infants. *Pediatrics* 131, 902–918 (2013).

19. Adamson, L. B. & Frick, J. E. The still face: A history of a shared experimental paradigm. *Infancy* 4, 451–473 (2003).

20. Hardin, J. S., Jones, N. A., Mize, K. D. & Platt, M. Parent-training with kangaroo care impacts infant neurophysiological development & mother-infant neuroendocrine activity. *Infant Behav Dev* 58, 101416 (2020).

21. Esposito, G., et al. Infant calming responses during maternal carrying in humans and mice. *Curr Biology* 23, 739–745 (2013).

22. Williams, L. R. & Turner, P. R. Infant carrying as a tool to promote secure attachments in young mothers: Comparing intervention and control infants during the still-face paradigm. *Infant Behav Dev* 58, 101413 (2020).

23. Ackerley, R., et al. Human C-tactile afferents are tuned to the temperature of a skin-stroking caress. *J Neurosci* 34, 2879–2883 (2014).

24. Gilchrist, I. *The Master and His Emissary* (Yale University Press, 2009).

25. Hardin, Jones, Mize, & Platt. Parent-training with kangaroo care impacts infant neurophysiological development & mother-infant neuroendocrine activity.

26. Brauer, J., Xiao, Y., Poulain, T., Friederici, A. D. & Schirmer, A. Frequency of maternal touch predicts resting activity and connectivity of the developing social brain. *Cereb Cortex* 28, 692 (2017); Ardiel, E. L. & Rankin, C. H. The importance of touch in development. *Paediatr Child Healt* 15, 153–156 (2009); Gursul, D., et al. Stroking modulates noxious-evoked brain activity in human infants. *Curr Biology* 28, R1380–R1381 (2018); Bagot, R. C., et al. Variations in postnatal maternal care and the epigenetic regulation of metabotropic glutamate receptor 1 expression and hippocampal function in the rat. *Proc Natl Acad Sci USA* 109, 17200–17207 (2012); Carozza, S. & Leong, V. The role of affectionate caregiver touch in early neurodevelopment and parent-infant interactional synchrony. *Front Neurosci* 14, 613378 (2020).

27. Charpak, N., et al. Twenty-year follow-up of kangaroo mother care versus traditional care. *Pediatrics* 139, e20162063 (2017); Takahashi, Y., Tamakoshi, K., Matsushima, M. & Kawabe, T. Comparison of salivary cortisol, heart rate, and oxygen saturation between early skin-to-skin contact with different initiation and duration

times in healthy, full-term infants. *Early Hum Dev* 87, 151–157 (2010); Moore, E. R., Anderson, G. C. & Bergman, N. Early skin-to-skin contact for mothers and their healthy newborn infants. *Cochrane Database Syst Rev* CD003519 (2007) doi:10.1002/14651858.cd003519.pub2; Handlin, L., et al. Effects of sucking and skin-to-skin contact on maternal ACTH and cortisol levels during the second day postpartum—Influence of epidural analgesia and oxytocin in the perinatal period. *Breastfeed Med* 4, 207–220 (2009).

28. Bergman, N., Linley, L. & Fawcus, S. Randomized controlled trial of skin-to-skin contact from birth versus conventional incubator for physiological stabilization in 1200- to 2199-gram newborns. *Acta Paediatr* 93, 779–785 (2004); Luong, K. C., Nguyen, T. L., Thi, D. H. H., Carrara, H. P. O. & Bergman, N. J. Newly born low birthweight infants stabilise better in skin-to-skin contact than when separated from their mothers: A randomised controlled trial. *Acta Paediatr* 105, 381–390 (2015).

Chapter 7. When Your Baby Is Crying, Clinging, Withdrawn, or Melting Down: Nurturing Stress

1. Grubb, C. Our Story. The Beyond Sleep Training Project. https://thebeyondsleep trainingproject.com/our-story.

2. Bell, S. M. & Ainsworth, M. D. S. Infant crying and maternal responsiveness. *Child Dev* 43, 1171 (1972).

3. Eshel, N., Daelmans, B., Mello, M. C. de & Martines, J. Responsive parenting: Interventions and outcomes. *B World Health Organ* 84, 991–998 (2006); Tamis-LeMonda, C. S. & Bornstein, M. H. Maternal responsiveness and early language acquisition. *Adv Child Dev Behav* 29, 89–127 (2002); Bakeman, R. & Brown, J. V. Early interaction: Consequences for social and mental development at three years. *Child Dev* 51, 437–447 (1980); Beckwith, L., Rodning, C. & Cohen, S. Preterm children at early adolescence and continuity and discontinuity in maternal responsiveness from infancy. *Child Dev* 63, 1198–1208 (1992); Shaw, D. S., Keenan, K. & Vondra, J. I. Developmental precursors of externalizing behavior: Ages 1 to 3. *Dev Psychol* 30, 355–364 (1994); Dunst, C. J. & Kassow, D. Z. Caregiver sensitivity, contingent social responsiveness, and secure infant attachment. *J Early Intensive Behav Intervention* 5, 40–56 (2008); Harries, V. & Brown, A. The association between baby care books that promote strict care routines and infant feeding, night-time care, and maternal–infant interactions. *Maternal Child Nutrition* 15, e12858 (2019); Brown, A. & Arnott, B. Breastfeeding duration and early parenting behaviour: The importance of an infant-led, responsive style. *Plos One* 9, e83893 (2014).

4. Nachmias, M., Gunnar, M., Mangelsdorf, S., Parritz, R. H. & Buss, K. Behavioral inhibition and stress reactivity: The moderating role of attachment security. *Child Dev* 67, 508–522 (1996); Gunnar, M. R. Quality of early care and buffering of neuroendocrine stress reactions: Potential effects on the developing human brain. *Prev Med* 27, 208–211 (1998); Hostinar, C. E., Johnson, A. E. & Gunnar, M. R. Early social deprivation and the social buffering of cortisol stress responses in late

childhood: An experimental study. *Dev Psychol* 51, 1597–1608 (2015); Perry, R. E., Blair, C. & Sullivan, R. M. Neurobiology of infant attachment: Attachment despite adversity and parental programming of emotionality. *Curr Opin Psychology* 17, 1–6 (2017).

5. Lillas, C. & Turnbull, J. *Infant Child Mental Health Early Intervention: A Neurorelational Framework for Interdisciplinary Practice* (Norton, 2009).

6. Lillas & Turnbull. *Infant Child Mental Health Early Intervention.*

7. Lillas & Turnbull. *Infant Child Mental Health Early Intervention.*

8. Chess, S. & Thomas, A. *Temperament: Theory and Practice* (Routledge, 1996) doi:10.4324/9780203766170.

9. Chess & Thomas. *Temperament.*

10. Chess & Thomas. *Temperament.*

11. Film. *The Wisdom of Trauma* (2022). https://thewisdomoftrauma.com/.

12. LeMoyne, T. & Buchanan, T. Does "hovering" matter? Helicopter parenting and its effects on well-being. *Sociol Spectrum* 31, 399–418 (2011); Locke, J. Y., Campbell, M. A. & Kavanagh, D. Can a parent do too much for their child? An examination by parenting professionals of the concept of overparenting. *Aust J Guid Couns* 22, 249–265 (2012); Odenweller, K. G., Booth-Butterfield, M. & Weber, K. Investigating helicopter parenting, family environments, and relational outcomes for millennials. *Commun Stud* 65, 407–425 (2014); Schiffrin, H. H. & Liss, M. The effects of helicopter parenting on academic motivation. *J Child Fam Stud* 26, 1472–1480 (2017).

13. Circle of Security International. www.circleofsecurityinternational.com.

14. Esposito, G., et al. Infant calming responses during maternal carrying in humans and mice. *Curr Biology* 23, 739–745 (2013).

15. McKenna, J. J., Middlemiss, W. & Tarsha, M. S. Potential evolutionary, neurophysiological, and developmental origins of sudden infant death syndrome and inconsolable crying (colic): Is it about controlling breath?: Biocultural model of SIDS and inconsolable crying. *Fam Relat* 65, 239–258 (2016).

16. Gunnar, M. R. & Donzella, B. Social regulation of the cortisol levels in early human development. *Psychoneuroendocrinology* 27, 199–220 (2002).

17. Porges, S. W. Social engagement and attachment: A phylogenetic perspective. *Ann NY Acad Sci* 1008, 31–47 (2003); Porges, S. W. Polyvagal Theory: A biobehavioral journey to sociality. *Compr Psychoneuroendocrinology* 7, 100069 (2021); Porges, S. W. Polyvagal theory: A science of safety. *Frontiers Integr Neurosci* 16, 871227 (2022).

Chapter 8. When Your Baby Is Drowsy and Sleeping: Nurturing Sleep

1. Xie, L., et al. Sleep drives metabolite clearance from the adult brain. *Science* 342, 373–377 (2013); Dudai, Y., Karni, A. & Born, J. The consolidation and transformation of memory. *Neuron* 88, 20–32 (2015); Kim, T. W., Jeong, J.-H. & Hong, S.-C. The impact of sleep and circadian disturbance on hormones and metabolism. *Int J Endocrinol* 2015, 591729 (2014); Mostaghimi, L., Obermeyer, W. H., Ballamudi, B., Martinez-Gonzalez, D. & Benca, R. M. Effects of sleep deprivation on

wound healing. *J Sleep Res* 14, 213–219 (2005); Irwin, M. R. Sleep and inflammation: Partners in sickness and in health. *Nat Rev Immunol* 19, 702–715 (2019).

2. Crossley, N. A., et al. The hubs of the human connectome are generally implicated in the anatomy of brain disorders. *Brain* 137, 2382–2395 (2014); Cao, M., Huang, H. & He, Y. Developmental connectomics from infancy through early childhood. *Trends Neurosci* 40, 494–506 (2017); Wen, X., et al. First-year development of modules and hubs in infant brain functional networks. *Neuroimage* 185, 222–235 (2019); Lerner, R. E., et al. The Association between mother-infant bed-sharing practices and infant affect and behavior during the still face paradigm. *Infant Behavior and Development* 60, 101464 (2020); Barry E. S. Using complexity sciience to understand the role of co-sleepimg (bedsharing) in mother-infant co-regulatory processes. *Infant Behavior and Development* 67, 101723 (2022).

3. Shinar, Z., Akselrod, S., Dagan, Y. & Baharav, A. Autonomic changes during wake–sleep transition: A heart rate variability based approach. *Autonomic Neurosci* 130, 17–27 (2006).

4. Philbrook, L. E. & Teti, D. M. Associations between bedtime and nighttime parenting and infant cortisol in the first year. *Dev Psychobiol* 58, 1087–1100 (2016); Philbrook, L. E., et al. Maternal emotional availability at bedtime and infant cortisol at 1 and 3 months. *Early Hum Dev* 90, 595–605 (2012); White, B. P., Gunnar, M. R., Larson, M. C., Donzella, B. & Barr, R. G. Behavioral and physiological responsivity, sleep, and patterns of daily cortisol production in infants with and without colic. *Child Dev* 71, 862–877 (2000); Beijers, R., Riksen-Walraven, J. M. & Weerth, C. de. Cortisol regulation in 12-month-old human infants: Associations with the infants' early history of breastfeeding and co-sleeping. *Stress Amsterdam Neth* 16, 267–277 (2012).

5. Xie, L., et al. Sleep drives metabolite clearance from the adult brain. *Science* 342, 373–377 (2013); Dudai, Y., Karni, A. & Born, J. The consolidation and transformation of memory. *Neuron* 88, 20–32 (2015); Kim, T. W., Jeong, J.-H. & Hong, S.-C. The impact of sleep and circadian disturbance on hormones and metabolism. *Int J Endocrinol* 2015, 591729 (2014); Mostaghimi, L., Obermeyer, W. H., Ballamudi, B., Martinez-Gonzalez, D. & Benca, R. M. Effects of sleep deprivation on wound healing. *J Sleep Res* 14, 213–219 (2005); Irwin, M. R. Sleep and inflammation: Partners in sickness and in health. *Nat Rev Immunol* 19, 702–715 (2019).

6. Gettler, L. T., McKenna, J. J., McDade, T. W., Agustin, S. S. & Kuzawa, C. W. Does cosleeping contribute to lower testosterone levels in fathers? Evidence from the Philippines. *PLOS One* 7, e41559 (2012).

7. Cassels, T. & Rosier, J. G. The effectiveness of sleep training: Fact or fiction? *Clin Lact* 13, 65–76 (2022).

8. Loutzenhiser, L., Hoffman, J. & Beatch, J. Parental perceptions of the effectiveness of graduated extinction in reducing infant night-wakings. *J Reprod Infant Psyc* 32, 282–291 (2014).

9. Cassels, T. & Rosier, J. G. The effectiveness of sleep training: Fact or fiction? *Clin Lact* 13, 65–76 (2022); Douglas, P. S. & Hill, P. S. Behavioral sleep interventions in the first six months of life do not improve outcomes for mothers or infants: A

systematic review. *J Dev Behav Pediatrics* 34, 497–507 (2013); Galland, B. C., et al. Anticipatory guidance to prevent infant sleep problems within a randomised controlled trial: Infant, maternal and partner outcomes at 6 months of age. *BMJ Open* 7, e014908 (2017); Gradisar, M., et al. Behavioral interventions for infant sleep problems: A randomized controlled trial. *Pediatrics* 137, e20151486 (2016); Hall, W. A., et al. A randomized controlled trial of an intervention for infants' behavioral sleep problems. *BMC Pediatr* 15, 181 (2015).

10. Mantua, J. & Spencer, R. M. C. Exploring the nap paradox: Are mid-day sleep bouts a friend or foe? *Sleep Med* 37, 88–97 (2016).

11. Rosenwasser, A. M. & Turek, F. W. Neurobiology of circadian rhythm regulation. *Sleep Medicine Clin* 10, 403–412 (2015).

12. Joseph, D., et al. Getting rhythm: How do babies do it? *Arch Dis Child Fetal Neonatal Ed* 100, F50–54 (2014).

13. Huang, Z.-L., Urade, Y. & Hayaishi, O. The role of adenosine in the regulation of sleep. *Curr Top Med Chem* 11, 1047–1057 (2011).

14. Watamura, S. E., Donzella, B., Kertes, D. A. & Gunnar, M. R. Developmental changes in baseline cortisol activity in early childhood: Relations with napping and effortful control. *Dev Psychobiol* 45, 125–133 (2004); Weerth, C. de, Zijl, R. H. & Buitelaar, J. K. Development of cortisol circadian rhythm in infancy. *Early Hum Dev* 73, 39–52 (2003); Larson, M. C., Gunnar, M. R. & Hertsgaard, L. The effects of morning naps, car trips, and maternal separation on adrenocortical activity in human infants. *Child Dev* 62, 362–372 (1991).

15. Hirshkowitz, M., et al. National Sleep Foundation's sleep time duration recommendations: Methodology and results summary. *Sleep Heal* 1, 40–43 (2014).

16. Pennestri, M.-H., et al. Uninterrupted infant sleep, development, and maternal mood. *Pediatrics* 142, e20174330 (2018); Goodlin-Jones, B. L., Burnham, M. M., Gaylor, E. E. & Anders, T. F. Night waking, sleep-wake organization, and self-soothing in the first year of life. *J Dev Behav Pediatrics* 22, 226–233 (2001); Scher, A. Attachment and sleep: A study of night waking in 12-month-old infants. *Dev Psychobiol* 38, 274–285 (2001); Anders, T. F. & Keener, M. Developmental course of nighttime sleep-wake patterns in full-term and premature infants during the first year of life. I. *Sleep* 8, 173–192 (1985); Anders, T. F. Home-recorded sleep in 2- and 9-month-old infants. *J Amer Acad Child Psychiatry* 17, 421–432 (1978); Armstrong, K. L., Quinn, R. A. & Dadds, M. R. The sleep patterns of normal children. *Medical J Australia* 161, 202–206 (1994); Scher, A. A longitudinal study of night waking in the first year. *Child Care Heal Dev* 17, 295–302 (1991); Wooding, A. R., Boyd, J. & Geddins, D. C. Sleep patterns of New Zealand infants during the first 12 months of life. *J Paediatr Child H* 26, 85–88 (1990); Baumgartner, C. Psychomotor and social development of breast-fed and bottle-fed babies during their first year of life. *Acta Paediatr Hung* 25, 409–417 (1984); Paavonen, E. J., et al. Normal sleep development in infants: Findings from two large birth cohorts. *Sleep Med* 69, 145–154 (2019).

17. Bonnet, M. H. & Arand, D. L. EEG arousal norms by age. *J Clin Sleep Medicine* 3, 271–274 (2007).

18. Duncan, J. R., Ramirez, J.-M., Ramirez, S. & Anderson, T. M. Sudden infant death syndrome, sleep, and the physiology and paraphysiology of the respiratory network. In *SIDS: Sudden Infant and Early Childhood Death: The Past, the Present and the Future* (University of Adelaide Press, 2018), 615–640. doi:10.20851/sids-27.

19. Pennestri, M.-H., et al. Uninterrupted infant sleep, development, and maternal mood. *Pediatrics* 142, e20174330 (2018); Mindell, J. A., Leichman, E. S., DuMond, C. & Sadeh, A. Sleep and social-emotional development in infants and toddlers. *J Clin Child Adolesc Psychology* 46, 236–246 (2016); Price, A. M. H., Wake, M., Ukoumunne, O. C. & Hiscock, H. Five-year follow-up of harms and benefits of behavioral infant sleep intervention: Randomized trial. *Pediatrics* 130, 643–651 (2012).

20. Mileva-Seitz, V. R., Bakermans-Kranenburg, M. J., Battaini, C. & Luijk, M. P. C. M. Parent-child bed-sharing: The good, the bad, and the burden of evidence. *Sleep Med Rev* 32, 4–27 (2015).

21. Scammell, T. E., Arrigoni, E. & Lipton, J. O. Neural circuitry of wakefulness and sleep. *Neuron* 93, 747–765 (2017).

22. Hoyniak, C. P., et al. Child sleep and socioeconomic context in the development of cognitive abilities in early childhood. *Child Dev* 90, 1718–1737 (2018).

23. Anders, T. F. & Keener, M. Developmental course of nighttime sleep-wake patterns in full-term and premature infants during the first year of life. I. *Sleep* 8, 173–192 (1985); Mindell, J. A., Sadeh, A., Wiegand, B., How, T. H. & Goh, D. Y. T. Cross-cultural differences in infant and toddler sleep. *Sleep Med* 11, 274–280 (2009).

24. Rijt-Plooij, H. H. C. V. D. & Plooij, F. X. Infantile regressions: Disorganization and the onset of transition periods. *J Reprod Infant Psyc* 10, 129–149 (1992).

25. Mindell, K., et al. The evaluation and treatment of sleep disturbances in young children. *J Child Psychol Psychiatry* 34, 521–533 (1993).

26. Hoyniak, C. P., et al. Child sleep and socioeconomic context in the development of cognitive abilities in early childhood. *Child Dev* 90, 1718–1737 (2018).

27. Rosen, R. C., Rosekind, M., Rosevear, C., Cole, W. E. & Dement, W. C. Physician education in sleep and sleep disorders: A national survey of U.S. medical schools. *Sleep* 16, 249–254 (1993); Gruber, R., Constantin, E., Frappier, J. Y., Brouillette, R. T. & Wise, M. S. Training, knowledge, attitudes and practices of Canadian health care providers regarding sleep and sleep disorders in children. *Paediatr Child Healt* 22, 322–327 (2017).

28. Richardson, C., Ree, M., Bucks, R. S. & Gradisar, M. Paediatric sleep literacy in Australian health professionals. *Sleep Med* 81, 327–335 (2020).

29. Yates, J. Perspective: The long-term effects of light exposure on establishment of newborn circadian rhythm. *J Clin Sleep Medicine* 14, 1829–1830 (2018).

30. Yates. Perspective; Gilbert, S. S., Heuvel, C. J. van den, Ferguson, S. A. & Dawson, D. Thermoregulation as a sleep signalling system. *Sleep Med Rev* 8, 81–93 (2004); Someren, E. J. W. V. Mechanisms and functions of coupling between sleep and temperature rhythms. *Prog Brain Res* 153, 309–324 (2006); Barrett, J., Lack, L. & Morris, M. The sleep-evoked decrease of body temperature. *Sleep* 16, 93–99 (1993); Okamoto-Mizuno, K. & Mizuno, K. Effects of thermal environment on sleep and circadian rhythm. *J Physiol Anthropol* 31, 14 (2012).

31. Jeon, M., Dimitriou, D. & Halstead, E. J. A systematic review on cross-cultural comparative studies of sleep in young populations: The roles of cultural factors. *Int J Environ Res Public Health* 18, 2005 (2021); Bruni, O., et al. Longitudinal study of sleep behavior in normal infants during the first year of life. *J Clin Sleep Medicine* 10, 1119–1127 (2014); Mindell, J. A., Lee, C. & Sadeh, A. Young child and maternal sleep in the Middle East. *Sleep Med* 32, 75–82 (2017).

32. McKenna, J. J. & Gettler, L. T. There is no such thing as infant sleep, there is no such thing as breastfeeding, there is only breastsleeping. *Acta Paediatr* 105, 17–21 (2015).

33. White, B. P., Gunnar, M. R., Larson, M. C., Donzella, B. & Barr, R. G. Behavioral and physiological responsivity, sleep, and patterns of daily cortisol production in infants with and without colic. *Child Dev* 71, 862–877 (2000).

34. Moon, R. Y., et al. Sleep-related infant deaths: Updated 2022 recommendations for reducing infant deaths in the sleep environment. *Pediatrics* 150 (2022).

35. Sullivan, R., Perry, R., Sloan, A., Kleinhaus, K. & Burtchen, N. Infant bonding and attachment to the caregiver: Insights from basic and clinical science. *Clin Perinatol* 38, 643–655 (2011); Prochazkova, E. & Kret, M. E. Connecting minds and sharing emotions through mimicry: A neurocognitive model of emotional contagion. *Neurosci Biobehav Rev* 80, 99–114 (2016); Feldman, R., Magori-Cohen, R., Galili, G., Singer, M. & Louzoun, Y. Mother and infant coordinate heart rhythms through episodes of interaction synchrony. *Infant Behav Dev* 34, 569–577 (2011); Richard, C. A. & Mosko, S. S. Mother-infant bedsharing is associated with an increase in infant heart rate. *Sleep* 27, 507–511 (2004).

36. McKenna, J. J., Ball, H. L. & Gettler, L. T. Mother-infant cosleeping, breastfeeding and sudden infant death syndrome: What biological anthropology has discovered about normal infant sleep and pediatric sleep medicine. *Am J Phys Anthropol* Suppl 45, 133–161 (2007); McKenna, J. J., Mosko, S., Dungy, C. & McAninch, J. Sleep and arousal patterns of cosleeping human mother/infant pairs: A preliminary physiological study with implications for the study of sudden infant death syndrome (SIDS). *Am J Phys Anthropol* 83, 331–347 (1990); Mosko, S., McKenna, J., Dickel, M. & Hunt, L. Parent-infant cosleeping: The appropriate context for the study of infant sleep and implications for sudden infant death syndrome (SIDS) research. *J Behav Med* 16, 589–610 (1993); Hauck, F. R., et al. Sleep environment and the risk of sudden infant death syndrome in an urban population: The Chicago Infant Mortality Study. *Pediatrics* 111, 1207–1214 (2003).

37. Mosko, S., Richard, C. & McKenna, J. Maternal sleep and arousals during bedsharing with infants. *Sleep* 20, 142–150 (1997); Mosko, S., Richard, C. & McKenna, J. Infant arousals during mother-infant bed sharing: Implications for infant sleep and sudden infant death syndrome research. *Pediatrics* 100, 841–849 (1997).

38. Mosko, S., McKenna, J., Dickel, M. & Hunt, L. Parent-infant cosleeping: The appropriate context for the study of infant sleep and implications for sudden infant death syndrome (SIDS) research. *J Behav Med* 16, 589–610 (1993); Shinohara, H. & Kodama, H. Relationship between duration of crying/fussy behavior and actigraphic sleep measures in early infancy. *Early Hum Dev* 88, 847–852 (2012).

39. Hofer, M. A. & Shair, H. Control of sleep-wake states in the infant rat by features of the mother-infant relationship. *Dev Psychobiol* 15, 229–243 (1982); Reite, M. & Short, R. A. Nocturnal sleep in separated monkey infants. *Arch Gen Psychiat* 35, 1247 (1978).

40. Morgan, B. E., Horn, A. R. & Bergman, N. J. Should neonates sleep alone? *Biol Psychiat* 70, 817–825 (2010).

41. Feldman, R., Weller, A., Sirota, L. & Eidelman, A. I. Skin-to-skin contact (kangaroo care) promotes self-regulation in premature infants: Sleep-wake cyclicity, arousal modulation, and sustained exploration. *Dev Psychol* 38, 194–207 (2002).

42. Nishitani, S., et al. The calming effect of a maternal breast milk odor on the human newborn infant. *Neurosci Res* 63, 66–71 (2008); Shenfield, T., Trehub, S. E. & Nakata, T. Maternal singing modulates infant arousal. *Psychol Music* 31, 365–375 (2003).

43. Baddock, S. A., Galland, B. C., Bolton, D. P. G., Williams, S. M. & Taylor, B. J. Differences in infant and parent behaviors during routine bed sharing compared with cot sleeping in the home setting. *Pediatrics* 117, 1599–1607 (2006).

44. Richard, C. A. & Mosko, S. S. Mother-infant bedsharing is associated with an increase in infant heart rate. *Sleep* 27, 507–511 (2004); Gunnar, M. R. Social buffering of stress in development: A career perspective. *Perspect Psychol Sci* 12, 355–373 (2017); Uvnas-Moberg, K., Handlin, L. & Petersson, M. Self-soothing behaviors with particular reference to oxytocin release induced by non-noxious sensory stimulation. *Front Psychol* 5, 1529 (2014).

45. Gunnar. Social buffering of stress in development; Middlemiss, W., Granger, D. A., Goldberg, W. A. & Nathans, L. Asynchrony of mother-infant hypothalamic-pituitary-adrenal axis activity following extinction of infant crying responses induced during the transition to sleep. *Early Hum Dev* 88, 227–232 (2012).

46. Lewin, M., et al. Early life trauma has lifelong consequences for sleep and behavior. *Sci Rep* 9, 16701 (2019).

47. Feng, P., Vurbic, D., Wu, Z. & Strohl, K. P. Brain orexins and wake regulation in rats exposed to maternal deprivation. *Brain Res* 1154, 163–172 (2007).

48. Mosko, S., Richard, C. & McKenna, J. Maternal sleep and arousals during bedsharing with infants. *Sleep* 20, 142–50 (1997).

49. McKenna, J. J., Mosko, S., Dungy, C. & McAninch, J. Sleep and arousal patterns of cosleeping human mother/infant pairs: A preliminary physiological study with implications for the study of sudden infant death syndrome (SIDS). *Am J Phys Anthropol* 83, 331–347 (1990); Mosko, S., McKenna, J., Dickel, M. & Hunt, L. Parent-infant cosleeping: The appropriate context for the study of infant sleep and implications for sudden infant death syndrome (SIDS) research. *J Behav Med* 16, 589–610 (1993); Tsai, S.-Y., Barnard, K. E., Lentz, M. J. & Thomas, K. A. Mother-infant activity synchrony as a correlate of the emergence of circadian rhythm. *Biol Res Nurs* 13, 80–88 (2010).

50. Keller, M. A. & Goldberg, W. A. Co-sleeping: Help or hindrance for young children's independence? *Infant Child Dev* 13, 369–388 (2004); Okami, P., Weisner, T. & Olmstead, R. Outcome correlates of parent-child bedsharing: an eighteen-year longitudinal study. *J Dev Behav Pediatrics* 23, 244–253 (2002).

51. Forbes, J. F., Weiss, D. S. & Folen, R. A. The cosleeping habits of military children. *Mil Med* 157, 196–200 (1992).

52. Gilmour, H., Ramage-Morin, P. L. & Wong, S. L. Infant bed sharing in Canada. *Health Rep* 30, 13–19 (2019); Bombard, J. M., et al. Vital signs: Trends and disparities in infant safe sleep practices—United States, 2009–2015. *MMWR Morbidity Mortal Wkly Rep* 67, 39–46 (2018).

53. Philbrook, L. E. & Teti, D. M. Associations between bedtime and nighttime parenting and infant cortisol in the first year. *Dev Psychobiol* 58, 1087–1100 (2016); Philbrook, L. E., et al. Maternal emotional availability at bedtime and infant cortisol at 1 and 3 months. *Early Hum Dev* 90, 595–605 (2012).

54. Philbrook & Teti. Associations between bedtime and nighttime parenting and infant cortisol in the first year; Philbrook et al. Maternal emotional availability at bedtime and infant cortisol at 1 and 3 months.

Chapter 9. How to Nurture Your Changing Parent Brain

1. Lillas, C. & Turnbull, J. *Infant Child Mental Health Early Intervention A Neurorelational Framework for Interdisciplinary Practice* (Norton, 2009).

2. Porges, S. W. Social engagement and attachment: A phylogenetic perspective. *Ann NY Acad Sci* 1008, 31–47 (2003); Porges, S. W. Polyvagal theory: A biobehavioral journey to sociality. *Compr Psychoneuroendocrinology* 7, 100069 (2021); Porges, S. W. Polyvagal theory: A science of safety. *Frontiers Integr Neurosci* 16, 871227 (2022).

3. Prochazkova, E. & Kret, M. E. Connecting minds and sharing emotions through mimicry: A neurocognitive model of emotional contagion. *Neurosci Biobehav Rev* 80, 99–114 (2016); Waters, S. F., West, T. V. & Mendes, W. B. Stress contagion: physiological covariation between mothers and infants. *Psychol Sci* 25, 934–942 (2014).

4. Tang, Y.-Y., H.lzel, B. K. & Posner, M. I. The neuroscience of mindfulness meditation. *Nat Rev Neurosci* 16, 213–225 (2015).

5. Noroña-Zhou, A. N., et al. The effects of a prenatal mindfulness intervention on infant autonomic and behavioral reactivity and regulation. *Psychosom Med* 84, 525–535 (2022); Epel, E., et al. Effects of a mindfulness-based intervention on distress, weight gain, and glucose control for pregnant low-income women: A quasi-experimental trial using the ORBIT model. *Int J Behav Med* 26, 461–473 (2019).

6. Volz, K. G. & Cramon, D. Y. von. What neuroscience can tell about intuitive processes in the context of perceptual discovery. *J Cognitive Neurosci* 18, 2077–2087 (2006).

7. Saper, C. B. & Lowell, B. B. The hypothalamus. *Curr Biology* 24, R1111–R1116 (2014).

8. Surget, A. & Belzung, C. Adult hippocampal neurogenesis shapes adaptation and improves stress response: A mechanistic and integrative perspective. *Mol Psychiatr* 27, 403–421 (2021).

9. Masento, N. A., Golightly, M., Field, D. T., Butler, L. T. & Reekum, C. M. van. Effects of hydration status on cognitive performance and mood. *Brit J Nutr* 111, 1841–1852 (2014).

10. Bratman, G. N., Hamilton, J. P., Hahn, K. S., Daily, G. C. & Gross, J. J. Nature experience reduces rumination and subgenual prefrontal cortex activation. *Proc Natl Acad Sci USA* 112, 8567–8572 (2015); Hedblom, M., et al. Reduction of physiological stress by urban green space in a multisensory virtual experiment. *Sci Rep* 9, 10113 (2018).

11. Sowndhararajan, K. & Kim, S. Influence of fragrances on human psychophysiological activity: With special reference to human electroencephalographic response. *Sci Pharm* 84, 724–751 (2016).

12. Katerndahl, D. A., Bell, I. R., Palmer, R. F. & Miller, C. S. Chemical intolerance in primary care settings: Prevalence, comorbidity, and outcomes. *Ann Fam Med* 10, 357–365 (2012).

13. Micheli, L., Ceccarelli, M., D'Andrea, G. & Tirone, F. Depression and adult neurogenesis: Positive effects of the antidepressant fluoxetine and of physical exercise. *Brain Res Bull* 143, 181–193 (2018).

14. Liu, P. Z. & Nusslock, R. Exercise-mediated neurogenesis in the hippocampus via BDNF. *Front Neurosci* 12, 52 (2018).

15. Xie, L., et al. Sleep drives metabolite clearance from the adult brain. *Science* 342, 373–377 (2013); Dudai, Y., Karni, A. & Born, J. The consolidation and transformation of memory. *Neuron* 88, 20–32 (2015); Krause, A. J., et al. The sleep-deprived human brain. *Nat Rev Neurosci* 18, 404–418 (2017).

16. Uvnas-Moberg, K., Handlin, L. & Petersson, M. Self-soothing behaviors with particular reference to oxytocin release induced by non-noxious sensory stimulation. *Front Psychol* 5, 1529 (2014).

17. Kyeong, S., Kim, J., Kim, D. J., Kim, H. E. & Kim, J.-J. Effects of gratitude meditation on neural network functional connectivity and brain-heart coupling. *Sci Rep* 7, 5058 (2017).

18. Creswell, J. D., Way, B. M., Eisenberger, N. I. & Lieberman, M. D. Neural correlates of dispositional mindfulness during affect labeling. *Psychosom Med* 69, 560–565 (2007); Lieberman, M. D., et al. Putting feelings into words: Affect labeling disrupts amygdala activity in response to affective stimuli. *Psychol Sci* 18, 421–428 (2007).

19. Lee, A., et al. Maternal care in infancy and the course of limbic development. *Dev Cogn Neuros* 40, 100714 (2019); Strathearn, L., et al. Long-term cognitive, psychological, and health outcomes associated with child abuse and neglect. *Pediatrics* 146, e20200438 (2020); Vachon, D. D., Krueger, R. F., Rogosch, F. A. & Cicchetti, D. Assessment of the harmful psychiatric and behavioral effects of different forms of child maltreatment. *JAMA Psychiat* 72, 1135 (2015); Dobson, O., Price, E. L. & DiTommaso, E. Recollected caregiver sensitivity and adult attachment interact to predict mental health and coping. *Pers Indiv Differ* 187, 111398 (2022).

20. Tang, Y.-Y., H.lzel, B. K. & Posner, M. I. The neuroscience of mindfulness meditation. *Nat Rev Neurosci* 16, 213–225 (2015).

21. Yackle, K., et al. Breathing control center neurons that promote arousal in mice. *Science* 355, 1411–1415 (2017); Sevoz-Couche, C. & Laborde, S. Heart rate variability and slow-paced breathing: When coherence meets resonance. *Neurosci Biobehav Rev* 135, 104576 (2022); Magnon, V., Dutheil, F. & Vallet, G. T. Benefits from one

session of deep and slow breathing on vagal tone and anxiety in young and older adults. *Sci Rep* 11, 19267 (2021).

22. Nair, S., Sagar, M., Sollers, J., Consedine, N. & Broadbent, E. Do slumped and upright postures affect stress responses? A randomized trial. *Health Psychol* 34, 632–641 (2015).

23. Kyeong, S., Kim, J., Kim, D. J., Kim, H. E. & Kim, J.-J. Effects of gratitude meditation on neural network functional connectivity and brain-heart coupling. *Sci Rep* 7, 5058 (2017); Kini, P., Wong, J., McInnis, S., Gabana, N. & Brown, J. W. The effects of gratitude expression on neural activity. *Neuroimage* 128, 1–10 (2016); Takano, R. & Nomura, M. Neural representations of awe: Distinguishing common and distinct neural mechanisms. *Emotion* 22, 669–677 (2022).

24. Covey, S. R., Merrill, A. R. & Merrill, R. R. *First Things First* (Simon and Schuster, 1995).

25. Creswell, J. D., Way, B. M., Eisenberger, N. I. & Lieberman, M. D. Neural correlates of dispositional mindfulness during affect labeling. *Psychosom Med* 69, 560–565 (2007); Taylor, J. B. *My Stroke of Insight: A Brain Scientist's Personal Journey* (Penguin, 2009).

26. Lindsey Lockett. Personal communication, 2022. https://lindseylockett.com.

Conclusion

1. Brito, N. H., et al. Paid maternal leave is associated with infant brain function at 3 months of age. *Child Dev* 93, 1030–1043 (2022).

2. Heckman, J. J., Moon, S., Pinto, R. R., Savelyev, P. A. & Yavitz, A. The rate of return to the High/Scope Perry Preschool Program. *SSRN Electron J* (2009) doi:10.2139/ssrn.1501969; Karoly, L. A. Toward standardization of benefit-cost analyses of early childhood interventions. *SSRN Electron J* (2010) doi:10.2139/ssrn.1753326; Karoly, L., Kilburn, M. & Cannon, J. *Early Childhood Interventions: Proven Results, Future Promise* (RAND Corporation, 2005) doi:10.7249/mg341; Cunha, F., Heckman, J. J., Lochner, L. & Masterov, D. V. Chapter 12. Interpreting the evidence on life cycle skill formation. *Handb Econ Educ* 1, 697–812 (2006); Cunha, F. & Heckman, J. J. The technology of skill formation. *SSRN Electron J* (2007) doi:10.2139/ssrn.958713; Heckman, J. J. Schools, skills, and synapses. *Econ Inq* 46, 289–324 (2008); Karoly, L. A. Toward standardization of benefit-cost analysis of early childhood interventions. *J Benefit-Cost Analysis* 3, 1–45 (2012).

RESOURCES

Chapter 4

POSTPARTUM DEPRESSION (PPD), POSTPARTUM ANXIETY (PPA), AND POSTPARTUM PSYCHOSIS RESOURCES

Postpartum International: www.postpartum.net

Postpartum Depression: www.postpartumdepression.org/postpartum -depression/

Search on the internet for "Edinburgh Postnatal Depression Scale."

POSTPARTUM MENTAL HEALTH PLAN

1. Family members, friends, or professionals who will support you and/or your partner in your home if either of you experience a perinatal mood issue.

    Person 1 name and phone number:

    Person 2 name and phone number:

    Person 3 name and phone number:

2. A perinatal mental health professional who can provide regular therapeutic sessions with you and/or your partner.

    Perinatal mental health professional name and phone number for you:

    Perinatal mental health professional name and phone number for your partner:

3. A psychiatrist or doctor who can provide a prescription to you and/or your partner as needed.

    Psychiatrist or physician name and phone number for you:

Psychiatrist or physician name and phone number for your partner:

4. Many hospitals have a perinatal mood program for anyone who qualifies as high risk for a perinatal mood issue. If there is a special program at your local hospital, check to see if you qualify to be part of it.

Name of the hospital program and phone number:

Chapter 5

TOPICS TO DISCUSS WITH CAREGIVERS

1. Face-to-face interactions, when your baby is alert and ready to communicate.
2. No shaming or name-calling, acceptance of all emotional expressions.
3. Nurtured empathy to link behavior, feelings, and needs.
4. Co-regulation at all times of day when baby is experiencing stress.
5. Co-regulation to fall asleep and upon all wakings.
6. Close sleep in a safe sleep environment.

Chapter 6

BABYWEARING RESOURCES

Carrying Matters: https://www.carryingmatters.co.uk

NINO—Neuroscience for Improved Neonatal Outcomes: https://ninobirth.org

Kangaroo Mother Care: http://kangaroomothercare.com

Chapter 8

NORMAL INFANT SLEEP RESOURCES

Little Sparklers (home of The Beyond Sleep Training Project) https://www.littlesparklers.org

Basis: www.basisonline.org.uk/

Dr. James McKenna: cosleeping.nd.edu/

La Leche League International: https://www.llli.org

UNICEF UK—Caring for Your Baby at Night: www.unicef.org.uk

/babyfriendly/baby-friendly-resources/sleep-and-night-time
-resources/caring-for-your-baby-at-night/

Lullaby Trust: www.lullabytrust.org.uk/

IDEAL DAY FOR INFANT SLEEP

This is a guide that outlines an ideal day for nurtured infant sleep for a baby about six months old. Take from it what will work for your life.

Morning: Baby wakes up naturally to sunlight and goes outside for a fifteen-minute walk. Feeds outside or near a window, explores and plays on the floor in natural light.

First nap: Parent observes tired cue of rubbing eyes and change of mood. Does a fast sleep routine of diaper change, sing a song, and feed to sleep. Blinds stay open to continue natural light (no blackout blinds). Baby wakes from nap on their own.

Awake time: Happens near natural light or outside, includes nurtured connection, nurtured stress, play, exploration, feeding, movement, books, socializing.

Second nap: Parent observes tired cues. Fast sleep routine. Rocking to sleep. Blinds stay open to continue natural light (no blackout blinds). Baby wakes from nap on their own.

Awake time: A midday walk or playtime outside for fifteen minutes. Happens near natural light, includes nurtured connection, nurtured stress, play, exploration, feeding, movement, books, socializing.

Third nap: Parent observes tired cues. Puts baby in a carrier and goes for a one-hour walk. Transfers baby to a bed when they get home. Baby's windows stay open to continue natural light (no blackout blinds). Baby wakes on their own.

Awake time: Happens near natural light, includes nurtured connection, nurtured stress, play, exploration, feeding, movement, books, socializing.

Evening: As the sun goes down, lights are dimmed.

Bedtime: Parent observes tired cues, does a longer sleep routine, changes diaper, pajamas, book, singing, and feeding to sleep.

Night waking one: Parent, who has not yet gone to sleep, sees baby wake on the monitor, nurtures back to sleep by feeding and rocking.

Night waking two: Parent has gone to sleep. Baby sleeps on a sidecar bed, parent puts hand on baby and they fall back to sleep.

Night waking three: Baby joins breastfeeding mom in bed, feeds and falls back to sleep.

Morning: Baby wakes naturally to sunlight.

Chapter 9

SAMPLE STRESS JOURNAL

For each event, use self-awareness to reflect on your stress state and create a stress rating with 1 being low stress and 10 being high stress. Be curious about your emotions, thoughts, and body sensations. Use Growing SPACE and I CARE to make a plan to bring you to a safety state in high-stress experiences, and enjoy low-stress experiences.

EVENT	STRESS RATING	EMOTIONS	THOUGHTS	BODY SENSATION	SPACE Plan	I CARE Plan
Morning Routine	7/10 Fight State	Irritated	I want to run away	Tense Heart racing	Feel it, Shake it out, Breathe	Water, breakfast, breathing
Playtime	0/10 Safety State	Loving, calm, playful, amused	I love being with my baby	Relaxed, Smiling	Feel it	Aware of emotions
Baby Class	9/10 Freeze State	Overwhelmed, detached	I want to disappear	Low energy hard to speak	Stand up and sway with baby	Aware of emotions

Find additional blanks on my website: www.nurture-neuroscience.com.

YOGA NIDRA RECORDING

See www.nurture-neuroscience.com.

DOMESTIC VIOLENCE RESOURCES

1. Canada
   - Government of Canada—Stop Family Violence: www.canada
     .ca/en/public-health/services/health-promotion/stop-family
     -violence.html
2. United States
   - Department of Justice—Domestic Violence: www.justice
     .gov/ovw/domestic-violence
   - National Coalition Against Domestic Violence—Resources:
     https://ncadv.org/resources
3. UK
   - Gov.uk—Domestic Abuse: How to Get Help: www.gov.uk
     /guidance/domestic-abuse-how-to-get-help
4. Australia
   - WA.gov.au—Family and Domestic Violence Services
     and Resources: www.wa.gov.au/organisation/department
     -of-communities/family-and-domestic-violence-services
     -and-resources
5. Other countries
   - On the internet search for "domestic violence" and the name
     of your country. Contact emergency services or local groups
     supporting survivors of domestic violence.

APPENDIXES

FEELINGS INVENTORY

The following are words we use when we want to express a combination of emotional states and physical sensations. This list is neither exhaustive nor definitive. It is meant as a starting place to support anyone who wishes to engage in a process of deepening self-discovery and to facilitate greater understanding and connection between people.

There are two parts to this list: feelings we may have when our needs are being met, and feelings we may have when our needs are not being met.

Feelings When Your Needs Are Satisfied

Affectionate

compassionate	openhearted	warm
friendly	sympathetic	
loving	tender	

Engaged

absorbed	enchanted	intrigued
alert	entranced	involved
curious	fascinated	spellbound
engrossed	interested	stimulated

Hopeful

expectant	encouraged	optimistic

Confident

empowered	proud	secure
open	safe	

Appendix

Excited

amazed	dazzled	invigorated
animated	eager	lively
ardent	energetic	passionate
aroused	enthusiastic	surprised
astonished	giddy	vibrant

Grateful

appreciative	thankful
moved	touched

Inspired

amazed	awed	wonder

Joyful

amused	happy	tickled
delighted	jubilant	
glad	pleased	

Exhilarated

blissful	enthralled	rapturous
ecstatic	exuberant	thrilled
elated	radiant	

Peaceful

calm	fulfilled	serene
clearheaded	mellow	still
comfortable	quiet	tranquil
centered	relaxed	trusting
content	relieved	
equanimous	satisfied	

Refreshed

enlivened	renewed	restored
rejuvenated	rested	revived

Feelings When Your Needs Are Not Satisfied

Afraid

apprehensive	mistrustful	suspicious
dread	panicked	terrified
foreboding	petrified	wary
frightened	scared	worried

Annoyed

aggravated	displeased	impatient
dismayed	exasperated	irritated
disgruntled	frustrated	irked

Angry

enraged	indignant	outraged
furious	irate	resentful
incensed	livid	

Aversion

animosity	disgusted	horrified
appalled	dislike	hostile
contempt	hate	repulsed

Confused

ambivalent	hesitant	puzzled
baffled	lost	torn
bewildered	mystified	
dazed	perplexed	

Disconnected

alienated	detached	removed
aloof	distant	uninterested
apathetic	distracted	withdrawn
bored	indifferent	
cold	numb	

Appendix

Disquiet

agitated	restless	uncomfortable
alarmed	shocked	uneasy
discombobulated	startled	unnerved
disconcerted	surprised	unsettled
disturbed	troubled	upset
perturbed	turbulent	
rattled	turmoil	

Embarrassed

ashamed	flustered	mortified
chagrined	guilty	self-conscious

Fatigue

beat	lethargic	weary
burnt out	listless	worn out
depleted	sleepy	
exhausted	tired	

Pain

agony	grief	miserable
anguished	heartbroken	regretful
bereaved	hurt	remorseful
devastated	lonely	

Sad

depressed	discouraged	hopeless
dejected	disheartened	melancholy
despair	forlorn	unhappy
despondent	gloomy	wretched
disappointed	heavy-hearted	

Tense

anxious	distressed	edgy
cranky	distraught	fidgety

frazzled	nervous	stressed out
irritable	overwhelmed	
jittery	restless	

Vulnerable

fragile	insecure	sensitive
guarded	leery	shaky
helpless	reserved	

Yearning

envious	longing	pining
jealous	nostalgic	wistful

Source: © 2005 by Center for Nonviolent Communication | Website: www.cnvc.org |
Email: cnvc@cnvc.org | Phone: +1.505.244.4041

NEEDS INVENTORY

The following list of needs is neither exhaustive nor definitive. It is meant as a starting place to support anyone who wishes to engage in a process of deepening self-discovery and to facilitate greater understanding and connection between people.

Connection

acceptance	consideration	security
affection	consistency	stability
appreciation	empathy	support
belonging	inclusion	to know and be
cooperation	intimacy	known
communication	love	to see and be seen
closeness	mutuality	to understand and
community	nurturing	be understood
companionship	respect/self-respect	trust
compassion	safety	warmth

Physical Well-Being

air	rest/sleep	shelter
food	sexual expression	touch
movement/exercise	safety	water

Honesty

authenticity	integrity	presence

Play

joy	humor

Peace

beauty	equality	order
communion	harmony	
ease	inspiration	

Autonomy

choice	independence	spontaneity
freedom	space	

Meaning

awareness	creativity	mourning
celebration of life	discovery	participation
challenge	efficacy	purpose
clarity	effectiveness	self-expression
competence	growth	stimulation
consciousness	hope	to matter
contribution	learning	understanding

Source: © 2005 by Center for Nonviolent Communication | Website: www.cnvc.org | Email: cnvc@cnvc.org | Phone: +1.505.244.4041

EMOTION AND NEEDS INQUIRY FOR PARENTS

Here is a practice to help you begin to be aware of your emotions and understand that often there are needs underlying your emotions. The next time you feel a big emotion, positive- or negative-feeling, try: Feel it, move it, name it, and plan it.

Feel it: Close your eyes, breathe into your belly, and feel the emotion. Pay attention to the sensations in your body for about ninety seconds as you breathe. If you have thoughts, direct your attention back to the sensations in your body and your breath. Note: Where do you feel this in your body: your chest, your throat, your stomach? What happens when you experience it and breathe? If your baby is around, you can tell them, "I'm feeling a big emotion. I'm going to breathe as I feel it."

Move it: You might need to express these emotions. You might need to move to express your emotions. You can run, jump, lie down, give yourself a hug, get a hug, have a nap. If your emotion could make a sound and have a movement, what would they be? If your baby is around, you can tell them, "I'm going to move my emotions." Make sure you are clear that you are expressing your feelings, and your baby is not causing your feelings.

Name it: Name your emotions and needs. Use an emotions list (page 269) and identify the names of the emotions that you're feeling. You can say them out loud, write them down, or tell someone how you're feeling. Then look at a needs list (page 274). You can tell your baby, "I'm going to move to express how I'm feeling or I'm going to write down my feelings." See if you can identify what needs might be underlying your behavior and emotions. Do you need something physical like food, water, movement, rest, safety, touch? Do you need something emotional like connection, empathy, nurture, peace, choice, freedom, space, reflection, time? If your baby is there, you can tell them, "I'm feeling sad. I need a big glass of water, a nap, and some time with my best friend."

Plan it: Once you know your needs, you can create a plan to meet your needs. This is essential to charge your "nurture reservoir" so you are set up to nurture yourself and your baby. Make a plan as you answer these questions:

Can you meet your needs on your own?
If yes, how will you meet your needs today, this week, this month?
If not, who can you trust to help you meet your needs?
What will you say when you ask for support?
How will you feel when your needs are met?

Belly Breathing Resource

Guided recordings are available at www.nurture-neuroscience.com.

This exercise can be done standing up or sitting down, and pretty much anywhere at any time. All you have to do is be still and focus on your breath for a few breaths, or up to a few minutes. We are going to inhale and exhale through the nose.

1. Start by breathing in and out slowly from your nose.
2. Place a hand on your belly and a hand on your heart.
3. Notice how your breath feels on the inhale. Push out your belly like a balloon.
4. Notice how your breath feels on the exhale. Feel your hand move as your belly balloon deflates.
5. Breathe in and out, letting your breath flow effortlessly in and out of your body. Your belly expanding and relaxing like a balloon.
6. Notice how the breath gives you energy on the inhale.
7. Notice how the breath relaxes you on the exhale.
8. Let all thoughts go; let them drift away and come back to your breath.

GROWING SPACE RESOURCE

S—Self-awareness: Develop awareness to know when you're feeling a little stress, medium stress, or high stress.

P—Pause your immediate reaction: Use your breath, sing or speak in a low tone, or walk away to avoid being reactive.

A—Aware of the sensations: Feel the emotion; notice where the sensation is in your body; if you have thoughts, bring your attention back to your body for about ninety seconds. Relax your jaw and shoulders, shift your body posture from closed to open, expose your belly, and breathe as you feel it.

C—Create movement: This is bottom-up regulation—regulation from the body. Stay with the body. Move from there. How can you release your stress from your body?

Fight or flight

1. Move: Shake your body, dance, jump, do jumping jacks, run, do squats, yawn—movement uses the energy that is mobilized by the stress system to lower stress and make you feel calmer.
2. Embody your emotion: If your emotion had a physical movement or sound, what would it be?

Freeze

1. Music: Play your favorite song or play an instrument.
2. Singing or humming: Sing or hum your favorite song.
3. Movement: Sway slowly or dance.
4. Crossing your midline: Do shoulder taps or thigh taps across your body.

5. Body posture from closed to open: Expose your belly and breathe.
6. Put cold water on your face or body.

E—Emotion processing: This is top-down regulation—regulation from the thinking brain. It helps to have your body online first before moving to the thinking brain because the thinking brain can make up elaborate stories that you get stuck in. Feel the emotion and move from the body first and then name your feelings and needs. Use the lists on pages 269 and 274.

NURTURE IN PREGNANCY

1. Practice I CARE and Growing SPACE to manage your stress (see chapter 9).
   o Make a daily plan to practice I CARE.
   o Use Growing SPACE when you're feeling big emotions.
2. Meet your basic needs.
   o Clean water
   o Nourishing food
   o Nature and air
   o Movement
   o Sleep and rest
   o Touch and connection
   o Safety
3. Meet your emotional needs:
   o See The Center for Nonviolent Communication resources on pages 269 and 274.
4. Communicate with your baby—songs, reading, talking.
5. Connect with emotional support—doula, partner, friends, or family.
   o Look into doula support for your pregnancy, birth, and postpartum support.
   o Who in your life might support you emotionally? Who is nurturing?
6. Connect with physical support—doula, massage, acupuncture, body work, pelvic floor physiotherapy.
   o Invest in taking care of your physical body, find practitioners who specialize in perinatal care.

7. Find trauma-informed care providers—midwives, obstetricians.
   o Does your care provider understand trauma-informed care, consent in care, and your emotional experience?
8. Find a trauma-informed therapist.
   o Invest in taking care of your emotional and mental health in pregnancy, postpartum, and your child's early years.
   o Meet several therapists and choose someone who you connect with.
9. Find education for pregnancy, birth, postpartum, infant sleep, infant feeding.
   o Educate yourself before your baby arrives when you are able to focus on learning and integrating information.
10. Make a postpartum plan for mental health, infant feeding support, pelvic floor physiotherapy, postpartum doula.
    o Fill out your postpartum mental health plan (see page 261).
    o Find an IBCLC to support you prenatally and postpartum.
    o Create a postpartum plan—who will take care of you when you bring your baby home?

NURTURE IN BIRTH

1. Find trauma-informed medical professionals—midwife, doctor, nurse.
   - Does your care provider understand trauma-informed care, consent in care, and your emotional experience?
2. Get emotional and physical support in birth—doula, partner, friends, or family.
   - Emotional and physical support in birth reduces interventions and trauma, and helps you be regulated to meet your baby and start nurturing.
3. Find the birthing location that feels safest to you—hospital, birthing center, home birth.
   - Use your intuition to decide to birth in the place that feels safest to you.
4. Aim for zero separation—baby skin-to-skin as soon as possible and as long as possible on the mother or birthing person, father or parent.
   - Baby's default position is skin-to-skin.
5. Limit time in a bassinet—default position is on a person skin-to-skin under a blanket.
6. Have all medical procedures done while baby is skin-to-skin.
   - Advocate for your baby to be on your chest for all procedures.
7. Breastfeed, chestfeed, or bottle feed on cue.
   - Advocate to feed your baby on cue.
   - Plan to provide human milk to your newborn baby, by breastfeeding or chestfeeding, pumping, or donor milk.

8. Baby sleeps on mother or birthing person, or father.
    o Use a wrap to have baby sleep on your body, or set up a safe bedsharing, sidecar bed, or crib right beside your bed.
9. Meet your basic needs and emotional needs.
    o Plan support so you have time for yourself.
10. Process your birth story.
    o Tell your birth story to your doula, friends, family, or support group. Include how you felt, what you wish you could have said or done, what you were happy about, what you were sad or angry about.

NURTURE IN THE NICU

1. Babies and parents in the NICU benefit tremendously from as much skin-to-skin holding as possible.
   - Skin-to-skin means that the baby is naked except for a diaper and held vertically on the naked chest of a parent. This is possible and beneficial for almost all babies in the NICU, including the youngest premature infants.
   - Advocate by telling the NICU doctors and nurses you need to hold your baby skin-to-skin as much as possible, the majority of the time you are there. When parents are resting, other adults, like family members or friends, can hold your baby skin-to-skin.
   - Advocate to hold your baby skin-to-skin (with breastfeeding/ chestfeeding if available) for all painful medical procedures.
2. Babies in the NICU benefit from reduced sensory input.
   - Advocate by communicating your need for dim lights, quiet voices, muting of unnecessary beeping or loud sounds.
3. Babies benefit from drinking human milk in the NICU.
   - If your goals are to breastfeed/chestfeed or pump milk from your body, find an IBCLC to support your feeding in and out of the hospital.
   - If breastfeeding/chestfeeding is possible, advocate to breastfeed/chestfeed your baby as much as possible. This is possible and beneficial to almost all babies in the NICU, including the youngest premature babies.
   - If pumping milk is possible, advocate to feed your baby pumped milk as much as possible.

- o If you are not producing milk, advocate for your baby to receive human milk from a milk bank or a milk donor.

4. Babies benefit from your smell when you are resting.
    - o When you are resting out of the NICU, leave your scent with your baby. You can leave behind a worn T-shirt, or you can put a baby blanket on your skin and wrap your baby in it when you leave. If breastfeeding/chestfeeding, you can put your milk on your baby's sheets or their hat so they can smell it.
    - o Ask for your baby to sleep on their stomach when alone. This is only safe in the NICU as babies' vitals are monitored, but it is not safe to put a baby on their stomach for sleep at home.

5. Parents benefit from meeting their needs.
    - o Make sure you have plenty of water and healthy food.
    - o Rest in or out of the NICU is vital for you. If you can't sleep in the NICU, go home to sleep.
    - o Take your pain medication on time if applicable.

WHEN YOU GET HOME FROM THE NICU

Touch: Invest in a stretchy newborn wrap and wear your baby skin-to-skin as much as possible. Hold your baby for naps. Hold your baby as much as possible. Can be done by parents, family, and friends.

Sleep: Set up a safe sleeping surface right next to your bed, as close to you as possible, where your baby can hear your breathing and smell you. Allow your baby to sleep on cue, whenever they are tired. Find resources and support for normal infant sleep (see www.nuture-neuroscience.com /network).

Feed: Feed your baby on cue. Continue your support with an IBCLC for breastfeeding/chestfeeding or bottle feeding. Learn paced bottle feeding if using a bottle.

Play: When your baby is alert and awake, hold them close and speak to them, repeat their sounds, make faces, copy the faces they make. When they look away, give them a break; they will look back when they are ready to play again.

Environment: Use minimal beauty products and choose unscented products so your baby can smell you; remove any artificial scents from the home. Use a HEPA air filter.

Nurture Postpartum and Infancy

1. Rest and sleep as much as you can.
   o Set up safe sleep environments where you and your baby can get optimal rest.
   o Consult an infant and family sleep specialist if you need support (see my website).

2. Meet your basic needs and emotional needs.
   o Practice I CARE and Growing SPACE.
3. Ask for help—food, cleaning, laundry, walking the dog.
   o Practice asking family and friends for help, or hire professionals.
4. Get support from IBCLC regardless of how you feed your baby.
   o Connect with an IBCLC or lactation professional to optimize and support infant feeding.
5. Process your birth—tell your birth story.
   o Connect with a postpartum doula, a professional specializing in narrative therapy, or a support group to process your conception, pregnancy, birth, and postpartum experiences.
6. Assess if you need or your baby needs to see a professional.
   o For parents: mental health, wound healing, pelvic floor, massage.
   o For baby: feeding and digestion, physical discomfort.
7. Keep your baby skin-to-skin as much as possible.
   o Your baby can sleep on you, feed on you, play on you; you are their home.
8. Let your baby feed when they show hunger cues.
9. Give your baby sleep opportunities when they show tired cues, and sleep close.
10. Give your baby opportunities for baby chats when they are awake and alert.

ACKNOWLEDGMENTS

My passion for neuroscience and the art of nurture comes from the people in my life who were simultaneously nurturers and influenced by low nurture. I want to thank my parents, Fern and Lorne; my brother, Asher; my grandparents, Marcia, Moe, Anne, and Sol; my aunts and uncles; my friends who have been family; and all of my ancestors for the resilience, experience, knowledge, and heartbreak that lives in me.

Fern—my mom, you started a cycle of intergenerational nurture in our family and guided me on a path to study and embody the power of nurture. You nurtured me day and night, breastfed me through all of infancy, and bedshared with me. This set me up to know in my body the benefits and power of nurture. You guided me to study neuroplasticity of the infant brain, which led to the greatest gift of all—a lifelong passion and purpose to speak for the babies.

Bubbie Marce—you are my unconditional nurturer. I started my life in your womb and spent my life in your arms. You are my warm fuzzy loving person and continue to hold me to this day. You have been gone for more than half my life, yet the way you made me feel has been present for every single day of my life.

Josh—my *bashert*, husband and love of my life. I knew we were meant to be together the second that I met you. You are fierce, loving, passionate, and determined. Nothing I do would be possible without your partnership and support. You believe in me, understand me, and share my awe of ideas, creativity, humor, art, beauty, nature, and life. Thank you for our life of adventure, for constantly growing with me, and for the freedom of pursuing our passions and our hearts.

Oschin—my son, I had been wishing for you my whole life, and you

Acknowledgments

are more incredible than I could have ever imagined. You are loving, curious, kind, hilarious, and thoughtful. You are free, you hold nothing back, and I hope you never do. I am lucky to be your mama and wake up next to your gorgeous face and your snuggles every single morning of our lives. You are my healer, my teacher, my heart. Just by being beautiful you, you have reshaped me in the most beautiful ways to love, be, play, and feel. You are my medicine and my inspiration.

Cthulhu Red Peppers—my baby girl and dog doula. You show up for me with love, acceptance, play, and comfort every single day. You've been my emotional support and my best friend through the hardest days in my life. You make me laugh every day and you are my constant antidepressant furball baby.

My science family, who nurtured my mind and spirit and grew my curiosity and confidence. At Dalhousie University: Dr. Richard Brown, Dr. Jennifer Stamp, Dr. Kazue Semba, Dr. Dennis Phillips. At the University of Toronto: Dr. John Roder, Dr. Laleh Sinai, Dr. Tatiana Lipina, Dr. Steven Clapcote, Dr. Steven Duffy, Dr. Viviane Labrie, Dr. Bechara Saab. At Columbia University: Dr. Alex Dranovsky, Dr. David Leonardo, Dr. Miriam Navarro Sobrino, Dr. Alvaro Garcia Garcia, Dr. Esther Kim, Dr. Qingyuan Meng.

The knowledge in this book sits on the shoulders of many giants. It is a culmination of the tireless work and sacrifice of the thousands of scientists in the citations and thousands beyond—scientists who give everything to the pursuit of knowledge with the goal of helping humanity. Fund science: It's important for all of us.

Doulas, friends, and families who have invited me into their lives— you have taught me nurture and enriched my spirit and my mothering. You invited me into the world of the divine feminine, and rehabilitated me with compassion, vulnerability, and connection.The women who nurtured my son in my home and in preschool, you made the village to raise my son.

When I left academia, I was determined to write this book and set out on a path of new experiences. This path led me to meet Stephanie

290

Tade, my agent; and Colleen Martell, my collaborator. Stephanie—you immediately understood my message and you guided me through the whole process with support, compassion, and great wisdom. Colleen— while writing this book we dove deep into the nuances of babies and motherhood while nurturing our own babies, nurturing ourselves, and learning a ton along the way. You are brilliant, beautiful, and talented beyond belief. Thank you for everything we've shared, your friendship, your honesty, your humor, and going above and beyond over and over to use your talents to make this all shine. Georgia Webber— thank you for drawing the illustrations and infusing your brilliance into each and every image. Dr. Tracy Cassels, Dr. Rocio Zunini, and Kaitlin Klimmer—thank you for your valuable feedback. Nana K. Twumasi, my editor—thank you for seeing the potential of my ideas and being the welcoming home for my book. Thank you for your wisdom, guidance, and most of all for bringing this book into the world.

INDEX

NOTE: *Italic page locators* indicate figures

Index

Index

ABOUT THE AUTHOR

Greer Kirshenbaum, PhD, is a neuroscientist, doula, infant and family sleep specialist, and educator. She has a BSc in neuroscience from Dalhousie University and a PhD from the Institute of Medical Science at the University of Toronto. At Columbia University, Greer was a Canadian Institutes of Health Research postdoctoral fellow and research scientist in integrative neuroscience.

Greer lives with her husband, son, and tiny dog in the countryside outside of Toronto, Canada. She is always working on new ways to educate and support families to grow the nurture revolution. You can find out what she's doing next on her website, www.nurture-neuroscience.com.